CHESHIRE
Unusual & Quirky

Andrew Beardmore

HALSGROVE

ALSO BY ANDREW BEARDMORE:

Our English counties are full of glorious countryside, historic buildings and thriving cities, towns and villages. However, lurking not far beneath their surface is a host of oddities and peculiarities that turn the apparently staid and conventional into something much more intriguing…

Derbyshire: Unusual & Quirky: Find out about Derbyshire's Gretna Green, the Devil of Drakelow, and T'owd Man, and see what Muggles and Full-Blood Princes have to do with Ashbourne's Shrovetide football!

Or how about the World Head Balancing Champion and Naked Racing; and not forgetting award-winning urinals, the man who crossed the English Channel in a bath, and the woman who lived in a bacon box!

Nottinghamshire: Unusual & Quirky: Find out which Notts villages are home to a lethal Roman curse, an 8 foot trumpet and the Black Pig Dancers, and which one swapped sides of the Trent in the 16th century.

Or how about an *oven* made of gravestones, or the Flying Bedstead, while not forgetting a pub chair that increases fertility, plus a village which puts cows on thatched roofs to keep them topped up on straw!

Leicestershire and Rutland: Unusual & Quirky: Find out which Leicestershire villages had a beer-swilling fox, a wig-detecting phantom, and a parson who tied 58 bulldogs to 58 apple trees to prevent scrumping!

Or what about which Leicestershire village was hit by a meteorite, and which one still fights annually over a hare pie. Alternatively, find out which Rutland village had a 14th century rector involved in serious organised crime, which one is twinned with Paris, and which one is home to a truly mind-blowing historical revelation.

Staffordshire: Unusual & Quirky: Find out which Staffordshire town has a noisy peace memorial, or which Staffs villages are home to Britain's unluckiest church, and the man who danced for a dozen days.

Then there's the largest non-nuclear explosion on British soil, and the town which saw its brand new canal lock destroyed by the very cannon that was supposed to be heralding its grand opening! Alternatively, find out which ancient customs involve one thousand year-old reindeer horns, teapots, brass statues and a goose!

Lincolnshire: Unusual & Quirky: Find out which Lincolnshire town was the capital of England in the early 11th century, and which one is home to the first ever carving of an ursine musician! Alternatively, you'll need a strong stomach to read of the Hideous Happening in Holbeach, while you'll be amazed at some of the bizarrest Lincolnshire customs – such as the one involving a virgin in mourning garb, another which involves setting fire to a Fool, and yet another which involves the local vicar, a whip and 30 pieces of silver!

If you think you know these counties, read these fascinating and profusely illustrated books and think again…

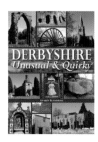  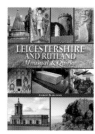 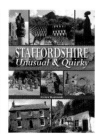 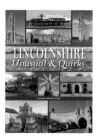

First published in Great Britain in 2018

Copyright © Andrew Beardmore 2018

British Library Cataloguing-in-Publication Data
A CIP record for this title is available from the British Library

ISBN 978 0 85704 323 8

HALSGROVE
Halsgrove House,
Ryelands Business Park,
Bagley Road, Wellington, Somerset TA21 9PZ
Tel: 01823 653777 Fax: 01823 216796
email: sales@halsgrove.com
website: www.halsgrove.com

Printed and bound By Parksons Graphics, India

Cheshire – Unusual and Quirky

Welcome to *Cheshire – Unusual and Quirky*. This is the sixth book in the 21st century series that calls to mind that classic series of travel books called *The King's England*, written in the 1930s by Arthur Mee, since each volume in Mee's series was suffixed with "*There have been many books on <insert county>, but never one like this…*" Well the very same tag line could be applied to this book, as some of its elements are certainly unique. Having said that, the book still has plenty to offer in terms of conventional reference, but it delivers large parts of this in a lateral and humorous format never seen before.

Essentially, then, the book is comprised of two main sections which are called *Conventional Cheshire* and *Quirky Cheshire*. The *Conventional* section kicks off with county maps along with key facts and figures relating to the county – such as county town, population, highest point, key industries and famous sons and daughters. The facts are then followed by a history of the Cheshire *area* from the Stone Age to the 11th century – by which time Cheshire, along with most of England's counties had been officially formed – after which the last one thousand years of county history is covered, bringing us up-to-date and into the 21st century.

Nevertheless, in keeping with the title of the book, the *County History* also has a number of appropriately historical "Quirk Alerts" interspersed. Like a paragraph about the mean-spirited Cheshire parson who cut down Shakespeare's mulberry tree and demolished his house just to spite the people of Stratford, or an anecdote about an ancient Chester custom involving four giants, a camel and 16 naked boys. Alternatively, there are Quirk Alerts on The Alderley Wizard, Little Fanny Bush, White Nancy – and Maggotty Johnson, the fiddling, stilt-walking 18th century Cheshire dramatist from Gawsworth.

The *Conventional* section then hands over to the *Quirky* section…and it is here that we really begin to earn the "*…but never one like this…*" tag line – as the whole section is driven by a quirky poem known as a Shire-Ode! Told in rhyming verse, the Shire-Ode portrays imaginary inhabitants of Cheshire but, as an extra twist, the poem contains dozens of place-names found within the historic county, each subtly woven into the tale – and it is these place-names upon which the *Quirky* section focuses. Firstly, the places have their location pin-pointed via a map. A series of chapters then follow in (largely) alphabetical order for each place featured in the Shire-Ode – and it is here that the strangest and most interesting facts and features about each place are explored. As a result, you get a random

almanac of places that would never ordinarily appear together – along with population figures, earliest place-name recording and origins, famous sons and daughters, historic trivia, Quirk Alerts…and lots of accompanying photographs, too.

So, feel free to commence your obscure Cheshire fact-digging; to read about some very famous people and their Cheshire exploits, to read about ancient battles and, quite frankly, some ridiculous legends, too…but to hopefully have a little chuckle along the way. For example, find out which Cheshire village has a library in a telephone kiosk, which one was once home to the largest sub-post office in England, and which one has a connection with farmer's wives and a big chest! Or discover which former Cheshire village is home to the Wizard's Milestone and which one used to be called Bullock Smithy. Then there's the former Cheshire town that is home to the most successful water polo team in history, another the oldest book in the world containing the rules of rugby, and another which lends its name to a famous Agatha Christie character.

From a historical perspective, find out which Neolithic Cheshire monument should have been one of Britain's most impressive, why the Bronze Age Murder Stone is so-named, and which Macclesfield object is just plain *wrong*! Read about the 89 year-old knight who took on the Spanish Armada, which 16th century hall was built using *timbers* from the Armada, and which Royalist officer was beaten to death with his own wooden leg in 1649. Or simply read of glorious Roman and medieval Chester, of terrible atrocities committed in Cheshire during the English Civil War or, from a more uplifting aspect, look at photos of the stunning architectural delights of Port Sunlight, and awesome engineering feats such as the Anderton Boat Lift.

Finally, check out *The Witches of Keckwick*, the quirky Shire-Ode that drives the idiosyncratic *Quirky Cheshire* section and learn how a trio of white witches overcome the wicked Northwich!

Anyway, that's the introduction completed. As you have probably gathered by now, this book is indeed "unusual and quirky"…so it's time to prime the quirkometer and pull up a pew at St Strangeways – oh, and did I mention the village that had nine vicars in nine years, the squire who squeezed 11 boys into one tree, and the 6ft 6in Cheshire convict who escaped and became an aboriginal chief for 32 years? Or what about which Cheshire hall was built around an oak tree, which Cheshire church is featured in an album called *Urge for Offal*, which Cheshire lake is rumoured to be bottomless and home to a mermaid every Easter …

Contents

Cheshire Facts and Figures

County Status:	Ceremonial county and former non-metropolitan county
County Town:	Chester
County Population:	1,028,600
County Population Rank:	19th out of 48
Cities:	Chester
Largest Settlement:	Historic Cheshire: Birkenhead; Modern Cheshire: Warrington
Largest Settlement Populations:	39. Warrington (165,456); 50. Birkenhead (142,968); 53. Sale (134,022); 74. Stockport (105,878); 100. Chester (86,011); 127. Crewe (71,722)
National Parks:	Peak District
Other Areas:	Delamere Forest, Mid-Cheshire Ridge/Sandstone Trail
County Area:	905 miles² (2,343 km²)
County Area Rank:	25th out of 48
Highest Point:	Pre-1974: Black Hill, 1,909ft (582m); Post-1974: Shining Tor, 1,834ft (559m)
Longest Rivers:	The Mersey is 70 miles long (112km), a large part of which forms the Cheshire border with Merseyside and Greater Manchester. Slightly behind is the Dee at 68 miles, roughly half of which defines Cheshire's border with Wales. Meanwhile, the Weaver is contained entirely within Cheshire and is 60 miles long (96km).
Football Clubs:	Crewe Alexandra (League Two); Chester F.C., Macclesfield Town (National League); Altrincham, Stalybridge Celtic, Stockport County (National League North); Nantwich Town, Warrington Town (Northern League Premier Division); Hyde United, Mossley (Northern League Division 1 North); Northwich Victoria, Witton Albion (Northern League Division 1 South)
Rugby Union Clubs:	Sale Sharks (Premiership); Macclesfield (National League 1); Chester, Sale, (National League 2 North); Lymm, Wirral, Stockport (National League 3 North); Altrincham, Birkenhead Park, Northwich, Warrington, Wilmslow (North 1 West)
Rugby League Clubs:	Warrington Wolves, Widnes Vikings (Super League)
Industries (Present):	Agriculture, Aircraft, Cars, Bio-technology, Chemicals, Cheese, Commerce, Financial Services, Information Technology, Oil, Railways, Retail, Salt, Services, Tourism
Industries (Past):	Agriculture, Cheese, Chemicals, Railways, Salt, Shipbuilding, Silk, Wool
Born in Cheshire:	**CHE:** Russ Abbot, Nigel Adkins, Jonathan Agnew, Ben Ainslie, Randle Ayrton, Sir George Back, Joan Bakewell, Gary Barlow, David Beatty, Ian Blair, Emma Bossons, Ian Botham, Adrian Boult, William Bowman, Margaret Burbidge, Tim Burgess, Sarah Burton, Paul Butler, Hall Caine, Randolph Caldecott, Lewis Carroll, James Chadwick, Leonard Cheshire, David Coleman, Danny Collins, Lewis Collins, Henry Cotton, Steven Cousins, Daniel Craig, Tim Curry, Peter Davenport, Matt Dawson, Dixie Dean, David Dickinson, John Douglas, Richard Egington, Doug Ellis, Ben Foden, Alan Garner, John Gerard, Andy Goldsworthy, Leo Gradwell, Wilfred Grenfell, John Gummer, Lady Emma Hamilton, Paul Heaton, Tom Heaton, Malcolm Hebden, Dame Wendy Hiller, Eaton Hodgkinson, Raphael Holinshed, A. S. Hornby, Stephen Hough, David Hughes, Tom Hughes, Tim Hunt, John Ireland, Sandy Irvine, Glenda Jackson, Megs Jenkins, Norman Cyril Jones, Kerry Katona, Conor Kostick, Matt Langridge, Lee Latchford-Evans, Hugh Lloyd, Jason McAteer, George Mallory, John Marshall, Valerie Masterson, John Mayall, Bob Mills, Danny Murphy, Paul O'Grady, Michael Owen, Fred Perry, Ronald Pickup, Daniel Poole, Eileen Power, Paula Radcliffe, Basil Radford, Shanaze Reade, I. A. Richards, Nick Robinson, George Rodger, Tom Rolt, Dame Patricia Routledge, George Sampson, Pat Sanderson, Cyril Scott, Ryan Shawcross, May Sinclair, John Speed, John Steiner, Nigel Stonier, Shirley Strong, William Swainson, Richard Synge, Anthony Thwaite, Beatrice Tinsley, Stuart Tomlinson, Stuart Turner, Martin Tyler, Sir Joseph Whitworth, Helen Willetts, Frederic Williams, Arthur Woodward *Pre-1974:* **LAN:** Charles Barkla, Ian Brown, Chris Evans, Sue Johnston, Pete Postlethwaite *Post-1974:* **GMR:** Sarah Storey; **MER:** Taron Egerton, David Thompson

Cheshire Maps

Administrative Counties of England 1889 to 1965

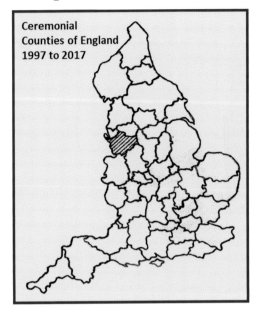

Ceremonial Counties of England 1997 to 2017

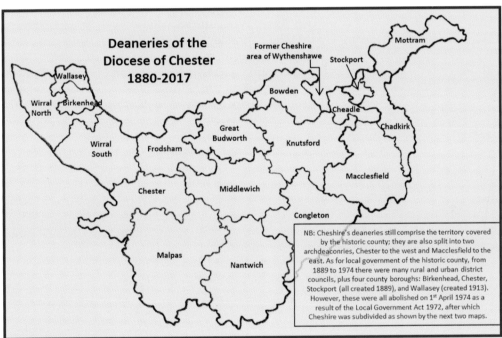

Deaneries of the Diocese of Chester 1880-2017

Former Cheshire area of Wythenshawe

Mottram

Stockport

Wallasey

Wirral North

Birkenhead

Bowden

Cheadle

Chadkirk

Wirral South

Frodsham

Great Budworth

Knutsford

Macclesfield

Chester

Middlewich

Congleton

Malpas

Nantwich

NB: Cheshire's deaneries still comprise the territory covered by the historic county; they are also split into two archdeaconries, Chester to the west and Macclesfield to the east. As for local government of the historic county, from 1889 to 1974 there were many rural and urban district councils, plus four county boroughs: Birkenhead, Chester, Stockport (all created 1889), and Wallasey (created 1913). However, these were all abolished on 1st April 1974 as a result of the Local Government Act 1972, after which Cheshire was subdivided as shown by the next two maps.

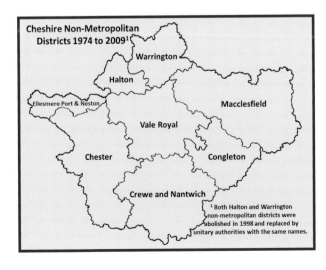

Cheshire Non-Metropolitan Districts 1974 to 2009[1]

Warrington

Halton

Ellesmere Port & Neston

Macclesfield

Vale Royal

Chester

Congleton

Crewe and Nantwich

[1] Both Halton and Warrington non-metropolitan districts were abolished in 1998 and replaced by unitary authorities with the same names.

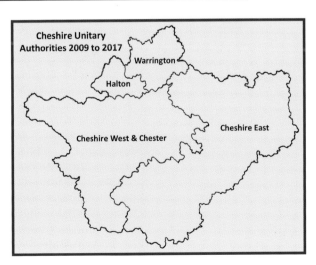

Cheshire Unitary Authorities 2009 to 2017

Warrington

Halton

Cheshire West & Chester

Cheshire East

Cheshire County History

Prehistory

The county of Cheshire is believed to have been created by Edward the Elder in around 920, although the name isn't recorded in print until 980, when the *Anglo-Saxon Chronicle* name it as *Legeceasterscir*. The name is derived directly from Chester, which was recorded as *Legacæstir* in 735, and means "city of the legions" – this, of course, referring to the ancient Roman city of Chester, that was recorded as *Deoua* in c.150, but which had been set up as *Deva Victrix* in the year AD 79 by the Roman *Legio II Adiutrix* during the reign of the Emperor Vespasian. The origins of the name *Deva*, however, are not certain: it may have been named after the goddess of the River Dee, while the river-name is of uncertain origin, and was named by the Celtic *Cornovii* people who lived in the area at the time of the Roman invasion.

Of course, the *area* of Cheshire goes back much further than Roman times – although despite there being evidence of humans inhabiting the British Isles from as long ago as 200,000 years, the first evidence of man in Cheshire dates from around 12,000 BC – this being in the east of the county along the western edge of the Pennines. These people probably lived in caves in the Peak District but would have hunted well into the Cheshire Plain, particularly in the extensive forests that existed then, as well as the many meres. By 6000 BC, we start to find flint and chert implements at Alderley Edge while excavations at Tatton Mere have revealed a settlement dating from this time. Other prehistoric settlements are thought to have been at Oakmere in Delamere Forest and in the mossy areas of north Wirral, while a number of prehistoric finds on Hilbre Island off the north-western corner of the Wirral suggest a settlement there; indeed, there is also evidence of settlement along the north coast of the Wirral peninsula, from Hilbre Island to New Brighton, from around 5000 BC.

By the end of the Mesolithic (Middle Stone Age) period, which ran from 10,000 to 4500 BC, the first permanent settlements appeared and trees would have been cleared for the first farming; evidence of the latter has been dated to around 5000 BC, such as that discovered near Tarvin. Systematic forest clearance began during the Neolithic period (4500 BC to 2000 BC), thus enabling arable farming and evidence has been found of cereal crop growing at Hatchmere in Delamere Forest between 4200 and 3500 BC.

The finest ancient Neolithic monument in Cheshire is the Bridestones, which are located at 820 feet (250m) above sea level on the county border with Staffordshire around 3 miles east of Congleton. Dating from 3500 to 2400 BC, the Bridestones are a Neolithic burial chamber, or chambered cairn, of which the most striking element are the two upright portal stones after which the place is named, that stand like a couple of massive sentries over the one surviving chambered tomb. These two 8-9ft high stones once supported a massive capstone, and the whole structure was covered by an earthen mound. Its design suggests high-status burials.

However, striking though the Bridestones are today, they once formed part of a much larger structure that,

Rostherne Mere is the largest of Cheshire's many natural lakes that were formed by retreating glaciers at the end of the last glacial period. It was also around these meres that prehistoric man hunted from around 12,000 BC.

Blakemere Moss (above) in Delamere Forest and Budworth Mere (below) just north of Northwich are also areas where prehistoric man hunted.

had it survived, would have been one of the most impressive Neolithic monuments in Britain. Strong evidence indicates that it was a vast chambered tomb with a paved crescent of a forecourt and a portholed stone dividing the main chamber. An 18th century study, carried out when the monument was considerably more intact, states that in addition to the 20ft by 9ft (6m by 2.7m) main chamber which still survives, a further two subsidiary chambers were also part of the structure – but of which no trace survives today. However, an 18th century plan of the Bridestones by Henry Rowlands shows that the sandstone cairn was once flanked to the east by an impressive stone circle. This included four portal stones, two either side of the tomb entrance – the southerly pair of which survive as today's Bridestones – and twelve 12ft stone pillars of which only one

survives. These latter stones would have formed a pear shape, spreading out eastwards from the front of the chamber, and they would also have been capped, thus forming an area of about 30ft by 45ft.

Interestingly, it is believed that the Bridestones – a chambered tomb with a crescentic forecourt – is similar and contemporary to monuments found in western Scotland, Northern Ireland and the Isle of Man, but *not* with any other examples on the English mainland – thus suggesting cultural links between Cheshire and these other areas. Furthermore, the Bridestones also has a portholed stone, a characteristic usually associated with chambered tombs from the Cotswolds and Severn Regions, and similar to the Devil's Ring and Finger around 15 miles to the south-west in Staffordshire. As to why so little of this monument survives today, this is

The Bridestones on the Cheshire border with Staffordshire 3 miles east of Congleton, are Cheshire's finest surviving Neolithic monument. Dating from between 3500 and 2400 BC, these remaining two portal stones and chambered cairn (behind the Bridestones) were once part of a far larger monument that, had it remained intact, would have been one of Britain's finest prehistoric monuments.

Quirk Alert: *Erratic Science*

Shown right is a c.30-ton granite boulder in Macclesfield's West Park which is actually a glacial erratic, carried south from Cumbria by advancing glaciers around 12,500 years ago. The boulder was presented to the people of Macclesfield in their new public park in 1857, having been discovered during excavations nearby. It took a team of eight horses to move it the 1km to its current location, after which a wonderful brass plaque was affixed to the stone, proclaiming its date of placement and its origin – the latter claiming it had been carried south by "an iceberg from Cumberland" – an interesting insight into how science and English county geography has since changed! As for the origin of the name "erratic", it derives from the  *Latin "errere", meaning "error" or "wanderer" – so in this case, a rock that shouldn't be there as it has totally different characteristics to the rock strata around it. They were once thought to have been deposited by a great flood, which in a way they sort of were!*

because thousands of tons of stone were taken from the cairn in order to construct the nearby turnpike road in 1764, while further stones were used to build the adjacent house and farm, and yet more were used to construct an ornamental garden in Tunstall Park. Furthermore, a number of the standing stones from the 'circle' forming the forecourt have also been removed over the years, including the top half of the portholed stone. The best example of this sad disregard for our heritage was by one of the construction engineers of the Manchester Ship Canal. He used one of the largest portal stones in order to effect a demonstration with a detonator, and which resulted in great damage to the stone. Thankfully, the stone was cemented back together again during excavations in the 1930s.

The origin of the name "Bridestones" is now lost. However, there are the usual legends. One suggests that a newly married couple (possibly Vikings) were murdered at the site and the stones were laid around their resting place. Another theory is that they could have been named after the Celtic fertility goddess *Brigantia* (otherwise known as Brighid or Bridie), while another suggests the Old English word for birds, which was *brides* – so the stones in their original form could have resembled birds, thus leading to "the Brides

stones". Alternatively, it may have been named after the Celtic *Brigante* tribe who inhabited this area in the first century AD.

The only other significant Neolithic site in Cheshire is a suspected long barrow at Somerford, known as Somerford Bridge barrow – although its mound is now covered by oak trees. However, a number of Neolithic stone axes have been found around the county, but which originated from other parts of the country – typically from the Lake District, but also from North Wales and Cornwall – and which also therefore indicates some form of primitive trade between Cheshire and other areas of Britain. Other discoveries of Jadeite axes from this period, suggest trade with even farther afield, as these axes could only have originated from foreign shores.

In terms of Bronze Age evidence (2100 to 700 BC), Cheshire is home to around one hundred Bronze Age burial chambers. A large proportion of them are to be found on the eastern edge of the Peak District, particularly around Rainow, while Macclesfield is surrounded by around twenty. Other clusters of Bronze Age sites can be found near to Wincle, and at Lyme Handley, where you will also find the Murder Stone, a tear-shaped Bronze Age standing stone that was so-named as this was the location of the murder of William Wood

BRONZE AGE BEESTON CRAG

This is a view of the heavily-wooded Beeston Crag in late summer, as seen from the eastern approach. The 328ft (100m) high crag was the location of a late Bronze Age hillfort which was only accessible from the east.

View from the top of Beeston Crag looking towards the north-east. The ground falls away almost vertically from here to 300ft below.

View from Beeston Crag to the west towards the Welsh hills with a similar near-vertical drop down to the plains below.

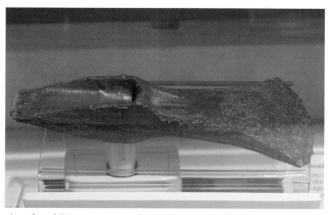

A socketed Bronze Age axe-head discovered at Beeston Crag.

of Eyam in 1823. There are also further clusters of Bronze Age barrows further west in the Delamere Forest area, and over in the south-west of the county, including those at Bickerton, Carden, Coddington and Horton. Meanwhile, to the west of Macclesfield is Engine Vein copper mine which was used as an open-cast mine for copper and other minerals from the early Bronze Age.

During the Bronze Age, a hillfort was built around the top of the sandstone crag at Beeston, and was a favoured site because the lowland areas were badly drained and marshy and the 328ft (100m) cliffs there made the crag virtually inaccessible except from the east. The Bronze Age hillfort was a defended enclosure of a bank of stone and earth with a timber palisade constructed on top of the hill. Timber roundhouses were built inside the enclosure in order to provide housing, storage and workshops. The inhabitants would have made pots from local clay, and tools from local stone which would have been used, for example, to grind corn; the corn would have been grown on the lowlands around the base of the crag. Meanwhile, the surrounding woods would have been ideal for hunting.

Of course, the inhabitants also made their own bronze weapons, tools and jewellery thanks to the copper ore found at the foot of Beeston Crag – making the site an important centre for metalworking during these times. Hence a number of highly-prized Bronze Age artefacts have been found here, including two socketed axe-heads made of an alloy of copper, lead and tin, while moulds and crucibles for smelting have also been found. In total, five socketed axes with decorative ribs have been found at Beeston, along with one socketed axe decorated with flat facets, a socketed knife, a spearhead with a leaf-shaped blade, and fragments of two sword blades – the only definite examples found in Cheshire. These artefacts are thought to date from between 900 and 800 BC, just prior to the advent of ironworking, and comprise one of the most important Bronze Age collections in England. The majority were found in the outer ward, while the two aforementioned socketed axe heads appear to have been deliberately placed beneath the bank of the prehistoric defences – perhaps as part of some ancient ritual. Other finds at Beeston are from further afield and confirm trade with other areas of Britain, such as high quality flints imported from Yorkshire and Lincolnshire.

The Iron Age in Britain ran from around 700 BC to the 1st century AD, and Beeston Crag continued to be inhabited during this period, with the Bronze Age enclosure gradually being converted into an Iron Age hillfort. Elsewhere, salt extraction from the Weaver Valley in the 5th century BC was being used at the hill-fort on the Wrekin – which was the capital of the terri-tory of the Celtic *Cornovii* tribe at that time – and over the next 500 years, that territory spread northwards to envelop the area of Cheshire.

Iron Age Hillfort (Location)	Features and Remains
Beeston Crag hillfort (Beeston on central Cheshire ridge)	Between c.650 to 450 BC, the existing Bronze Age bank (dated to 1270-830 BC) was enlarged and an accompanying external ditch was constructed, and between c.450 BC to AD 40, a huge earthwork bank was internally strengthened with stone rubble and topped with a wooden palisade. Seven circular buildings have also been iden-tified as either late Bronze Age or early Iron Age in origin.
Bradley hillfort (Kingsley on central Cheshire ridge)	Only natural defences to the north survive, with the other man-made defences damaged or erased by ploughing. Bradley is unusual in that it is largely surrounded by high ground, and hence doesn't command the fine views that its counterparts do. The fort was positioned to exploit the steep banks of a tributary of the River Weaver which runs past the north face.
Burton Point (Neston on the Wirral peninsula)	This promontory fort consisted of an arc of earthworks protecting a former headland overlooking the Dee Estuary – which has since become land-locked due to navigation improvements on the Dee in the 18th century. Surviving earthworks are largely tree-covered, while the northern defences have been eradicated by sandstone quarrying.
Eddisbury hillfort (Delamere on central Cheshire ridge)	The largest and most complex of the mid-Cheshire ridge hillforts was originally concentrated on the eastern side of the hill on a steep-sided sandstone projection. The initial univallate (single rampart and ditch) build dates from around 200 BC, but was expanded westward between 1 and 50 AD, such that the hillfort followed the contours of the entire hill, growing to 660ft by 1250ft (200m by 380m). This increased the enclosed area from 5.5 acres (22,000m²) to 7 acres (28,000m²). This later build was also bivallate with a 33ft (10m) ditch in between the two ramparts that was 1.6ft deep (0.5m). Eddisbury hillfort was slighted by the Romans in the 1st century AD.

Helsby hillfort (Helsby Hill on central Cheshire ridge)	Helsby hillfort was built on the steep-sided sandstone projection known as Helsby Hill, which has a summit of 463ft (141m), and incorporates steep cliffs on the northern and western sides, thus providing a natural semi-circular defence. Double rampart earthworks were built on the southern and eastern faces of the hill with a single ditch in between. The hill commands fine views on all sides.
Kelsborrow promontory fort (Delamere on central Cheshire ridge)	A univallate promontory fort which exploits the steep sides to the south and a curving bank and ditch to the north. The fort overlooks the Cheshire Plain to the south and west, with higher ground to the east. The site is largely surrounded by a 100ft-wide (30m) artificial bank and ditch, and encloses a 7.25 acre (2.93ha) site. Some surviving parts of the bank are still 6ft (1.8m) high.
Maiden Castle Larkton Hill on central Cheshire ridge)	Maiden Castle was built in around 600 BC on a slight promontory at the highest point of a plateau on Larkton Hill at 694ft (212m). The hillfort was naturally defended to the north, west and south by a steeply sloping escarpment where the hillfort has a commanding view of the Cheshire Plain. The eastern side was defended by two 40ft-wide (12m) artificial banks, set 35ft (11m) apart. The defences cover about 1.66 acres (6,700 m²) out of the entire 3 acres (12,000 m²) of the Maiden Castle site.
Oakmere hillfort (Oakmere on central Cheshire ridge)	A low-lying promontory site, built on a triangular area of land projecting westwards into Oak Mere. Ramparts were built in an arc around the remaining eastern side of the fort, and a ditch was constructed in front of the rampart which was thought to be around 50ft (15m) wide. Today, the bank stands at around 6ft (1.8m) high and, at its deepest point the ditch is now a symmetrical 6ft deep – although it was originally 10ft (3.0 m) deep in places.
Peckforton Mere promontory fort (Peckforton on central Cheshire ridge)	A smaller defensive settlement of c.0.35ha located on a ridge, with Peckforton Mere to the south-west and marsh to the northwest and southeast. The fort occupied a promontory on the east side of Peckforton Mere, and had a bank and external ditch which curved around the promontory on the north and south sides, with the west side defended by the mere and the old course of the River Gowy. Only 180m of the original earthworks are now visible thanks to centuries of ploughing.
Rainow hillfort (Rainow in the Peak District)	This is the only known Iron Age hillfort in the Peak District part of Cheshire, probably because the Pennines were a peripheral zone between the lands of the *Cornovii* to the west and the *Corieltauvi* to the east. However, all traces of the hillfort's earthworks have long-since disappeared.
Woodhouse hillfort (Frodsham on central Cheshire ridge)	Another promontory hillfort that sits at 449ft (137m) at the northern end of the mid-Cheshire ridge. The hillfort was defended on its western and southern sides by steep cliffs, and by ramparts to the north and east where the ground slopes more gently. Excavations in 1951 showed that the rampart was originally 4m high and revetted with stone on both sides.

One other site that was also populated throughout Iron Age Britain was at Meols on the northern edge of the Wirral peninsula, and coins dating from around 500 BC to the mid-1st century AD have been found here, with some of the coins originating from as far afield as Brittany and Carthage. Meols therefore appears to have been an important trading settlement between Iron Age Britain and continental Europe and the Mediterranean.

The indigenous population of the British Iron Age were Brythonic Celts, and Cheshire was largely home to the Celtic *Cornovii* tribe. The territory of the *Cornovii* stretched from the northern tip of the Wirral all the way down to northern Herefordshire and Worcestershire, and across from much of Cheshire and Staffordshire, through Shropshire to parts of eastern Powys,

Flintshire and Wrexham. This meant that most of later Cheshire territory belonged to the *Cornovii*, with northern and eastern parts belonging to the *Brigantes* and *Corieltauvi*, respectively. The *Cornovii* capital of pre-Roman Britain, was probably a hillfort on The Wrekin in Shropshire, while Ptolemy's 2nd century *Geography* names two *Cornovii* towns: *Deva Victrix* (modern-day Chester), and *Viroconium Cornoviorum* (modern-day Wroxeter); the latter became the *Cornovii* capital under Roman rule. What is also interesting about the territory of the *Cornovii*, is the border area to the east with the *Corieltauvi* – for in the Middle Ages, this area was known as The Lyme, a name which survives in a belt running from Ashton-under-Lyne in the north (*Asshton under Lyme*, 1305), down through Lyme Park and Lyme

FOUR CHESHIRE IRON AGE HILLFORTS

Above left: *View to the north-west from Larkton Hill in south-west Cheshire, where the Iron Age hillfort now known as Maiden Castle was built in around 600 BC. This hillfort had natural defences to the north, west and south, courtesy of cliffs which rise steeply from the Cheshire Plain to a summit of 694ft. Meanwhile, the eastern approach* (above right) *was defended by impressive earthworks of two banks with a ditch in between.*

Above left: *This ground-level view of Eddisbury hillfort near to Delamere doesn't do it justice. From the air, the view is spectacular demonstrating the ramparts and ditches which surround the hill of what was Cheshire's largest Iron Age hillfort.* Above right: *The north-eastern corner of the Eddisbury hillfort reveals some of the surviving ramparts, the extensive views and some interesting residents!*

Long view on Helsby Hill which rises to a height of 463ft on the south shore of the Mersey estuary, and sits at the northernmost end of the mid-Cheshire ridge. The northern and western faces provided a natural defence; the eastern and southern approaches were defended by a double rampart and ditch. Above right: *View from the trig point on top of Helsby Hill.*

Above left: *View towards the south-facing ramparts of the former Iron Age hillfort at Burton Point.* Above right: *View from the same point, looking southwards on what would have been the Dee estuary in Iron Age times*

Green to Newcastle-under-Lyme in Staffordshire. This area between the plain and the upland was heavily forested back then, and it is a possibility that the name "Lyme" derives from the Celtic word for "elm". This may also account for why there is only one known Iron Age hillfort in this area, but dozens of pre-dating Bronze Age barrows – as The Lyme was probably a disputed frontier ground during the Iron Age – in this case between the *Cornovii* and the *Corieltauvi*.

Finally, the *Cornovii* were probably relatively wealthy, courtesy of their control of the south-Cheshire salt mines, which are known to have been worked in pre-Roman Britain. Their economy, however, was mainly pastoral, with some evidence of cereal crop cultivation, while they also created a network of paved and semi-paved roads which would have supported their product distribution.

Romans, Anglo-Saxons and Vikings

The Romans invaded Britain in AD 43, and by AD 45 they had constructed the Fosse Way, which ran all the way from Exeter (*Isca Dumnoniorum*) in the south-west to Lincoln (*Lindum Colonia*) in the mid-east. For a few years, the Fosse Way – which ran some way to the south of Cheshire – was thought to mark the temporary frontier of the embryonic province of *Britannia*, with all areas to the south and east of that line under Roman control. However, the Romans certainly operated beyond that line under the second and third Roman governors of *Britannia*, Publius Ostorius Scapula (AD 47 to AD 52) and Didius Gallus (AD 52 to AD 57), both of whom slowly brought parts of Cheshire under Roman control. There were certainly a number of Roman camps at this time in what is now western Staffordshire, as it was from these bases that the Romans pushed westwards towards Wales, along the ancient Brythonic grassy trackway that they named as Watling Street, and which soon connected London (*Londinium*) to the Roman capital of *Cornovii* territory at Wroxeter (*Viroconium Cornoviorum*). Nevertheless, by AD 57, most of Cheshire's territory was still in Celtic hands, although it was bordered to the west, south and east by Roman-controlled *Britannia*. Cheshire had therefore been spared up to this point, as the conquest of Wales was of top priority to the Romans, courtesy of rich Flintshire lead and silver deposits. Having said that, one school of thought suggests that the first Roman fort at Chester was constructed as early as AD 60 – although there is no archaeological evidence to support this theory. But it would make sense if this were true, as Chester made an ideal Roman base as part of their quest to pacify the troublesome *Deceangli* of North Wales and the *Ordovices* of Mid-Wales. However, it was probably nearer to AD 70 before this happened, as evidenced by Roman pottery found in the Chester area that dates to the late AD 60s.

It was certainly in AD 71, though, that the Romans launched two major offensives – one into Wales to stamp out the last resistance of the *Deceangli* and *Ordovices*, and the other north into *Brigante* territory. In order to do this, the Cheshire area was of key strategic importance, and this was the point at which the first *known* fortress at Cheshire was constructed to use as a base for both campaigns, and to block any attempt of one tribe coming to the aid of the other. The 62 acre fortress (25ha) was constructed on the north bank of the River Dee, on a sandstone ridge overlooking the lowest potential bridging point before the Dee opened out into its estuary, and also the point up to which the river was then navigable. This meant that the fortress was also located close to the natural harbour which is today occupied by the Chester Racecourse, and which therefore offered natural protection to the south and the west. The fortress was completed by around AD 79, and comprised a ditch, a turf rampart topped by a palisade, and wooden towers. The ramparts were around 20ft-wide (6m) and were comprised of turf laid over sand, clay, rubble, and layers of logs, while the ditch system was 10ft wide (3m) and 5ft deep (1.5m). In shape, the fortress was rectangular with rounded corners, and had dimensions of 1950ft by 1360ft (594m by 415m), while four gates were situated to the north, east, south and west. The fortress was the largest constructed in Britain during the AD 70s.

This early fortress was initially home to the *Legio II Adiutrix* (auxiliary), and the legion would have comprised around 5000 to 6000 soldiers. Their barracks

The remains of the Roman amphitheatre in Chester (Deva Victrix).

The foundations of the Roman south-east tower of Deva Victrix.

Left: *What are known as the Roman Gardens in Chester at the southern edge of the former Roman town of Diva Victrix.* Right: *In the Roman Gardens is this replica construction of the under-floor heating system of the Roman baths, known as a* hypocaust. *Some of the sandstone pillars in the construction are genuine articles, discovered in one of the rooms of the* sudatoria *(a sauna or sweat room) in 1863, and which probably date to a refurbishment in the 4th century.*

were located inside the fortress along with the military headquarters (*principia*), granaries (*horrea*), workshops, an unsheltered exercise yard (*palaestra*) and the legionary Roman baths (*thermae*), which were completed in around AD 79. This early bath complex included an entrance room (*vestibulum*), an exercise hall (*basilica thermarum*), a cold room with a cold pool (*frigidarium*), a warm room (*tepidarium*), a sweating room (*sudatorium*), and a hot room with a hot plunge bath (*caldarium*). The baths had mosaic floors and were heated by a sophisticated heating system known as a *hypocaust* – with the floors raised on columns of tiles (*pilae*) which allowed the hot air from the furnace to circulate beneath and up through flues in the walls. These baths would have been in operation 24 hours a day, and required around 850,000 litres of water each day, which was supplied from the springs to the east of Chester in Boughton. The water was supplied to the fortress through underground lead pipes linked to the main aqueduct near the east gate, and which was then held in large tanks with concrete foundations before being fed through the complex.

The Romans named their fortress *Deva* from the Latin word *dea* or *diva* (meaning "goddess"), thus referring to the goddess of the River Dee – although an alternative theory suggests that the place was named after the Celtic name for the river.

In around AD 87, the *Legio II Adiutrix* was forced to leave their base at *Deva* to assist on campaigns in Dacia, in the lower Danube area of mainland Europe. After this point, the city was home to the *Legio XX Valeria Victrix*, with the "Valeria" part of the name thought to be named after their commander, Marcus Valerius Messalla Messallinus, and the "Victrix" part deriving from the Latin word for "victory". It was therefore from around this time that the fortress became known as *Deva Victrix*, and which continued to be home to the 20th legion for the next 300 years or so.

The first task of the 20th legion, however, was to commence a rebuild of the fortress, replacing the timber walls with stone ones. These walls were 4.5ft thick (1.36m) at the base and 3.5ft thick (1.06m) at the top, while some 22 towers were also built at regular intervals of around 200ft (60m), and which were sized at around 21ft (6.5m) square. The defensive ditch was refreshed to a width of 25ft (7.5m) and a depth of 8ft (2.45m), while the timber barracks were also replaced by superior stone successors. This incarnation of the fortress was thought to be complete by AD 105, and used local sandstone quarried across the river to the south of the fortress at Handbridge. And whereas the first fortress covered around 60 acres, the second covered around 100 acres.

The Roman fortress at *Deva Victrix* occupied much the same area as the medieval city did a thousand years later, while a civilian settlement or *canabae* sprang up to the east of the fortress during the 2nd century and eventually spread out, encircling the fortress to the south and west, too. The settlement probably started out as a collection of huts belonging to traders who had become wealthy trading with the fortress. However, as legionaries from the fortress retired, many of them settled in the *canabae*, effectively making it a veteran colony – or *canabae legionis* – and a number of these

Chester's city walls were built by the Romans in the 2nd century, and were re-fortified and extended by Æthelfæda in 907 since when their line has been unchanged. Here we see a section of the south wall alongside the Dee.

retired legionaries probably became members of the elected council which administered the settlement separately from the fortress. As the settlement developed, shops would have fronted the roadside for about 300 metres beyond the fortress walls, while the legion's parade ground was located to the east, the civilian baths to the west, and a large coaching house or *mansio* for travelling government officials to the south. Meanwhile, cemeteries were located beyond the *canabae legionis*, alongside the roads leading to the settlement, and around 150 of these tombstones can be found today in Chester's Grosvenor Museum – the largest collection of Roman tombstones from a single site in Britain.

To the south of the settlement was the amphitheatre, part of which also survives today. Excavations have revealed that *Deva's* amphitheatre was built in two phases, with the first constructed from timber and probably during the AD 70s. The second build was larger than the first and measured 314ft by 286ft (95.7m by 87.2m), although only the seating area was extended; the arena remained the same size. The second build was also a two-tier structure, capable of housing between 8000 and 10,000 spectators, making it the largest known military amphitheatre in Britain. Its

attendance capacity also hints at the large size and wealth of *Deva's* civilian population, who would have enjoyed attending events involving acrobats and wrestlers as well as professional gladiators. The amphitheatre would also have been used by the resident legion for weapons training.

A number of artefacts have also been discovered over the years, with links to the amphitheatre, including part of a 2nd century slate frieze depicting a net-fighter, which was discovered in 1738, and which possibly once decorated the tomb of a gladiator. Also discovered was a small bronze statuette of a gladiator, parts of a Roman bowl depicting scenes from a gladiatorial contest, and part of a gladius sword handle. Alas, much of the amphitheatre masonry was later reused in the construction of St John's church and the monastery of St Mary, but what does remain today is a Scheduled Ancient Monument.

Also surviving in Edgar's Field at Handbridge, is another Scheduled Ancient Monument – a remarkable statue of the goddess Minerva, which was carved into the face of a sandstone quarry in the early 2nd century. This Grade I listed statue is the only in-situ, rock-cut Roman shrine that remains in its original location, not

THE FABULOUS GROSVENOR MUSEUM
(All of the following images are the copyright of The Grosvenor Museum, Chester)

Above left are two lengths of lead piping that were used to transport water into the fortress at Deva from the springs to the east of the city at Boughton. The inscription on the upper pipe tells us that it was made when the Emperor Vespasian was consul for the ninth time (AD 79), while the lower length bears the name of Gnaeus Julius Agricola, Governor of Britannia from 77 to 84 AD. Above right: These Roman tombstones were found in Chester in the 19th century. Most of them had been re-used during the 4th century rebuild of the city walls of Deva Victrix.

Roman box-flue tiles.

Roman pottery found at nearby Holt.

only in Britain, but in Western Europe, too. Minerva was the Roman goddess of war, knowledge and craftsmanship.

One interesting theory about *Deva Victrix* is that it was initially intended to be used as the base for a potential invasion of Ireland, and perhaps, thereafter, become the capital of the unified British Isles under Rome. This is based upon the fact that the fortress was built to be twenty per cent larger than other Roman fortresses in Britain, such as that at *Eboracum* (York) plus it also contained a mysterious and unique elliptical building not found during the excavations of other legionary fortresses, and which may have been intended as the headquarters of the governor of Britain. In fact, there were

Minerva's Shrine can be found in Edgar's Field in Handbridge and dates from the early 2nd century.

two elliptical buildings, the second having been built on top of the first, as discovered during building work in 1939. It is fairly certain that the first elliptical building dates from the original fort, this thanks to a length of lead piping which was discovered and which was stamped with the name of Emperor Vespasian (AD 69 to AD 79). The first building measured 172ft (42.4m) by 103ft (31.45m), and had at its centre, an oval courtyard with a central water feature which measured 46ft (14m) by 30ft (9m). In turn, the courtyard was surrounded by twelve wedge-shaped rooms which had large arched entrances, 13ft (4m) wide, and at least 18ft (5.5m) high. It is not certain if the first building was ever completed, but it had certainly been destroyed by the AD 90s and the site was subsequently used as the fortress rubbish dump for some considerable time. The second elliptical building was then built on top of the first in around AD 220, its build date confirmed by the discovery of a coin of Emperor Elagabalus (218-222), which was found beneath one of the pavement slabs. The second building used the same foundations as the first, although the layout was slightly modified to give it a slightly broader look, and this building probably lasted until the Roman departure from Britain in the early 5th century. The elliptical buildings also had their own baths along with a range of store rooms around the outside; again, two sets of baths are

unusual. It was probably the finest building in the fortress, but its function remains unknown – although another theory suggests it was a temple, with its twelve alcoves perhaps housing images of the twelve primary gods of the Roman pantheon.

So, *Deva Victrix* was twenty percent larger than other fortresses, had the mystery elliptical building, and also had a stone curtain wall that was constructed without mortar, using large sandstone blocks – a technique usually reserved for the most important buildings of the Roman Empire, as it required the greatest amount of skill and effort. *Deva Victrix* also contained a commercial area with a flourishing market along with an important craft and industrial sector, while the river was home to wharves, jetties and warehouses – all witness to the fact that Chester was a major military and commercial centre. Given its developed port, *Deva Victrix* was therefore also potentially the perfect location from which to invade *Hibernia* (Ireland) – a known intention of the 1st century Roman governor of Britain, Gnaeus Julius Agricola (77-84 AD) – while there is also that length of lead piping bearing his name. So perhaps this building was indeed scheduled to become his administrative headquarters, and hence the capital of a *Britannia* poised to invade *Hibernia*. As it turned out, though, it was around this time that the Roman policy switched from one of expansion to consolidation – and *Londinium*, rather than *Deva*, became the capital of *Britannia*.

Nevertheless, *Deva Victrix* expanded throughout the 2nd and 3rd centuries as the population increased. It is also thought that an extensive *prata legionis* (meadows of the legion) existed around the fortress and *canabae*, which provided food and other supplies for the garrison. This included important quarries at Storeton on the Wirral, and the Peckforton Hills to the south-east, while satellite communities appeared in this area at Heronbridge and Saltney on the west side of the River Dee, and at Tilston (possibly *Bovium*), Holt and Malpas a little further south, with Holt containing workshops that provided most of

Part of a Roman water-pipe.

Roman altar stones.

All of the following images are the copyright of Middlewich Library

  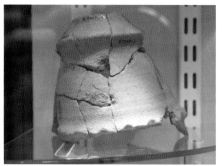

Left to right: A mixing bowl, known as a mortarium. The bowl dates from AD 60-90, and is marked ALBINVS (the potter's name) on the rim; A highly decorated high-status Samian Ware bowl, dating from c.120 AD. Samian Ware was the fine tableware of the Romans which was made in Gaul; Pieces from a Roman chimney pot probably made at Middlewich.

Left: Early 2ⁿᵈ century Roman pottery, including the cremation urn in the background and a single-handed container in the foreground. These artefacts were discovered near to Kinderton Old Hall between 1820 and 1866 by Benjamin Llewellyn Vawdrey.

Right: Fragments of a 2ⁿᵈ century Roman brick (bottom left) and part of a Roman diploma (bottom right). Also visible on the shelf above are pieces of a domestic metal cauldron, part of a folding camp stool, 3ʳᵈ or 4ᵗʰ century iron shears used for shearing sheep, and part of the upper half of a set of rotary quern stones from around 150 AD. The latter were used domestically for grinding corn.

the pottery to the garrison at *Deva* prior to AD 120. Also present at this time was a small fortlet to the north of *Deva Victrix* at modern-day Ince on the River Mersey, and which has been dated to AD 80-100.

Despite the continual population increase, the actual fortress at *Deva Victrix* went into something of a decline during the 2ⁿᵈ century. This was largely due to part of *Legio XX Victrix* being constantly redeployed to fight battles elsewhere, and thus leaving parts of the fortress abandoned which subsequently fell into disrepair. However, *Deva Victrix* was rebuilt again in the early 3ʳᵈ century under Septimius Severus, and some of these walls survive to this day, having been built into later medieval buildings. Alas, the last of the four fortress gateways associated with this build, the Eastgate, was demolished in 1786 – although thankfully, William Stukeley had recorded the details of the structure in 1725.

It seems likely that the fortress of *Deva Victrix* was abandoned by the legions sometime in the late 4ᵗʰ century, and which may have been triggered when the Dee is known to have silted up in 383. In the same year, it is thought that the garrison was removed by Magnus Maximus as part of his invasion of Gaul. So even if there were still military units there, it would only have been for a few more years anyway, as the Romans retreated from British shores for good in around 410.

We have already mentioned the surviving remnants of the east and north walls, the amphitheatre, and the Minerva goddess. However, a large area of the baths also survived until 1863, but was destroyed by building

works, while more was destroyed during the construction of the Grosvenor Shopping Mall in 1963. Thankfully some remnants of these ancient relics survived. These include a section of a hypocaust in the cellar of 39 Bridge Street, and some 2.5ft-wide (0.75m) sandstone columns from the exercise hall of the baths, which can be found in the Roman Gardens off Pepper Street. These columns would originally have stood at a height of 19ft (5.9m).

Moving away from *Deva Victrix*, there was still much Roman influence elsewhere, for when they first arrived in Cheshire territory, they found ready-made Iron Age salt-works in the central Cheshire area, and they continued to exploit these throughout their occupation. A Roman fort was therefore built at Northwich (*Condate*) in the late 1ˢᵗ century, close to where the east-west route from Manchester to Chester crossed the north-south route through Cheshire territory. However, at Middlewich (*Salinae*), an important Roman town grew up around the salt-works there, too, and the town became another hub of Roman Cheshire, with the Whitchurch (*Mediolanum*) to Manchester (*Mamucium*) route passing through from south-west to north-east, and the Chesterton to Wilderspool route passing through from south-east to north-west. However, Middlewich was also crossed on an east-to-west bearing, on a route that linked Buxton (*Aquae Arnemetiae*) to Chester (*Deva Victrix*). A late 1ˢᵗ century military enclosure on the northern edge of the Roman town also suggests that Middlewich was of strategic military importance as well.

The third hub of Roman salt-works was at Nantwich, while other rural salt springs were exploited in the south of the county, running from the Wych Valley in the south-west and eastwards through Shavington and Sandbach. The other hub of Roman industry in today's Cheshire territory was at Wilderspool in south Warrington, where late 20th century excavations have revealed the site of a large industrial and trading centre, built in the late AD 70s. Wilderspool was a trans-shipment point for the import and export of goods, with lead transported up the Mersey from Flintshire to be worked here, and product output including pans for the Cheshire salt-works. It is thought that glass and bronze was also worked here, with the latter providing equipment for the military in their campaigns further north. There were also iron-works and potteries here with those late 20th century excavations revealing the remains of Roman furnaces and large timber buildings which were probably smiths' workshops, while their pottery was distributed

---

Quirk Alert: *In Memoriam*
When the north wall of Chester (Deva Victrix) was repaired in the 4th century, hundreds of tombstones from the nearby Roman cemeteries were used as part of the construction!

---

as far north as Hadrian's Wall. Wilderspool therefore became the first industrial town of the North West, while nearby Runcorn was also home to lead smelting. By the 3rd century, though, the importance of Wilderspool and Runcorn had begun to decline.

In terms of the Roman road network, the main approach into Cheshire territory was via Ryknield Street. This road ran from Derby (*Derventio*) to Chesterton in north-west Staffordshire before entering Cheshire territory and then splitting, with the left-hand fork terminating at Chester (*Deva Victrix*), and the right-hand fork providing the route north into *Brigante* territory via Middlewich (*Salinae*), Northwich (*Condate*) and Warrington. However, Chester was the clear focal point and hub of the area, with roads heading southwards to Whitchurch (*Mediolanum*) via Tilston (*Bovium*), east-wards to Northwich (*Condate*), north-eastwards to Wilderspool and Warrington, northwards to Ince, north-westwards to the Wirral and Meols, and west-wards into Wales. To the south, Whitchurch (*Mediolanum*) was linked by a Roman road to Middlewich (*Salinae*), while the road from Chester to Northwich continued north-eastwards to Manchester (*Mamucium*). There were also a number of smaller roads, most of which are outlined on the map below.

One aspect of Roman Britain that Cheshire seems to have lacked was opulent villas, although this may have been due to its frontier-based location. The only defi-

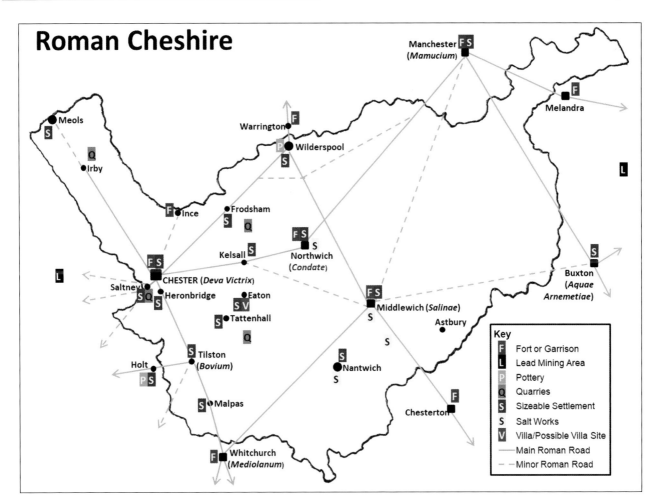

Roman Cheshire

nite site is at Eaton, near to Tarporley, although others are possible at nearby Tattenhall, and at Crewe Hall near Farndon. As for Roman governance, this largely included living in harmony with the local tribes-people, encouraging them to live their lives as they always had before the Roman invasion. As a result, the Romans had a reasonably willing workforce in their salt and lead mines, as well as out in the fields, while the Britons were able to live in a safer and more civilised manner, largely protected by the Roman garrisons; a clear step forward from Iron Age hilltop forts constantly under threat from rival tribes.

Quirk Alert: *Mersey Mystery*

An interesting theory is offered by James Stonehouse in his 1869 book, The Streets of Liverpool. *In his chapter called "The Silent Highway" (meaning the River Mersey), he suggests that the Mersey Estuary didn't exist in Roman Britain, theorising that a "stream" flowed between Biston and Wallasey hills. He also points out that there is no mention of such a significant estuary in the Antonine Itinerary (the 2nd or 3rd century register of Roman stations and distances), while he also mentions Ptolemy's map of Britain in about 150AD, which also fails to recognise the Mersey. He then goes on to theorise that the estuary was formed during the Dark Ages.*

What we do know, though, is that there was certainly an ancient forest growing from Meols on the north Wirral coast towards Formby, as tree stumps and roots were submerged in Liverpool Bay, as shown by photographs taken at very low tides at the end of the 19th century. However, the Mersey was almost certainly formed during the last Ice Age when deep glaciers moved inland from the Irish Sea, carving iceways later occupied by the Mersey and the Dee.

Finally for Roman Britain, although the legions had departed from Chester by 410, the civilian settlement continued largely as before, probably with some Roman veterans staying behind with their wives and children. Over time, many buildings would have fallen into disrepair, but some of the larger structures were maintained and are known to have survived for some time; indeed Bede (672-735) refers to Chester as a *civitas* in his works, indicating that the town remained an important centre. The town almost certainly retained its military and administrative control of the region, and the inhabitants of the Chester fortress probably continued to use its defences as protection from Celtic raiders from Wales and Ireland. All of this enabled a sub-Roman culture to survive throughout the 5th and 6th centuries, and possibly even into the 7th century in the area of Chester, as amphorae and archaeological remnants of a local Romano-British culture from this time have been found.

The sea-front at Meols on the north coast of the Wirral which had been an important port during Britain's Iron Age and was thought to be equally important in the century after the Romans departed from Britain.

The surviving heads of former Anglo-Saxon crosses at St John the Baptist church, Chester.

Overall, though, the Roman departure had a severe effect on Britain's economy which didn't return to similar levels until the late Anglo-Scandinavian period. It is thought that the Roman bureaucratic system designed to maintain Roman laws and to levy taxes, soon disintegrated. Naturally, this had a negative effect on trading and the economy reverted overwhelmingly back to agriculture, while the towns – which had essentially been bastions of Roman government and administration – saw their importance drop dramatically in tandem with their populations. One place that may have bucked this trend, though, was Meols on the north coast of the Wirral peninsula. There is growing evidence to suggest that the place became a substantial trading port during the 6th and 7th centuries, with links to both Europe and North Africa, importing luxury goods – and therefore suggesting some level of sophistication and wealth was sustained for at least a few lucky post-Roman inhabitants of Cheshire territory.

Of course, Cheshire's salt-works continued to be exploited, eventually providing these places with their modern names, courtesy of the Anglo-Saxon suffix *–wīc*, meaning "trading or industrial settlement". This indicates that places such as Northwich, Middlewich and Nantwich had become urban as well as industrial prior to the Norman Conquest. However, the colonisation of Cheshire territory by Anglo-Saxons didn't happen until the mid-7th century – a good century or so after they first arrived and settled in Lincolnshire and East Anglia before spreading out into the Midlands. This fact is strongly supported by lack of evidence of pagan Saxon burials in Cheshire territory, suggesting that when they finally arrived in the area, they had already converted to Christianity – something that didn't happen until the 650s. This means that Cheshire territory remained largely under Celtic influence between the Roman departure in 410 and the Mercian encroachment of the 640s and 650s. There may even have been Celtic Christian worship before the Saxons arrived, as evidenced by Eccleston, just south of Chester. This is because the place-name includes the Celtic element "eccles" which is derived from the Celtic word *eglēs*, meaning "British-Romano Christian church". Indeed, some historians believe that Eccleston is the site of one of the very earliest Christian churches in Britain, as there is evidence of potential Christian burials from as early as 390 AD; so these would certainly be the earliest known Christian burials in Cheshire. Furthermore, given that Eccleston is only ten miles north of the important Celtic monastery at Bangor-on-Dee, it seems reasonable to suggest a link.

There are also other Celtic or Old Welsh-related place-names in historical Cheshire territory too, such as Landican on the Wirral – possibly meaning "church of the deacon" and deriving from the words *llan* and *diacon*, the former being the Old Welsh word for "church"; Alan Crosby, in *A History of Cheshire*, suggests the alternative *Llan-tegan*, as in "the church of St Tegan". Other possible early Cheshire church dedications to Celtic saints include those at Heswall and Wallasey, while there are also references to a synod at

Chester in 603 or 604, at which St Augustine is said to have debated with representatives of the Welsh church.

All of this evidence suggests that western Cheshire had strong links with the Celtic kingdom of Powys, which had emerged after the Roman departure and covered part of the lands previously occupied by the Romano-British *Cornovii* tribe. However, before the Mercians arrived, it is likely that the rest of Cheshire was part of the territory of the Romano-British *Wrēocensǣte* tribe – as documented by the *Tribal Hidage*, which was compiled in Anglo-Saxon England between the 7th and 9th centuries. *Wrēocensǣte* territory also stretched southwards to cover large parts of modern-day Shropshire – including Wroxeter, which was probably the tribal capital. The name, therefore, probably means "the Wrekin-dwellers", referring to the distinctive hill in mid-Shropshire, close to Wroxeter and the site of a former Iron-Age hillfort.

In around 616, though, it is thought that the *Wrēocensǣte* were defeated by King Æthelfrith and the Northumbrians at a battle fought at Chester between Northumbria and the Kingdom of Powys. It is therefore likely that Cheshire territory became subject to Northumbrian rule for a short period.

It was also a long-held theory that Æthelfrith's victory at Chester was of immense strategic importance to the Saxons, as it resulted in the separation of the Britons in Wales from those in the north. However, that theory is now disputed, as shortly afterwards (still in 616), Æthelfrith was killed in another battle in today's Nottinghamshire territory by King Rædwald of East Anglia, plus there is scant evidence of Anglo-Saxon settlement within either Lancashire or Cheshire during this period. By the 630s, though, the *Wrēocensǣte* had become firmly aligned to Mercia after the combined forces of Mercia and Gwynedd defeated the Northumbrians at the Battle of Hatfield Chase in 633. At this time, the Kingdom of Mercia was centred on the Trent Valley and its tributaries, with its capital sited at Tamworth. The most authentic source of information at this time is again from the early 8th century Northumbrian monk and scholar, Bede, who describes Mercia as being divided in two by the River Trent. However, as Mercia expanded north-westwards towards North Wales, it brought the kingdom into conflict with its former ally, Gwynedd. It is for this reason that it is thought that Mercia could no longer allow the *Wrēocensǣte* tribe their autonomy, and the whole area therefore became absorbed into Mercia sometime in the mid-7th century. The Mercians then began constructing border defences, initially in the early 650s, with Wat's Dyke running southwards for 40 miles (64km) from Basingwerk on the Flintshire side of the River Dee, to Maesbury in Shropshire, all the time maintaining a trajectory of a few miles west of the current Welsh border – a border which remained intact until after the Norman Conquest.

Now formally part of Mercia, the Cheshire area was a frontier zone and was therefore regularly subject to

England in around 600 AD

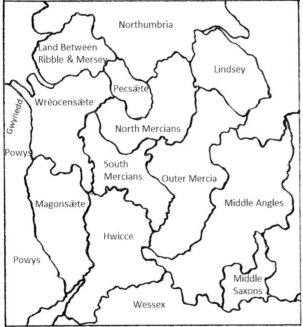

Chester's Seventh Century Saxon Churches and their Cathedral Successors

Pre-Saxon Era		
St Mary's		Thought to stand on the site of the Roman Christian basilica which is said to have been dedicated to St Peter and St Paul. Other conjecture is that it is located on the site of a Roman temple dedicated to Apollo, while 19th century Chester guide and author Thomas Hughes states that: "this temple had itself supplanted a still older fane of the superstitious Druids."
St John's		Possibly built on the site of an ancient 3rd or 4th century Celtic church, perched on a sandstone bluff high above the River Dee.
Saxon Era		
St Mary's	660	It is thought that a Saxon chapel was built on this site, probably by King Wulfhere of Mercia and, like its Roman predecessor, was also dedicated to St Peter and St Paul. It probably also incorporated part of its predecessor building, be that basilica or temple.
	875	The remains of St Werburgh (the niece of King Æthelred and daughter of King Wulfhere) were transferred from Hanbury church in Staffordshire, to the stronghold of Chester where they were buried. This was to safeguard the relics against Danish encroachment and likely desecration.
	907	Æthelflæd, Lady of the Mercians, re-dedicated the early Saxon church of St Peter and St Paul, to St Werburgh and St Oswald (the Northumbrian saint). The assumption is that the bones of St Werburgh were moved into the church at this point in time.
	907	In order to retain the dedication to St Peter, a new church at High Cross was dedicated to the saint.
	907	Chester is re-fortified by Æthelflæd against the Viking threat. Shortly afterwards, what is now St Werburgh's church was re-built and re-founded as a minster and collegiate church.
	958	King Edgar of England granted a charter and endowments to the church.
	975	A monastery was founded here and dedicated to St Werburgh and St Oswald.
	1057	Still a minster and collegiate church, St Werburgh's was restored by Earl Leofric of Mercia and his wife, Lady Godiva, and was also re-endowed.
St John's	689	A church dedicated to St John the Baptist was built here by King Æthelred of Mercia. Built of stone, it is thought that the church was also known as the Minster Church of West Mercia.
	973	As recorded by the *Anglo-Saxon Chronicle*, King Edgar of England held court at Chester in a palace located at what is now known as Edgar's Field and which is close to the Old Dee Bridge at Handbridge. He was then rowed up the Dee to St John's church by six tributary kings (some accounts say eight) where he received the homage of his vassal kings as *Rex Anglorum* (King of the English). At this time, King Edgar also gave grants and endowments to St John's.
	1057	Earl Leofric of Mercia re-endowed St John's.
Norman Era to Dissolution		
St Mary's	1090	Leofric's 1057-restored St Werburgh's church was razed to the ground by fire.
	1092	A Benedictine abbey was established in its place by Hugh D'Avranches (also known as Hugh Lupus), 1st Earl of Chester and nephew of William the Conqueror. It remained dedicated to St Werburgh and St Oswald and was constantly developed over the next two centuries.
	1250	The abbey church was rebuilt again from 1250 onwards in the Gothic style, and took around 275 years to complete. It is still dedicated to St Werburgh.
	1538	The abbey was dissolved and disbanded and the shrine of St Werburgh was desecrated.
	1541	St Werburgh's abbey was raised to the status of Chester Cathedral of the Church of England by order of Henry VIII, and the church dedication was changed to Christ and the Blessed Virgin. The probable reason for the cathedral status switch is that St Mary's was in a much better condition than St John's, at this time, due to its more recent rebuild.
St John's	1066	When the Normans conquered England, St John's became Chester Cathedral (but may already have been designated a cathedral during Saxon times).
	1075	Peter de Leia, Bishop of Lichfield, transfered his see from Lichfield to Chester.
	1075	Peter de Leia – the 1st Norman Bishop of Chester pulled down the Saxon minster church and commenced the build of his great Norman cathedral, which took around two hundred years to complete.
	1075	As well as being Chester Cathedral, St John's was also a collegiate church, and was known as the Cathedral and Collegiate Church of Chester until 1541.
	1102	The 2nd Norman Bishop of Chester, Roger de Limsey, removed himself to Coventry, but St John's retained its status as the northern centre of ecclesiastical jurisdiction and bishops retained their seat here, albeit principally residing in Lichfield. Inevitably, the build of St John's (still then known as Chester Cathedral) stalled, with the nave still without its roof.
	1190	Work resumed on St John's, but it isn't completed until the late 13th century.
	1348	Parts of St John's (Chester Cathedral) were described as *"comely and sumptuous fabric constructed of stone and wood of great breadth and length, but the same being ancient and decayed, repair was necessary or it would fall into irrevocable ruin"*.
	1468	The central tower fell down.
	1541	The college was dissolved and the bishops' seat was moved to the dissolved abbey of St Werburgh's which, in turn, was re-dedicated to Christ and the Blessed Virgin.

Welsh raids. This probably accounts for the economic stagnation that occurred in Cheshire territory during the 7th and 8th centuries, symbolically represented by the fact that Chester did not have a mint until 890. Nevertheless, it is known that an important religious institution was founded at Chester in 689, by King Æthelred of Mercia (675-704) and Bishop Wilfrid, and which later became the first Chester Cathedral in 1075. In fact, there were almost certainly *two* important Saxon churches in Chester as early as the 7th century, both with possible eye-opening predecessors, and both (rather confusingly) having successor churches which went on to become Chester Cathedral at different times. Today, the two churches are known as Christ and the Blessed Virgin Mary (the current Chester Cathedral and which we will refer to as St Mary's), and St John the Baptist church (the former Chester Cathedral and which we will refer to as St John's). The table shown left attempts to timeline their respective histories from the pre-Saxon era to the Dissolution of the Monasteries.

Returning now to the 7th century, and a number of other churches founded by the newly-converted Saxons were associated with St Chad, the Bishop of Lichfield from 669 to 672, including the chapel at Chadkirk near Stockport, which is thought to be one of the first Christian churches in Cheshire territory. Meanwhile, Welsh raids on Cheshire territory continued into the 8th century, and this eventually resulted in the construction of Offa's Dyke, thought to have been constructed by King Offa of Mercia (757-796), probably sometime during the 760s and 770s. Offa's Dyke was a large linear earthwork which still delineates much of the England/Wales border and, back then, delineated the Mercia/Powys border – although claims that it stretched from the Irish Sea to the Severn Estuary have been disputed in recent centuries. Also now disputed is

It is thought that these two ancient crosses in the centre of Sandbach market place were associated with one of the early Anglo-Saxon minster churches in the Cheshire area, and founded as early as the late 7th century. For many years, it was thought that the crosses were even older, and were erected to commemorate the conversion to Christianity in 653 of King Peada of Mercia. However, a more recent assessment has dated the larger cross to the early 9th century and the smaller to the mid-9th century. That still makes them around 1,200 years old, though – so small surprise that both cross shafts are scheduled ancient monuments and Grade I listed.

This ancient Anglo-Saxon cross is known as the Greenway Cross, and stands on the modern successor to an ancient trackway on the edge of the Peak District. From here, the road heads downhill from Shutlingsloe to Sutton Lane Ends, affording magnificent views across the Cheshire Plain. There were once many of these crosses in the western Peak District, but the Greenway Cross is one of very few that remains in its original position. Note the worn cross that has been carved onto the above facing side of the stone.

the date of construction of the earthwork, with recent excavations suggesting at least part of the structure was built much earlier than the 7th century, with some of the lower parts probably dating to early post-Roman Britain, some 300 years earlier. Regardless of the date of construction, the final earthwork was up to 65ft wide (20m) when including its flanking ditch, and 8ft high (2.4m). It was constructed across low ground, hills and rivers, always traversing around hills to the western (Welsh) side. The ditch of Offa's Dyke was also placed on the Welsh side with the displaced soil piled up into a bank on the Mercian side.

In addition to Offa's Dyke, the initial dating of Wat's Dyke to the 650s has also been disputed. Late 20th century scholars had suggested the later reign of King Æthelbald of Mercia (716-757), but excavations in the 1990s then once again theorised that lower-level construction took place in early post-Roman Britain, this thanks to evidence of a small fire site together with eroded shards of Romano-British pottery; quantities of charcoal discovered here have also been dated to between 411 and 561. Then in 2006, further excavations swung back to a much later date of 792-852, with the earlier date now thought to relate to a fire site which preceded the dyke. However, whatever the date of construction of both earthworks, they were: a) likely to have been constructed over many decades, b) would have been used by the Mercians to defend English territory, irrespective of who created them, and c) largely delineated England from Wales throughout the Anglo-Scandinavian period.

It was during the Mercian occupation of Cheshire territory that many of the county's villages were formed, numerous using the ubiquitous place-name suffixes of –tun/ton and –ham, deriving from the Anglo-Saxon words *tūn* (farmstead) and *hām* (homestead), respectively. Many of these places were located close to the courses of former Roman roads, which survived as trackways throughout the Anglo-Saxon period. A number of Anglo-Saxon settlements in Cheshire also formed around the focal point of ancient parishes where a mother or minster church presided over its parishioners – such as Eastham, Frodsham and Weaverham (note the –ham suffixes). Other place-names used the Anglo-Saxon suffix of –bury, deriving from the Old English word *burh*, meaning "fortified place or stronghold". Such places include Prestbury, Wrenbury and Wybunbury, all of which were the location of important early churches, too. It is reasonable to assume, therefore, that such places were the focus of the early Christian Church in the Cheshire area, and probably also centres of administration, too. The other main surviving evidence of Anglo-Saxon Cheshire are many decorative crosses, the most impressive of which are to be found in the town centre of Sandbach, while the remains of other crosses can be found in Sandbach St Mary's churchyard, Chester (St John's), Acton, Landican, Overchurch and Prestbury.

In 735, Chester was recorded as *Legacæstir*, the name meaning "city of the legions" with the latter part of the name deriving from the Old English word *cæster* (Roman town or city). The name was also to lend itself to the county name when it was created, probably by Edward the Elder in around 920 – although the name "Cheshire" doesn't appear until it shows up in the *Anglo-Saxon Chronicle* in 980, where it is recorded as *Legeceasterscir*.

In between those two recordings of 735 and 980, the county territory had endured the turmoil of constant Viking raids – although not to the extent of other more easterly areas of England. Nevertheless, Norse attacks on North Wales and Ireland began towards the end of the 8th century, and Danish raids on southern England followed shortly afterwards. However the major Danish incursions started in the 860s, a time which happened to coincide with the decline of Mercia as a major power in Britain. In 829, King Ecgbert of Wessex (802-839), defeated King Wiglaf of Mercia (827-829), and drove Wiglaf out of his kingdom, temporarily ruling Mercia himself for a year, before Wiglaf recovered the kingdom in 830 – albeit perhaps subject to Ecgbert's overlordship. It may even be that this was the point at which Mercia lost its kingdom status

---

Quirk Alert: *Hindsight*

According to legend, King Æthelred had a dream in 689, in which he was instructed by God to build a church in Chester "at the place where you see a white hind" – the latter being a beast symbolic of Christ and his presence on earth. In those days, the forest reached right up to the city walls and, sure enough, Æthelred spotted his white hind on the sandstone bluff above the River Dee – where the church of St John the Baptist was duly built.

The Chester monk Henry Bradshaw (d.1513) in his "Lyfe and History of St Werburghe" wrote the following verse about the founding of the church:

The yere of Grace syxe hundreth foure score and nyen,
As sheweth myne auctour a Bryton Giraldus, Kynge Ethelred,
myndynge most the blysse of Heven,
Edyfyed a College Church notable and famous,
In the suburbs of chester, pleasant and beautious,
In the honour of God, and the Baptyste Saynte John,
With help of bysshop Wulprye, and good exortacions.

completely as by the mid-to-late 9th century, Mercia was ruled by ealdormen serving under the throne of Wessex. The kingdom's weakness therefore meant that it was ripe for plunder when the Danes invaded in the late 860s. The *Anglo-Saxon Chronicle* describes "a great heathen army" which landed in East Anglia in 865, and over the next decade or so, took control of the majority of England's east coast and the East Midlands.

By 873, the Danes had established a base at Nottingham which left Mercia appealing to their old enemy, Wessex. Still the Danes pressed on, moving ever-closer to Cheshire territory. Under Ivar the Boneless they saw out the next winter of 873-874 further south-west at Repton in south Derbyshire, from where they subdued the surrounding countryside and destroyed the Mercian capital at Tamworth. King Burgred of Mercia was unable to dislodge them and was thus expelled by the Vikings who promptly installed Ceolwulf II as the new Mercian king. The Vikings then returned in 877 to partition Mercia with the west of the Mercian kingdom going to Ceolwulf II, while the eastern half was ruled directly by the Danes. Cheshire territory was now effectively under Viking control through their puppet-king, Ceolwulf II.

As the Danes established their control over Mercia, waves of settlers arrived from their homeland, and this is why so many Saxon settlements in the East Midlands underwent a transition from Saxon-ending *–tuns* and *–hams* to Danish-ending *bý* (farmstead, village or settlement), *thorp* (secondary settlement) and *holmr* (island or promontory). Very telling, though, is how few of these Danish suffixes are present in Cheshire territory, with the exception of a clutch of places on the Wirral peninsula, which is explained shortly. However, the Danes suffered a massive setback at the Battle of Eddington in 878 where they were defeated by King Alfred of Wessex. The Danes then agreed what has been termed both the Treaty of Wedmore and the Peace of Wedmore, perhaps in around 878 – although there is confusion as to the dates, with a later "Treaty of Alfred and Guthrum" possibly dating from as late as 886. Either way, the treaty essentially carved up England between Saxon and Dane – the south and the west to the Saxons of Wessex and Mercia, and the east to the Danes – and a temporary peace was established. Cheshire remained within Mercian territory, but was bordered to the north by the Danish Kingdom of York, while to the east was what became known as the Five Boroughs, the name deriving from the Old English word *burh* meaning "fortified place or stronghold", and the strongholds in question being at Derby, Nottingham, Lincoln, Leicester and Stamford. The Five Boroughs became occupied by separate divisions of the Danish army, and the Danes introduced their native law and customs known as the Danelaw, but with all Danish areas subject to their overlords in *Jorvik* (York).

Despite the Treaty of Wedmore, the Danes renewed their attacks on Mercia in the late 9th century. Cheshire's new position was therefore perilous, and the area

Above: *Fragments of Anglo-Saxon stones in St Mary's churchyard at Sandbach.*
Right: *These stunning Anglo-Saxon carvings can be found inside St Mary's church at Acton, near Nantwich.*

became subject to frequent Danish raids which culminated in the taking of Chester in 893 by Danes attacking from the east. On this occasion, King Alfred of Wessex marched north, seized all the cattle and laid waste to the surrounding land to drive the Danes out, and Chester was re-taken for Mercia in around 895. Archaeological investigation suggests that this was also the point at which Chester began to experience re-urbanisation. Unfortunately for the town's new inhabitants, a new wave of attacks were launched at this point, not from the Danes to the north or east, but from Irish Norsemen from the west. Expelled from Dublin at the turn of the 10th century, these people began to settle in the Wirral, west Lancashire and north Wales in around 902. Conscious of having to deal with threats on two fronts, the Mercians decided to broker a peace agreement with these Norsemen, and therefore allowed them to settle in the Wirral. This accounts for Danish place-names on the peninsula, such as Thingwall, which derives from the Old Scandinavian word *thing-vǫllr*, meaning "field where an assembly meets", while within five miles are Greasby, Frankby and Irby, all of which include the Danish-ending *bý* meaning "farmstead, village or settlement".

By this stage, Mercian links with Wessex had been cemented further by the marriage of Earl Æthelred of Mercia to Æthelflæd, daughter of King Alfred. In 907, Æthelflæd began converting Chester into a stronghold or Anglo-Saxon *burh*. The walls of the former Roman fortress were repaired and incorporated into new defences, almost certainly to the north and east of the city, with the River Dee providing the remaining defence as it had in Roman times. The walls were also extended and ended up enclosing an area of around 100 acres, whilst a castle was built overlooking the river in the south-west quarter.

As well as Chester, fortifications were built to the south of the River Mersey, which now marked part of the northern frontier between Anglo-Saxon and Danish England. In 914 a *burh* was constructed at Eddisbury and was followed in 915 by another at Runcorn, while Thelwall and Manchester were fortified in 919. Naturally, the Eddisbury fortress re-used the hill's former Iron Age hillfort as a military outpost for Chester, while the Runcorn fortress was built on Castle Rock, the prominent headland which projects into the Mersey at its narrowest point. At Runcorn, a new minster church was also founded and the *burh* had an administrative role, the intention probably being to give birth to a new urban centre – but which didn't quite happen at this time.

On Æthelred's death in 911, Æthelflæd ruled Mercia as the 'Lady of the Mercian's' and, as well as fortifying Cheshire territory, she also set about fortifying Mercia's eastern borders. By 913 she had established another *burh* at Tamworth, significantly on the edge of Danelaw territory. Along with her brother (Edward the Elder), Æthelflæd then launched her first offensive in July 917 and expelled the Danes from the fortress at Derby and annexed the whole region back into English Mercia – a region which, according to the *Anglo-Saxon Chronicle*, included Derby "together with the region which it controlled", and which is likely to have been much of what we know as the historic county of Derbyshire. This suggests that Cheshire was also a county in its own right by this stage; equally significant was that the immediate Danish threat to the east had now been removed.

At the same time, Edward the Elder of Wessex had re-captured East Anglia and by 918, Leicester and Nottingham had fallen to the Saxons as well. However, the year 918 also marked the death of Æthelflæd. She was succeeded as Lady of the Mercians by her daughter, Ælfwynn, but a few months later, in December 918, Edward the Elder deposed her and seized the Mercian throne for himself. His seizure of power caused discontent amongst the north Mercians, more so when he began to advance northwards into Lancashire and westwards into Wales in an attempt to consolidate his power. As a result, there was open revolt in Cheshire against Edward's rule between 922 and 924, and local insurgents allied themselves with the Welsh against whom Edward was attacking. Things could have turned pretty nasty for Cheshire at this point, but Edward rather conveniently died in 924, and at Farndon (in Cheshire), as it happens. Even more fortunate was that his son, Æthelstan, had been brought up in Mercia and was therefore more in tune with local feeling. There wasn't, therefore, the expected backlash, and he even went so far as to levy less tax on Cheshire than most other counties, thus helping to further integrate Cheshire into Mercia.

By 925, Cheshire was even more secure with the five *burhs* guarding the Mersey now part of a wider strategy which included the fortification of Rhuddlan, Bakewell

These two shafts of late Anglo-Saxon crosses are known as the Bowstones, and they stand in a remote position a mile or so south-east of Lyme Park.

and possibly Penwortham outside Preston. When in 926, York eventually fell to Edward's son and successor, King Æthelstan (924-927), Æthelstan became the first Saxon ruler since King Offa (757-796) to hold complete control of southern, central and northern England, and proclaimed himself "King of all Britain" – at which point, the Scots and Welsh presumably raised eyebrows!

During the 930s, there were occasional Norse raids, with the most prominent in 937 resulting in a big battle at *Brunanburgh*, commonly thought to be at Bromborough on the Wirral, and which was a crushing victory for the English. However, some of those defeated Norsemen actually settled and integrated with the Saxons and even benefitted them – as Cheshire began to undergo an economic revival in the mid-10th century with Chester, in particular, seeing a rapid increase in trade and population. It is also known that Æthelflæd set up a mint at Chester in the early 10th century and that this soon became one of the most important mints in England.

We've already touched on King Edgar (959-975), as he held court at Chester in 973, after which he was rowed up the Dee to the church of St John the Baptist. Here, eight kings from north and west Britain are said to have sworn fealty and allegiance to him, and among them it is thought were Kynath, king of the Scots, Malcolm, king of the Cumbrians, Maccus, king of several isles, and five others, called Dufnall, Siferth, Huwall, Jacob and Juchill. As he entered the church, Edgar is reported to have said that with so many kings' allegiance, his successors could surely boast themselves to be kings of the English. As for Chester, it is thought that this episode meant that it was regarded as a north-western capital of England, perhaps even of Britain.

King Edgar died in 975, and five years later in 980, Cheshire is formally recorded as a county in the *Anglo-Saxon Chronicle*. However, it is fairly widely accepted that most English counties were created towards the end of the reign of Edward the Elder (899-924). It was probably Edward who also secured the "Cheshire panhandle" for the county, this being the strip of land to the north-east of the county around Longdendale, and which separated Derbyshire from Lancashire until 1974. His likely reasoning was that by securing Longdendale for Cheshire – and hence for Saxon-controlled Mercia – this meant that a strategic route into Yorkshire was secured by which an invasion into Yorkshire could potentially have been launched.

The late 10th century saw a fresh outbreak of Danish military activity, with 980 in particular being a bad year for Viking raids. At around the same time, Ethelred II used Chester as a naval base to tackle renewed Norse attacks from the Irish Sea. However, his campaign bore little success, while his government delegated owner-ship of large royal estates around the country to a number of leading nobles. In the early 11th century, Cheshire was therefore under the control of Eadric Streona, Earl of Mercia, who governed from his head-quarters at Chester from 1007. The earl also governed Shropshire and Staffordshire, and these three counties thus began to build a separate identity towards the middle of the 11th century. Leofric of Mercia (1030-1057) was head of one of the most powerful noble houses in England during his tenure, and his rule of the three counties actually saw Leofric conducting his own foreign policy, including negotiations with the princes of north Wales – which meant that the king's direct writ was rarely recognised in Cheshire during these times. This autonomy was eventually challenged by the Godwins under Edward the Confessor (1042-1066), but in the time leading up to the Norman Conquest, Leofric's grandson, earl Edwin (1062-1070), still reigned supreme in Cheshire. His days of rule, however, were somewhat numbered!

Chester Castle, first built in 907 by Æthelflæd, and then re-built in 1070 as a hastily constructed timber fortress by Hugh d'Avranches, first Earl of Chester. It was later re-built in stone in the early 12th century.

Part of the surviving earthworks of Aldford Castle, built in stone during the early 12th century by Richard de Aldford.

From the Conquest to the Wars of the Roses

Following the Norman Conquest of 1066, most English counties were rapidly subjected to a ruthless overhaul of ruling class and high clergy. In other words, out went the previous Anglo-Scandinavian incumbents, to be replaced by Norman gentry and bishops. This wasn't the case in Cheshire, though, or in the rebellious north of England – at least not for another three to four years, anyway. Between 1066 and 1070, William the Conqueror meted out savage and barbarous acts as part of his "harrying of the north" strategy, with the worst atrocities committed in Yorkshire and Northumbria during the summer of 1069. Vast areas were ravaged, the aim being to lay waste to the northern shires in order to eliminate further rebellion. As well as fortified buildings, William's army also destroyed the homes, stock and crops of ordinary people, as well as the means of food production and many starved to death as a result. William's armies then crossed the Pennines into Cheshire where a rebellion had broken out in the autumn of 1069. The uprising was brutally crushed, and much of the county then devastated in a similar fashion to Yorkshire and Northumbria. William carried

on down into Staffordshire during 1070 delivering similar retribution, and in Cheshire and Staffordshire, the destruction was so widespread, that one chronicler records "a huge crowd of old men, young men, women and children wandering as far south as Evesham Abbey in search of food".

The most interesting commentary of Cheshire during these times comes from Domesday Book, which was compiled 20 years later in 1086 – as it describes many Cheshire places as *wasta* – meaning "abandoned or useless land" – quite literally, "wasteland". It is therefore almost certain that these were vast tracts of land laid waste by William's armies in 1069 and 1070, and which had still not recovered 16 years later. The other pointer to this almost certainly being the case is that estates were valued in Domesday Book for tax purposes, and the survey describes their worth in 1086 and their previous worth in 1066. The vast majority of places see their 1086 value only a fraction of that in 1066, reflecting a drastic reduction in value and produc-tivity. Furthermore, there is a visible audit trail of *wasta* heading down into the county from the north-east at Woodhead, along the Longdendale Valley and into Stockport and then Macclesfield, with the concentra-tion of devastation around the latter town particularly acute. It is likely, therefore, that the way of life in north-

This is what is known as the Agricola Tower, a stone gateway which is a surviving part of Chester Castle built by the Normans in the early 12th century. On the first floor of the Agricola Tower is a Norman chapel which is dedicated to St Mary de Castro.

then dole out the rest of the various manors to a number of prominent Norman nobles. What played into his hands here, though, was that the lands of Cheshire were already allocated to one person – namely, Edwin, Earl of Mercia – hence 1071 saw Cheshire effectively handed over from Edwin to Hugh – this after Edwin was killed by the Normans on attempting to flee to Scotland following the end of the Siege of Chester. Domesday Book confirms the landowning position, revealing that even in 1086, William I did not hold any land in Cheshire.

Hugh d'Avranches was also named by William as 1st Earl of Chester, and he and his successors wielded enormous power in English politics from the late 11th to the 13th century, leading to a gradual increase in privileges for the county that they ruled. The more granular government of Cheshire's parishes, though, still followed the model used by other counties, although the earls of Chester certainly retained powers that would be considered "royal" elsewhere. For example, local courts were led by the earl's justiciar; similarly, the earl's chancery and exchequer at Chester Castle enjoyed exemption from certain monetary and military obligations, plus they also enjoyed local powers of taxation, too.

Despite the brutal suppression of rebellion in the north, William's position was still in the balance during the early years of his rule. Therefore William commissioned the build of a series of Norman castles to which he could deploy garrisons that would be handily placed to quell any further uprisings. These castles were to become the most symbolic representation of Norman power, and unsurprisingly, the first of them in Cheshire territory was built at Chester – this in 1070 by Hugh d'Avranches, 1st Earl of Chester. This was a typical hastily-constructed, early Norman motte and bailey castle, using an earthen mound topped by a timber palisade and tower, and it was located on a rocky outcrop looking out over the River Dee, outside the old Roman fortress walls. The wooden castle was replaced by a stone one in the early 12th century, and its new stone tower became known as the Flag Tower; at the same time, a stone gateway to the inner bailey was also built. The stone gateway became known as the Agricola Tower, and survives today along with a chapel on its first floor which is dedicated to St Mary de Castro. Meanwhile in the 13th century, the walls of an outer bailey were built, the gateway in the Agricola Tower was blocked up and residential accommodation, including a Great Hall, was built along the south wall of the inner bailey.

It was also in the early 12th century that Chester's former Roman and Saxon city walls were re-fortified to the north and the east, while in the 1120s, a new southern stretch of the wall was built at the same time as the castle rebuild. The remaining western wall, which completed the 2-mile circuit, was built at the end of the 12th century, and the final fortification was guarded by ten towers. As for Chester Castle, royal apartments

east Cheshire was decimated for decades after 1070, an area of upland where farming was already as tough as it gets.

The other area of Cheshire that was acutely devastated by William I was the city of Chester. Again, there is evidence of destruction on a disastrous scale, with Domesday Book using the term "thoroughly devastated". Domesday Book also reveals that whereas in 1066 there were 487 houses, by 1071 there were only 282 houses – a number which hadn't increased by 1086. The prosperity of the city, therefore, was probably at its lowest ebb ever during those last four decades of the 11th century, and it would be of little consolation to its inhabitants that the city was the last in England to fall to the Normans, nearly four years after the Battle of Hastings.

Having asserted his control over these now-ravaged areas of England, William proceeded to dispossess the former landlords – most notably Edwin, Earl of Mercia – and handing ownership to his nephew, Hugh d'Avranches, also known as Hugh Lupus (Hugh the Wolf) and, somewhat more disparagingly, Hugh the Fat! The interesting thing about the land designation in Cheshire, though, is that it pretty much all went to Hugh d'Avranches, whereas other counties tended to see the king himself take large tranches of land and were added for Edward I (1272-1307) and Queen Eleanor towards the end of the 13th century, as the castle became a regular stopping point for the king in his wars with Wales. At the same time, a new gateway to the outer bailey was constructed, flanked by two half-drum towers along with a drawbridge over a 26ft deep moat (8m), while internally, a new chapel and stables were added.

Other early Norman motte and bailey castles were built close to the Welsh border at Aldford and Malpas – although back then, the border was actually further west than it is today. As with all early Norman castles, Aldford was rebuilt in stone in the early 12th century, and was built by the resident Norman lord, Richard de Aldford, overlooking a ford on the River Dee. Some fragments of the bailey stonework do survive today along with some prominent earthworks, with the motte visible to the north of St John's church – while the church itself stands on the site of the infilled bailey ditch. It is a similar story regarding the remains of Malpas Castle, too, with only earthworks surviving to the north of St Oswald's church.

In the years following the Norman Conquest, more than a dozen further motte and bailey timber-based castles were built in Cheshire territory. Many were simply for military and strategic purposes, so when the country began to settle down towards the end of the 11th century, a number of them were left as they were to eventually fall into disrepair. Like Chester and Aldford, though, a number of other more important castles were rebuilt in stone in the early 12th century, including those at Halton and Frodsham. Both of these castles still had a military and strategic role to play, with each perched on a prominent hill above the Mersey lowlands, guarding the ancient fords at Runcorn and Hale. Halton Castle was almost certainly built by the first Baron of Halton, Nigel de Cotentin, a title bestowed upon the barons not by the king, but by the effective ruler of Cheshire in the late 11th century, Hugh d'Avranches, 1st Earl of Chester. Again, the first castle was timber-based with the second sandstone-based and built in the early 12th century.

Also built on the coast was a castle at Shotwick,

around 4 miles north-west of Chester – again built by the first Earl of Chester. It is thought that this castle was actually built of stone the *first* time around, but a little later in the 11th century, perhaps around 1090. It was actually built right on the Dee estuary, protecting a quay which was used as an embarkation point for Ireland, whilst also guarding a tidal ford on the original course of the River Dee. Nothing remains today of the castle other than some prominent earthworks. However, excavations have revealed that the castle was hexagonal and possessed several circular towers along with a square keep, while it also possessed two large defensive ditches that became flooded at high tide. Not that its location is on the estuary today, though – this thanks to land reclamation in the 18th century after the Dee was diverted to the south along a man-made canalised section; so Shotwick's earthworks now lie around 3 miles inland! Shotwick Castle was also visited in 1284 by Edward I, but the castle soon lost its strategic importance and its surrounding land was turned into a royal deer park for Edward III (1327-1377) who used the castle as a hunting lodge.

Probably the best-known castle in Cheshire isn't Norman at all – this being Beeston Castle for which construction was commenced in 1220 by Ranulf de Blondeville, 6th Earl of Chester. It sits on top of the dramatic Beeston Crag in central Cheshire which rears up to 350ft (107m) above the Cheshire Plain. Unlike the other castles in Cheshire, this one wasn't built as a strategic castle in the wars against the Welsh, but was built well back from the frontier, probably as a symbol of Ranulf's power, but perhaps also to protect the route through the mid-Cheshire ridge against other aggressors. This was the age of baronial struggles, and Ranulf had supported King John during the First Baron's War of 1215 to 1217. Supporters of John had been granted land, goods and offices, and in Ranulf's case, this included becoming 1st Earl of Lincoln, too. By the 1220s, though, the Crown saw these gains as a threat to Royal authority, and they therefore became a target for the king's justiciar.

At the same time, Ranulf also very cannily arranged a truce with the Welsh prince, Llewellyn the Great

Part of the surviving remains of Halton Castle, originally constructed of wood in 1071, and then re-built in stone in the early 12th century.

Some of the surviving earthworks of Shotwick Castle built sometime around 1090, when Shotwick was still on the Dee estuary.

(1173-1240), before he departed to join the Fifth Crusade in 1218. On his return, he arranged for the marriage of Llewellyn's daughter, Helen, to his nephew and heir, John le Scot, and then set about building his castle – thus negating any threat to his lands from the west. The impressive gatehouses in the inner and outer ward were probably built during the 1220s along with the tower to the east of the gatehouse, and throughout this time, Ranulf was able to secure and retain most of his lands and possessions. However, these passed to John le Scot who later died without an heir – and hence all of the Earldom of Cheshire's possessions – including all of the aforementioned castles – passed to Henry III after all, on John's death in 1237. Henry then appointed John de Lacy, 2nd Earl of Lincoln as "custodian of the county", thus including the castles at both Beeston and Chester.

Of the numerous castles built in Cheshire during Norman times, many initially performed the main function of a military and strategic role. However, they gradually also became centres for administration as well, which in medieval times was based on the system of hundreds and lordships – as they were throughout the rest of England. At Domesday Book, Cheshire territory was divided up into ten hundreds, but back then, it also included two other hundreds that today are the other side of the Welsh border – these being the

BEESTON CASTLE.

hundreds of Atiscros and Exestan, territory which is now in Flintshire and Wrexham. It is also thought that these Norman hundreds were based on Anglo-Saxon hundreds that covered very similar territory and which were based on the great parishes of the early Saxon minster churches; some even believe that these parishes were based on even earlier Romano-British subdivisions. There were some later modifications to the hundred boundaries of Norman times, but they largely remained the same until the late 19th century. As for the land to the north of the Mersey, this is referred to in Domesday Book as *Inter Ripam et Mersam* ("land between Ribble and Mersey"). Interestingly, this area was included in the returns for Cheshire, although it is likely that the north Cheshire boundary was still the River Mersey, even in 1086. Any argument as to whether this territory belonged to Cheshire was finally closed down in 1182 when it was formally aligned to the new county of Lancashire.

We now return to Cheshire's *western* boundary, for during the reign of King Stephen (1135-54), a large portion of Cheshire's Duddestan Hundred on the English side of Offa's Dyke, was transferred to Wales, and later became known as Maelor Saesneg. As for Atiscross and Exestan, the majority of these hundreds became part of the new county of Flintshire when it was formed in 1284, this following Edward I's defeat of

Part of the outer curtain wall of Beeston Castle, built in the 1220s by Ranulf de Blondeville, 6th Earl of Chester.

View towards the inner ward of Beeston Castle, including the impressive gatehouse. The inner ward sits at the top of Beeston Crag.

The curtain wall survives to its full height here at the south-eastern corner of the inner ward.

Looking towards the south-eastern corner of the inner ward from the inside.

the Principality of Wales and the resulting Statute of Rhuddlan. Flintshire thus became formally under English control and the administrative system of this part of north Wales became anglicised. The effect on England was that it pushed her border further west; the effect on Cheshire was that its size was reduced by the loss of most of Atiscross and Exestan to Flintshire. It was also at this point that Flintshire took control of the southern part of the former Cheshire hundred of Dudestan to form the aforementioned detached part of the county known as Maelor Saesneg. However, in 1397, Maelor Saesneg was merged back into what by then had become the County Palatine of Cheshire, whilst the county itself was promoted to the rank of "principality". This was thanks to the support that the Cheshire Guard had given to King Richard II (1377-1399), with the king himself also taking on the additional title of "Prince of Chester". No other English county has ever been honoured in this way, although the title was lost after Richard's defeat to Henry Percy in 1399. As for Maelor Saesneg, its territory was included in a new incarnation of Flintshire in 1536, albeit as an exclave, surrounded by Cheshire, Shropshire and Denbighshire. This also explains why Flintshire appears twice on pre-1974 maps, because the Hundred of Maelor as it was originally known, later became known as "Flintshire Detached".

As well as the overhaul of gentry, the other big overhaul imposed following the Norman Conquest was of religious institutions. When William I became king in 1066, Cheshire was part of the diocese of Lichfield, which covered roughly the same area as pre-850 Mercia. The first Norman bishop of Lichfield was Peter de Leia, and he decided to move his see to Chester in 1075. This was therefore the point at which the collegiate church of St John's became re-designated as Chester Cathedral. Over the next two decades, the new Chester Cathedral was substantially rebuilt by Peter to ensure it was more in keeping with its new status. However, Peter's successor, Robert de Limesey, decided to transfer the see to Coventry in 1102 – probably influenced by Chester's remoteness and its proximity to potential Welsh trouble – and therefore the first diocese of Chester only lasted for 27 years. Thereafter, Chester was part of the diocese of Coventry and Lichfield, although the bishops of the new diocese still retained the title of Bishop of Chester as well. The bishops also retained a palace in Chester, and one thing that Domesday Book also reveals is that the bishop owned 56 houses in the city too – a questionably large number considering the dramatic reduction in Chester houses between 1066 and 1086, caused by the harrying of William I in 1070! By 1315, the archdeaconry of Chester – which covered Cheshire and south Lancashire – had acquired considerable independence from Coventry and Lichfield, largely due to the sprawling and unwieldy nature of the diocese.

As well as St John's, St Werburgh's and three other churches in Chester, Domesday Book reveals that there were 28 other churches in the county of Cheshire,

The late Norman chapel at Prestbury survives completely intact in the churchyard of St Peter's church. The frontage includes the Norman doorway (shown above) with typical Norman zigzags and beaked heads as well as a tympanum. Above the arch is a row of saints.

The remains of the original Norman church of St John the Baptist in Chester, ruins of which can be found to both the west and east of the later medieval St John the Baptist church.

although this is almost certainly not a definitive list. In addition, some unfortunate churches had been destroyed during the "harrying", particularly those down that north-eastern corridor, including those at Prestbury and Macclesfield. Meanwhile, pre-Norman crosses have been found at other churches, such as at Cheadle and Over, that *weren't* recorded in Domesday Book – so these churches may well have been destroyed, too. Of course, after 1066, new churches were also founded, such as those at Bromborough, Bruera, Christleton, Coddington, Nantwich and Shocklach, meaning that by 1200 there were at least 65 churches and chapels in Cheshire, while a much later survey of 1541 lists 94.

In terms of Cheshire's religious houses, there was a stark contrast between Cheshire in the north-west of England and Lincolnshire on the opposite east coast. The latter county was home to many dozens of both pre-Conquest and medieval religious institutions, of many different denominations, but Cheshire had relatively few. This is probably down to two factors. Firstly, the Cheshire area did not have a monastic tradition from Anglo-Scandinavian times, and secondly, because the county was ruled by largely one family throughout the medieval centuries – they being the Earls of Mercia pre-Conquest and the Earls of Chester post-Conquest – and sponsoring monastic foundations could have potentially undermined both their possessions and their wealth. That's not to say that they completely disregarded religious institutions. After it had been razed to the ground by fire in 1090, Hugh d'Avranches, 1st Earl of Chester, re-built the late 7th century collegiate church of St Werburgh's, starting in 1092, and transformed it into a Benedictine abbey. He also re-endowed St Werburgh's with major estates from the Chester vicinity, while his successors continued to donate property to the abbey as well. This enabled the abbey to take advantage of the wool industry and maritime trade with Ireland throughout the medieval period, while also operating lucrative fisheries on the River Dee. Its continued wealth meant that it was always in a position to rebuild and restore, when necessary, which ultimately led to St Werburgh's being raised to the status of "Chester Cathedral of the Church of England" by order of Henry VIII in 1541, this also being when the church dedication was changed to Christ and the Blessed Virgin. Of course, three years earlier it had fallen victim to the Dissolution and, with 28 monks and an income of almost £1100, it was by far the largest and wealthiest religious house in Cheshire.

Another small religious institution founded in Chester was the Benedictine nunnery of St Mary's, founded in the mid-12th century by Ranulf de Gernon, 4th Earl of Chester, and the nunnery survived thanks to the support of a number of prosperous local families whose daughters had joined St Mary's. It was far-from wealthy though, with some of the nuns having to beg for food by the mid-13th century when the nunnery fell into severe financial crisis. It survived though, again thanks to local donations. Donations were also responsible for sustaining the three medieval friaries in Chester as well, which belonged to the Carmelite, Dominican and Franciscan orders, the latter two institutions having been founded in the Watergate area of the city in 1236 and 1237, respectively.

Aside from the five Chester-based institutions, most other religious medieval institutions in Cheshire were very poor and not noted for their learning, with many folding or moving to other sites elsewhere in England. The three exceptions were the Savigniac/Cistercian Combermere Abbey in the south of the county, the Augustinian Norton Priory in the north, and the

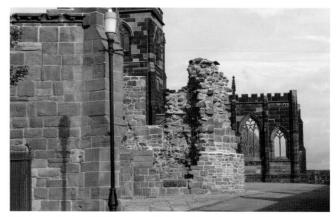

The remains of Birkenhead Priory, founded on this spot as a Benedictine monastery in the 1150s. It is the oldest-surviving building on Merseyside.

Cistercian Vale Royal Abbey in the centre, each of which were the only other Cheshire religious institutions with significant estates in the county.

Combermere Abbey was founded in 1133 by Hugh Malbank, Baron of Nantwich, and originally belonged to the Savigniac order, but which merged with the Cistercian order in 1147. Its initial endowments included several Cheshire villages, four churches in Cheshire and Staffordshire, land at Burleydam, various woods, and a mill and fishery at Chorley. Most important of all, though, was the grant of a quarter of Nantwich, including important salt-works, which kept the abbey afloat during the 13th century along with the wool it made from its sheep. Combermere continued to acquire assets in Cheshire and its surrounding counties up until the mid-13th century. However, it suffered from gross financial mismanagement in the late 13th and 14th centuries, and in 1275, the abbey was in such a state of debt that its management was moved from the abbot to the Lord Chancellor and Bishop of Bath and Wells, Robert Burnell, who contributed £213 towards the abbey's upkeep. Alas, from this point onwards, the abbey earned a reputation for poor discipline and violent disputes with both lay people and other abbeys, and it was frequently in royal custody. Despite this, the abbey was still Cheshire's third largest when it was dissolved in 1538.

The original Norton Priory was founded by William FitzNigel, Constable of Chester and 2nd Baron Halton, in 1115 on the south bank of the River Mersey where it narrows to form the Runcorn Gap – and therefore the only practical site where the Mersey could be crossed between Warrington and Birkenhead. However, in 1134 William fitz William, the 3rd Baron Halton, moved the priory to a site in Norton, a village three miles to the east of Runcorn. Norton Priory also had generous land endowments, including salt-works and local churches, but as well as in Cheshire, the priory also received land endowments in Lancashire, Nottinghamshire, Lincolnshire and Oxfordshire. It has been estimated that the original community would have consisted of 12 canons and the prior, but as the buildings expanded

THE FABULOUS NORTON PRIORY

All photographs shown here are © copyright of the Norton Priory Museum Trust.

Norton Priory at Runcorn is the site of the most important monastic remains in Cheshire, and the site is also the most excavated monastic establishment in Europe. The priory was originally founded by William FitzNigel in the early 12th century, while after the Dissolution of the Monasteries in the late 1530s the property fell into the hands of the Brooke family who converted much of the priory remains into their 16th century mansion. Today, the site is owned by the Norton Priory Museum Trust, who has done an outstanding job of preserving this very important historic establishment. The Trust has generously given permission to include various photographs of the priory remains and exhibits from their museum. Above left: *Surviving 13th century arches.* Above right: *This is a view of the surviving undercroft, built in the late 12th century. It would have been used to store food, drink and cloth and was looked after by the cellarer. The undercroft was later incorporated into the Tudor and Georgian buildings, while in 1868, Sir Richard Brooke, the 7th Baronet, converted it into the main entrance hall.* Below left: *Another view of Norton Priory's surviving undercroft.* Below right: *Surviving arches preserved in the Norton Priory Museum.*

Left and right are two Norman doorways – although only the one on the right is the original 12th century article; the one on the left was fashioned to lend symmetry to the porch in 1868, but which has been splendidly reproduced. Meanwhile, in the centre is a remarkable sculpture of St Christopher which is of international significance as it is one of the most outstanding examples of medieval sculpture anywhere in the world. It dates from between 1375 and 1400 and was probably made when the priory was raised to the status of an abbey in 1391. Post-Dissolution, the Brooke family maintained the statue down the centuries.

throughout the 12th century, this increased to around 26 members by the late 12th century, making it one of the largest houses in the Augustinian order.

Despite the major problems of the 14th century – such as sheep murrain, famine and the Black Death –

Norton Priory flourished to the extent that it was upgraded from a priory to an abbey in 1391. However, the abbey went into decline in the 15th century, with frequent floods reducing its income, and by 1429 the church and other abbey buildings were in a bad way.

After the Dissolution, the abbey was eventually purchased by Sir Richard Brooke in 1545, who built a Tudor house on the site, incorporating surviving parts of the abbey.

Finally, Vale Royal Abbey was founded considerably later in the 1270s, by Prince Edward, the future Edward I, and was intended to be an abbey on a sensational scale making it the largest Cistercian abbey in England. The reason for the ambition was due to the Prince having survived a terrible storm at sea, during which time he had vowed to God that if he survived, he would found an abbey of unprecedented size as thanks for his life. The original abbey site at Darnhall was moved to Whitegate in 1276. The finest royal masons of the day were engaged to build a huge and elaborate gothic church on the scale of a cathedral, while the now King Edward I greatly expanded the initial endowment and issued large donations of cash and materials. Alas, the schemes were too grand, while the king's coffers began to dwindle as he built his castles in Wales to cement his victory there. As a result, and despite a healthy abbey trade in wool and wine, the abbey church was never completed, although the monks managed to complete the east end of the church by the 1330s; the rest remained a shell. There was a brief resurgence of hope in the 1350s when the Black Prince took an interest and donated substantial funds, and work recommenced, starting with the nave. However, a terrible gale in 1360 destroyed the partially constructed nave, and thereafter, the finances of the abbey deteriorated dramatically. The abbey was dissolved in 1538, after which ownership passed to Thomas Holcroft who then built a large mansion on the site, incorporating the abbey's south and west cloister ranges, the abbot's house and the monks' dining hall along with their kitchen. The house was badly damaged during the English Civil War, and extensively altered and improved during the 19th century. Nothing remains of Edward I's great church.

Cheshire also had a number of religious hospitals, such as the leper institution founded as St Giles' at Broughton in the mid-12th century. The hospital eventually developed into almshouses for the poor and because of its good work, was spared during the Dissolution. Also in Chester was St John's Hospital, founded in 1190 by Ranulf de Blondeville, 6th Earl of Chester, and which actually survives today as almshouses – although not the medieval incarnation; that was destroyed during the English Civil War. Of the other medieval hospitals in the county, of particular note was the one at Denhall near Burton on the Wirral, which helped shipwrecked mariners and poor travellers from Ireland.

The Normans were well-known for their hunting, and most English counties had what were known as royal forests – areas outside the usual system of law and subject to the king's personal authority. In Cheshire, though, matters were slightly different as the forests didn't belong to the king – again down to this quirk from post-Conquest, whereby the Earls of Cheshire owned most of the land within the county. However, royal or not, the harsh forest laws still applied in Cheshire and were administered by the earl's officials in Chester, who presided over the three medieval hunting forests in the county: Delamere, Macclesfield and Wirral, and which, at their optimum period, covered around 40 per cent of the county. As the forestry offices were hereditary, this offered a platform for centuries of wealth for certain families, with the Grosvenors controlling the northern half of Delamere from the mid-12th century, while the Davenports held office in Macclesfield.

In terms of coverage, Delamere consisted of a northern and southern half, divided at Tarporley and Vale Royal, with the northern half (known as

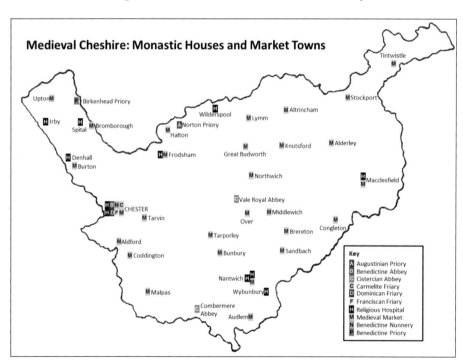

The above map shows the location of Cheshire's monastic houses and religious institutions. However, as these institutions are relatively sparse in Cheshire, the location of Cheshire's medieval markets has been included to flesh the map out a little. A number of these markets almost certainly existed pre-Conquest – such as those at Chester, Middlewich and Stockport – but most received their market charters during the 12th and 13th centuries, such as Alderley (1253), Aldford (1253), Congleton (1272) and Over (1280). However, Aldford, along with Coddington, didn't last long as they were too close to the commercial magnet of Chester; Tarvin suffered a similar fate much later in the 16th century. Other markets like those at Burton (1299) and Brereton (1368) soon folded, too.

Quirk Alert: *Key Monk Business*

In 1281, a feud between Combermere Abbey and the French abbey of Saint-Evroul in Orne, over the church at Drayton, culminated in the abbot and some of his monks being excommunicated for guarding the church "like a castle" and stopping the Archbishop of Canterbury from entering. Then in 1309, a dispute blew up between Richard of Fullshurst and the Abbot of Combermere which had to be mediated by Edward II. Fullshurst led two raids on the abbey, murdering the prior and assaulting the abbot, while buildings were burned and goods stolen. The attacks were repeated in 1344, while in 1360 it was the abbot who was accused of retaliating against Sir Robert Fullshurst. Then in 1365, monks from Combermere descended upon its daughter house at Whalley in Lancashire in an attempt to eject the latter's abbot. Furthermore, there were several outbreaks of theft in the late 14th century, while there were also several conflicts between the abbey and its tenants in the 15th century, with the most serious incident being the murder of Abbot Richard Alderwas in 1446, killed by an arrow. Finally, in 1520, a monk was murdered by the servant of the abbot, Christopher Walley.

Meanwhile at Vale Royal Abbey, the abbot was accused of rape in 1433, while in 1437 he was murdered by a large band of armed men at Over. Then at Norton Abbey in 1522, the abbot was accused of "wasting the house's resources, nepotism and relations with women", while the prior admitted to "fornication and lapses in the observation of the Rule". Next, in 1536, the abbot and brethren of Norton Abbey attacked the king's commissioners when it looked as though their abbey was about to be dissolved. But we'll leave the last word with Combermere again – for in 1414, its abbot, William Plymouth, was charged with the counterfeiting of gold coins, which he was presumably driven to produce as a result of the abbey's bankruptcy in 1410!

Mara) stretching north to the Mersey, and the southern half (known as Mondrem) stretching south to Nantwich; the eastern and western perimeters were defined by the Rivers Weaver and Gowy respectively. Macclesfield Forest stretched to the east of Macclesfield from Bosley in the south to Marple in the north, and hence the hunting-related names Cat's Tor, Wilboarclough and Wolf's Crag. Finally, Wirral Forest included the entirety of the peninsula – although it certainly wasn't entirely forested as it included extensive areas of heathland and grassland as well as settlements; indeed, the peninsula became totally deforested by 1384. However, the forest laws still applied, so any form of encroachment – be it buildings, hedges, fencing or even cultivation – and the penalties would be severe; as for poachers, if they were lucky, they'd just have their eyes gouged out, but it was usually a hanging for them!

As well as salt production, medieval industry in Cheshire was largely dominated by agriculture. In terms of arable farming, the predominant cereal crops were oats and barley thanks to their ability to better-tolerate the damp nature of the Cheshire weather and to thrive on the Cheshire Plains. However, as Cheshire's population grew throughout the 12th and 13th centuries, additional areas had to be brought into cultivation to increase production, and so woods were cleared and rough grazing land was ploughed. On the Wirral alone, 1000 acres of "new ploughings" were listed in a 1303 survey, while in Macclesfield Forest, virtually all the tenancies recorded in the early 14th century were of holdings cleared from waste – such as Disley, Pott Shrigley and Whaley (note the place-name suffix of –ley, derived from the Old English word *lēah*, meaning "woodland clearing"); meanwhile, in 1310, the abbot of Chester agreed to allow the enclosure of the heath in Tilston Fearnall and Alpraham. In fact, the demand for arable land was so great that by the early

14th century, even salt marshes at Frodsham were being ploughed.

Alas, agricultural progress and population growth came to a shuddering halt, country-wide, during the 14th century. A series of natural disasters were largely to blame, particularly during the crisis years of 1315 to 1322 when it is estimated that the national population declined by at least 15 per cent. This period was marked by widespread outbreaks of sheep murrain and poor, wet summers, with the latter resulting in poor harvests and subsequent famine. However, all of these setbacks were nothing compared with the Black Death which first arrived in England in 1349 and is estimated to have taken anything from a third to half of England's population, essentially returning it to its Domesday Book level of just over two million. One result of this series of catastrophes was that by the 1350s, thousands of Cheshire fields lay uncultivated as there weren't enough peasants to till the fields and those tenants who survived couldn't always manage the fields by themselves. Hence in 1372, the tenancies of eight properties in Macclesfield, for example, were confiscated because the land had been out of use for up to twelve years.

The other effect of the Black Death was that a number of hamlets and villages became depopulated. On the Wirral alone, these places include Barnston, Moreton, Poulton Lancelyn and Woodchurch, while at Meols on the coast, erosion and drifting sand is thought to have accelerated its economic decline. Some of the shrunken villages saw their land turned over to pasture, as happened at Aston-juxta-Mondrum in 1360, while at places as sizeable as Frodsham, over one third of the arable land on the estate was converted to pasture between 1350 and 1370. This shift from arable to dairy farming set the template for centuries to come, and in Macclesfield Forest, specialised *vaccaries*, or cattle-ranches, were operating from as early as the 1360s. By 1372, Cheshire cheese was being produced on

Above: *Chester Cathedral from the south-east.* Below: *Looking down the medieval nave of Chester Cathedral towards the east window. The building was gradually expanded between 1093 and the 16th century which resulted in its designation as a cathedral by Henry VIII in 1541.*

a commercial basis as dairying expanded to become a significant source of income – along with beef from the cattle as well.

Despite being largely agricultural, Cheshire did have its towns – with Chester, Northwich, Middlewich and Nantwich all thriving prior to the Conquest. They continued to grow into the 12th century and were joined by other towns that grew out of villages and which became formally recognised as towns via the granting of medieval borough charters. Congleton, for example, was a village at the time of Domesday Book, but by 1311, it had a mayor, burgesses and eighty burgage plots, along with its market (charter granted in 1272) and fairs, a watermill, a manor court-house and moot hall, while by 1350 it had a population of around 500 and two chapels – but no church, as it was still part of the parish of Astbury. Meanwhile, Macclesfield experienced a similar rate of growth thanks to the success of its early cloth and button industry, and a number of substantial buildings were built in the town by its wealthy gentry and burgesses; the town also received its market charter in 1261.

Meanwhile, Knutsford was effectively a medieval "new town" that was first laid out in the 1290s with one long main street (King Street) and a market place, but

not a church as it was part of the parish of Rostherne; it is also thought that Altrincham followed this pattern, being laid out after its market charter was granted in 1290. However, at Tintwistle, the project wasn't so successful. The rationale was that the place would thrive, being on the important route from Manchester and Cheshire through to Yorkshire, and a borough was established here before 1350. However, it was probably too remote to survive and in any case had competition from nearby Glossop. A total of 18 chartered boroughs are known of medieval Cheshire, with 12 going on to grow as urban centres.

Throughout these times, Chester remained the largest town in the North West, and after its harsh treatment by the early Normans and subsequent economic decline, it gradually began to reassert its prosperity. The population of the town grew in tandem with its burgeoning wealth, from around 1500 people in 1086 to around 3000 people by the mid-14th century. However, the aforementioned Black Death of the mid-14th century sent its population back to 1086 levels, triggering another period of economic decline which was exacerbated by the Dee estuary silting up and impeding access to Chester's port. As ever, the town regenerated, and during the 15th century it continued to be the commercial, political, ecclesiastical and social focus of Cheshire and the Welsh borderlands. The confines of the walled medieval town were dominated by the abbey of St Werburgh's taking up much of the northeastern quadrant and the castle located in the opposing south-western quadrant. The commercial centre was focused around the east gate, while the medieval cathedral – which was then the church of St John's – was actually located outside of the walls on the southeastern perimeter.

Perhaps the most famous feature of medieval Chester that survives today is what is known as the Rows – first-floor galleries through the centre of the town which provide a continuous upper-level walkway, and which are thought to be at least 700 years old. Historians believe that the ground-floor shops of today were once undercrofts, and that these buildings were gradually linked together at first-floor level throughout the medieval period, to provide a covered pedestrian walkway through the town centre. Their construction has been dated to the late 13th century due to the great fire of 1278 which destroyed much of Chester, and hence much of this area would have been rebuilt at this time. Ironically, it was probably the economic decline of Chester in the late 14th century which helped to preserve the Rows, as the depressed economy provided little incentive to see the town undergo a 15th and 16th century makeover – although despite the relatively depressed economy, Chester maintained its position as the leading port in the northern basin of the Irish Sea, and continued to source most of the maritime traffic to both Dublin and Belfast. This vital outlet was supplemented by the beginnings of trade with Brittany, south-western France and Spain,

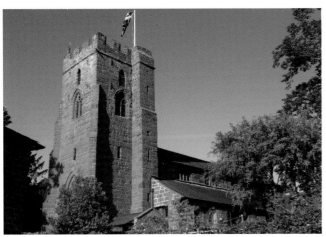

The three lower stages of the sandstone tower of St Chad's church in Farndon date from the 14th century.

Farndon Bridge over the River Dee dates from 1339.

with Chester importing large quantities of iron, oil, cork and foodstuffs, as well as wine from Gascony which was evident as early as 1275.

Medieval cloth manufacturing was important throughout Cheshire, particularly in the western half of the county where linen cloths were extensively produced along the River Dee where the damp lowlands were ideal for growing flax. The centre for this trade in the 1360s and 1370s was the Malpas area, and one inventory of 1371 demonstrates that among the goods of a Malpas mercer were Welsh woollen cloths and local linen. Of course, given the number sheep in the Pennines, the eastern part of Cheshire manufactured large quantities of woollen cloth, such as that produced by a fulling mill in Congleton from the late 12th century, while by the 16th century Macclesfield was renowned for its cloth-trading fairs. Woollen cloth was also produced in the Halton area from sheep which grazed the upland areas around Frodsham and Helsby.

Quirk Alert: *"A wheel, a wheel – two shillings for a wheel"*

During medieval times, there were regulations applied to the transport of Cheshire salt. For example, anyone who overloaded a salt-cart to the extent that it caused an axle to break, within one league of a Cheshire "wich", was fined two shillings. Interestingly, the same penalty was levied against anyone who so-overloaded a horse to the extent that he broke the poor creature's back – thus not defining any difference in importance between a wheel and a horse!

Of course, the salt industry has remained a major industry in Cheshire throughout the ages, but there were other minerals mined in the county during the medieval period. There were ironworkings in the Macclesfield area by the mid-14th century and it is recorded that there were 27 operational smelting hearths in the town in 1353, while near-surface coal was also being mined in the Cheshire Pennines. It may well

be that the copper deposits at Alderley Edge were already being worked during these times as well, although this is not for certain. As for Cheshire's medieval salt industry, Domesday Book provides a very clear commentary. For example, it shows that at Nantwich, in 1066, King Harold and the Earl of Mercia shared the income from the town's saltpit and eight salthouses. This suggests that the industry was well-established in Saxon times and explains the high Saxon status of Northwich, Middlewich and Nantwich, and their comparative wealth. In those days – and indeed all the way up to the 17th century – the method of salt extraction was one of evaporation from naturally-occurring brine, and hence the salt production had to be more or less co-located with the deposits – all advantageous to the three Cheshire *wich's*, of course. However, when in the 15th century, cheap sea-salt became available from the Atlantic coasts of Gascony and Aquitaine, the industry underwent a testing time, as the French salt – although of a relatively poor quality – sold at half the price of quality Cheshire salt.

Earlier, we talked about the special privileges bestowed upon the Earls of Chester by William I. By 1195, it was being suggested that Cheshire had so many special privileges that it had been set apart from the rest of England. This special dispensation was then taken further in 1215 when Cheshire's baronial lords secured a separate version of Magna Carta, not from King John, but from the Earl of Chester. However, in 1237, the last Norman Earl of Chester, John le Scot (1232-1237) died without a male heir, and Henry III thus stepped in to take control of this extremely powerful earldom. By 1241, the title of Earl of Chester had been surrendered to the king, and royal administrators took over the running of the county, while the king's judges began to preside over the county's courts. Then in 1253, the entire county was granted to the king's heir on the condition that it remained part of the crown's estate, and from this point onwards, the title of Earl of Chester has always been held by the eldest son of the monarch in conjunction with that of Prince of Wales; indeed, both honours were bestowed upon the current Prince

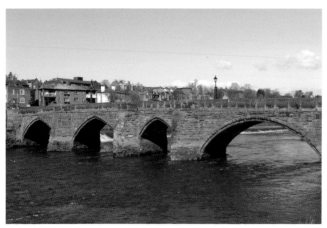

The Old Dee Bridge at Chester was built in 1387.

of Wales, Prince Charles, on 26th July 1958.

What this also meant was that Cheshire still effectively had a separate government, with its own courts, own procedures and own administration, thereby perpetuating the system previously controlled by the Norman Earls of Chester and before that, by the Saxon Earls of Mercia. By the 1290s, Cheshire had also been granted the status of county palatine, although this ratification of its special status wasn't officially used until the 14th century. However, this special status didn't mean the lot of the people of Cheshire was any better than in any other county. Indeed, there were many grievances over the years, such as those in the 1350s caused by the excessively high taxes levied by the Earl of Chester, also known as the Black Prince (Edward, Prince of Wales and eldest son of Edward III). Then in 1398, Cheshire was briefly promoted to a principality by King Richard II, who titled himself Prince of Chester – although this was reduced to an earldom the following year by King Henry IV. As for the independent palatinate jurisdiction of Chester, this survived until 1536, when Henry VIII brought the earldom more directly under the control of the Crown. However, the palatinate courts of Great Sessions and Exchequer actually survived until the reforms of 1830!

We return now to the late 14th century struggle for the Crown between Richard II (1377-1399) and Henry IV (1399-1413), which resulted in Richard's deposition by Henry in 1399. Shakespeare depicts the lead-up to these events as a period of misrule by Richard, leading to his deposition and, ultimately, to the Wars of the Roses – although modern historians no longer accept this interpretation. Whatever the truth, Cheshire became entangled in the struggle as early as 1387, when Richard toured England for support in his struggle against Parliament, and what he saw as an affront to his royal prerogative. Richard appointed his councillor and friend, Robert de Vere, as Justice of Chester, and he then set about creating a loyal military power base in Cheshire. However, on his return to London, Richard was confronted by his opponents (known as the Lords Appellant) while de Vere and his forces were routed at Radcot Bridge, with de Vere fleeing to France. Richard

had no choice but to comply with the demands of the Lords Appellant, and a fragile peace existed until the second crisis of 1397-1399 – during which time he elevated Cheshire to a principality. This second struggle, though, resulted in Henry IV's invasion of England and his march on Cheshire, which appeared to be the only English county opposed to him. Chester Castle was captured by Henry, and Richard surrendered at nearby Flint Castle on 19th August 1399. He was then brought to Chester Castle where he was briefly held prisoner in the crypt of the Agricola Tower. Thereafter, Richard returned to London, agreed to abdicate, and died in captivity the following year in unknown circumstances. That wasn't quite the end of it for Richard's Cheshire, though, as many of the gentry from the county fought against Henry IV in Harry Hotspur's rebellion which ended in defeat at the Battle of Shrewsbury on 21st July 1403. It was also during this period that a tower was built to fortify Chester's Dee Bridge.

Quirk Alert: *Mystery Plays*

What became known as the Chester Mystery Plays are thought to have started in the early 15th century, with the earliest record dating to 1422. The plays took place during the feast of Corpus Christi and were based on biblical texts that were enacted by guildsmen and craftsmen on stages that were moved around the city streets, with each company or guild performing one play.

Commencing in 1497, though, in years during which the mystery plays didn't occur, there took place what became known as the Chester Midsummer Watch Parade, whereby the people of Chester marched through the streets during the summer solstice, wearing costumes and carrying torches. Meanwhile, a similar event occurred on Christmas Eve, when a candlelit procession would walk from the mayor's house to the Common Hall where the keys to the city gates would be given to the mayor who, in turn, entrusted them to the watchmen who would keep the city safe over the festive season. We'll give the last word to the Chester Midsummer Watch Parade, though – for in 1564, it is recorded that the "costumes" comprised "4 giants, 1 unicorn, 1 dromedary, 1 fish, 1 camel, 1 dragon, 6 hobbyhorses…and 16 naked boys"!

During the Wars of the Roses of the late 15th century, the nearest battle to Cheshire occurred just over the border in Staffordshire in which many Cheshire gentry were killed. This was the Battle of Blore Heath on 23rd September, 1459, and in the lead-up to it, Queen Margaret of Anjou had visited Chester for the third time in seven years, rallying support for the Lancastrian cause and for King Henry VI, and issuing an emblem of a silver swan to knights and squires enlisted by her personally. A Yorkist force of around 5000 men, led by the Earl of Salisbury, were attempting

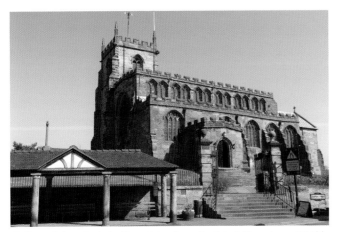

St James' church at Audlem dates from the late 13th century. Visible in the foreground is the old Buttermarket; Audlem's market charter was granted in 1295.

Saighton Gatehouse is a survivor of Saighton Grange, a medieval monastic grange belonging to St Werburgh's Abbey of Chester, and dates from the 15th century. All of the other monastic buildings which survived the Dissolution in the 16th century were demolished in 1861.

to link up with the main Yorkist army at Ludlow Castle in Shropshire, passing down through Cheshire and Staffordshire, and so Queen Margaret ordered Lord Audley to intercept them. However, despite Audley's superior force of around 10,000 men, the Lancastrian's were defeated and Audley himself mortally wounded. Once Audley had fallen, around 500 Lancastrians joined the enemy and began attacking their own side –

at which point the Lancastrians capitulated with many chased for miles across the countryside. Of the 2000 Lancastrians killed (against 1000 Yorkists), many belonged to the Cheshire gentry. After that, Chester received visits from successive kings from both sides: Edward IV in 1470, Richard III in 1484 and Henry VII in 1486, albeit one year before he was crowned King of England.

LATE MEDIEVAL CHESHIRE

Above left: *The timber-framed Marton church dates from the 14th century.*

Above right: *The Grade I listed St Oswald's church at Lower Peover, parts of which date from the 13th century. The stone tower dates from the 16th century while the medieval timber nave, aisles and chancel were heavily restored in the 19th century.*

Left: *This beautiful cottage in Haslington has a date of AD 1510 above the front door.*

Left: *The Hawk Inn in Haslington is located across the road from the cottage shown overleaf, and also dates from 1510. It also has old inscriptions around it (shown above) as well as some interesting faces. The above inscription reads: A JUG OF ALE A WHISPERED WORD CAN BE FOUND WITHIN THESE OLD WALLS.*

Above left: *A 17th century sundial in Acton churchyard. However, the central shaft is part of a medieval market cross.*
Above centre: *Gawsworth village cross is thought to be the remains of a medieval market cross.*
Above right: *The Grade II listed Woodhey Cross at Faddiley dates from the early 16th century.*

Far left: *Internal view of the timber-framed 14th century church at Marton.*

Left: *Also in Marton's church are a number of early medieval wall paintings, such as this one, which were discovered under plaster in 1930.*

Quirk Alert: *Oyez, Hagrid and Welsh Women!*

Shown right is Chester's town crier[1], standing in front of Chester High Cross where he makes his proclamations every Tuesday to Saturday, at midday. Behind him, are some of Chester's famous medieval Rows, the first floor galleries which provide a continuous upper-level walkway around the centre of the town, and are unique – as in nothing the same exists anywhere else in the world! The Rows rise above under-crofts – largely shops or restaurants today for which you have to walk down a few steps. The Rows first appeared in the 13th century along the four streets that radiate out from Chester High Cross. Around 20 of the medieval stone undercrofts survive today, but at the level of the Rows very little medieval fabric remains – as is demonstrated on the next page.

As for town criers, they originated in medieval England, where they were the chief means of news communication. Royal proclamations, local bylaws, market days and adverts were all proclaimed by a town crier. Also proclaimed were a number of offbeat issues such as the selling of loaves of sugar and the warning of prosecution for the poaching of salmon (that's the stealing of salmon, by the way, not the cooking of). It would also seem that some towns had separate bellmen and criers. For example, in 1792, Chester had a day and night bellman (John Yarwood) and a crier (William Ratcliffe), but by 1835 an economy of scale appears to have been realised, and only one multi-tasking position was held!

Town criers were also protected by the ruling monarch, because they sometimes brought bad news such as tax increases. To this day, any town crier in the British Commonwealth is protected under old English law in that they are not to be hindered or heckled while performing their duties. And indeed, in times past, to injure or to harm a town crier was seen as an act of treason against the ruling monarchy!

Finally, some more town crier snippets. For starters, as one of the few literate townspeople, the crier would not only deliver and read news, but also acted as a local scribe. As such, the term "Posting a Notice" originates from town criers, who having read their message to the townspeople, would attach it to the door post of the local inn. It is also for this reason that some newspapers were christened "The Post". As for the town crier, he was also the official ale tester in a number of towns, and thus after downing a flagon or two and finding it pleasing to the taste, he would nail an appropriate proclamation to the hitching post outside of the hostelry. And last, but by no means least, the town crier was also a protector of the Mayor, or Lord of the Manor, and was

not averse to using his heavy bell as a handy cudgel to ward off known troublemakers…and hence, apparently, the phrase "his face rings a bell". Which indeed it would under those circumstances!

[1]*Actually, this **isn't** Chester's town crier, but Shrewsbury's town crier, Martin Wood, who happened to be standing in for Chester's town crier on this particular week in the summer of 2012! Martin also happens to be the tallest town crier in the world, standing at 7ft 2in tall, while he was also the stunt double for Robbie Coltrane's Hagrid in the Harry Potter films. Anyway, on the day in question, he proceeded to ring his bell and shout Oyez (both are very loud, hence the little boy's fingers in his ears in the second photograph), and then issue the day's proclamations. He then invited visitors to the city to have a go – which is why the poor lady in the bottom photograph was asked to say a piece about Cardiff, having been built up by Martin on the grounds that "I've never yet met a woman from Wales who was lost for words!"*

MAGNIFICENT MEDIEVAL CHESTER (OR IS IT...)

This beautiful building on the corner of Foregate Street and Frodsham Street dates from 1921 when it was the Manchester and Liverpool District Bank.

Eastgate and the Eastgate Clock. However, this particular Eastgate was built in 1769 to replace its medieval predecessor. The clock dates from 1897.

View of Eastgate Street from the Eastgate bridge.

This stunning row of houses can be found on the corner of Eastgate Street and St Werburgh Street – but they were built between 1895 and 1897!

Northgate Street, with some of the Rows visible on the left. The Rows were first referenced in 1293 near High Cross. However, these particular timber-framed buildings were built in 1912-1913.

More Rows at Chester High Cross where the four medieval streets of Chester meet. The beautiful building on the corner, however, dates from 1888, and those on the right from 1889-1890 – although some medieval masonry exists at the rear.

Alas, this magnificent timber-framed building isn't medieval either; it was built between 1909 and 1911! Note the Rows again on the first floor.

This is Nine Houses in Park Street – although only six remain! And no, even these aren't medieval; they are almshouses dating from c.1650!

From the Dissolution to the Eve of the Industrial Revolution

It was during the 16th century that the commercial and economic structure of the North West began to change, and Chester – which for centuries had been the main town of the region – began to lose its dominant place to what would later become the giants of Liverpool and Manchester. Indeed, the administration of the entire county of Cheshire had lost most of its distinctive identity and privilege by the 17th century, and its palatinate status became increasingly irrelevant. The nature of its government changed, too, and by 1620, the gentry and the justices of the peace were leading the county's administration.

The gentry in question could largely trace their ancestry back to Domesday Book (1086), and included the Davenport, Legh, Mainwaring, Massey and Venables families; indeed all but 16 of the leading 106 families of mid-17th century Cheshire were well-established before the Reformation, while in the late 1630s, the active JPs of Cheshire were represented by 28 of these long-established families. Two exceptions were the Cottons and the Brookes – and here we find another difference between Cheshire and other counties of England. For in the aftermath of the Dissolution of the Monasteries, it was usually the long-established families who partook in a mad scramble to acquire the then-redundant buildings from the Crown. Those who inherited these religious institutions and their land substantially increased their social standing, thus strengthening their position which enabled many of them to continue to dominate local society for many more centuries to come, too. Hence it was that the Cottons and the Brookes bucked this trend in Cheshire, as they weren't members of recognised aristocratic families. However, they certainly reaped similar rewards, when they acquired the remains of the former abbey's at Combermere and Norton, respectively.

The abbey and the estates at Combermere were granted to Sir George Cotton in 1539, who completely demolished the church and most of the buildings. However, he converted part of the abbey – believed to be the abbot's house – into a country home, and indeed, the hammerbeam roof timbers of the Great Hall have recently been dated to 1502, therefore confirming the incorporation. The house was later re-modelled in 1563 by Sir George's son, Richard Cotton, altered in 1795 by Sir Robert Cotton, and given a Gothic overhaul between 1814 and 1821 by Stapleton Cotton. The house remained under Cotton ownership until 1919. Meanwhile, Norton Priory was dissolved in 1536, and the surviving buildings – along with the estates and manor of Norton – were eventually acquired by Sir Richard Brooke in 1545. Sir Richard also built a Tudor country house which incorporated part of the abbey, although this building was replaced in the 18th century by a Georgian house. Norton Priory remained under Brooke ownership until 1921, and the Georgian house was partially demolished

Gawsworth Old Hall at Gawsworth was built between 1480 and 1600 for the Fitton family, and replaced an earlier Norman manor house.

Moss Hall at Audlem was built in 1615 for the Massey family.

in 1928. As well as the surviving undercroft, subsequent excavations exposed further foundations and lower walls of the monastery buildings and the site is now a popular visitor attraction.

> **Quirk Alert:** *Bunbury Knights*
> *There are two interesting tombs in the church of Bunbury St Boniface. The first is of Hugh Calveley, a 14th century giant of 7 feet, of whom it was said he could "eat as much as two plain men and fight like ten". Meanwhile, Sir George Beeston was knighted following his exploits against the Spanish Armada in 1588 – at the grand old age of 89!*

The Dissolution of the Monasteries had nowhere near the impact in Cheshire as it had elsewhere, and this was primarily down to the limited number of religious institutions established in the county. That wasn't quite the case in Chester, though, which as well as being home to seven religious institutions which were dissolved, it also "profited" by being the centre of one of five new dioceses of the new Church of England. Created in August 1541, this new diocese took in the archdeaconry of Chester and the archdeaconry of Richmond (from York), with the abbey church of St Werburgh's becoming its cathedral. Its territory stretched from Malpas in south Cheshire to Workington in what was then Cumberland, meaning that its cathedral was anything but central. Alas, its finances were not good, while it suffered in its early years through clergy absenteeism, with only 20 of its 94 bishops' resident. Of those that were resident, many were criticised, while Bishop Downham (1561-1579) was publicly reprimanded on several occasions for the abject failure of his policies.

While the Cottons and the Brookes converted former monastic buildings into their homes in the 16th century, other landed families replaced earlier medieval manor houses, usually on the same site. For example, Haslington Hall was built by Admiral Sir Francis Vernon in 1545, and included parts of the original medieval manor house, thought to date back to 1480. Further alterations to the house were made in the 16th, 17th and 19th centuries. Meanwhile, Brereton Hall was built for Sir William Brereton in 1586. The building was built in red brick with stone dressings, originally in an E-plan, although the central wing of the E was demolished in the 19th century and replaced with a conservatory. The frontage includes a distinctive duel-turreted central gateway, with its octagonal turrets linked by a bridge.

Little Moreton Hall was built in the early 16th century for the Moreton family.

Lyme Park near Disley in north-east Cheshire was built in the mid-16th century for the Legh family.

> ## Quirk Alert: *Timberland*
> *It is claimed that some of the timbers used in the construction of Haslington House were salvaged from ships of the Spanish Armada in 1588! Meanwhile, Peover Hall was initially intended to be an H-shaped mansion when built for the Mainwaring family in 1585, but ended up being T-shaped when money ran short!*

One manor house already in place at the Dissolution, though, was Adlington Hall; in fact, the surviving Great Hall was built between 1480 and 1505, while the east wing was added much later in 1581. The occupants of this hall and its medieval predecessor dating back to the early 14th century were the aforementioned Legh family – apart from a short hiatus in the 1640s when the Royalist Leghs were ousted by Parliamentary troops during the English Civil War; the house sustained significant damage during two sieges. Further changes were made to the north wing in the mid-17th century, including encasing the Great Hall in brick, while in the 18th century Charles Legh built a new west wing, which incorporated a ballroom, and a south wing with a large portico.

Sticking with late medieval houses, the north wing of Lower Carden Hall also dates from the 15th century, perhaps earlier. However, a south cross-wing was added in the mid-16th century and the north wing was enlarged and re-fronted in the early 17th century. Meanwhile, one of the finest timber-framed Tudor houses in England is Little Moreton Hall, which is located around four miles south-west of Congleton.

The earliest parts of the house were built for William Moreton in the early 16th century, with the remainder constructed in stages, up until around 1610, by successive generations of the Moreton family; indeed, the house remained in the possession of the Moreton family for almost 450 years, after which it was taken over by the National Trust in 1938. Little Moreton Hall is also Grade I listed and is particularly noted for its highly irregular asymmetrical shape.

> ## Quirk Alert: *Captain Whitle's Wind*
> *The wind is so-named after one stormy day in the 16th century when Captain Whitle was being laid to rest in the churchyard of St Michael and All Angels at Mottram. The storm was so severe that one fury of wind wrested the coffin from the shoulders of the bearers as the procession moved up Mottram's steep hill.*

Also owned by the National Trust (since 1946) is Lyme Park near to Disley in north-eastern Cheshire, and which also belonged to the Legh family. The house is the largest in Cheshire, measuring 190ft (58 m) by 130ft (40 m) around a courtyard plan. The oldest part of the current house was built in the mid-16th century by

The Grade I listed Crown Hotel in High Street, Nantwich, dates from just after 1583 – this being the year of the Great Fire of Nantwich which destroyed the previous inn of the same name. The fire burned for twenty days and destroyed over 600 buildings.

Also in Nantwich, and also Grade I listed, is Churche's Mansion which dates from 1577 and is one of very few houses in the town to survive the Great Fire, six years later.

Piers Legh VII with east and north ranges; further additions were made throughout the 17th century. Then in the 1720s, a south range was added thus creating the courtyard plan, while other alterations were made, retaining some of its Elizabethan features but also introducing a mixture of Palladian and Baroque styles.

The Grade I-listed Crewe Hall was built a little later between 1615 and 1638 for Sir Randolph Crewe and is described by Nikolaus Pevsner as one of the two finest Jacobean houses in Cheshire. The hall was extended in the late 18th century and altered by Edward Blore in the mid-19th century. It was extensively restored by E. M. Barry after a fire in 1866, while the interior is renowned for its elaborate wood carving, chimney-pieces and plasterwork, some of which are still the originals. The park was landscaped during the 18th century by Lancelot "Capability" Brown and, in the 19th century, formal gardens were designed by W. A. Nesfield. The Grade II-listed stables quadrangle is contemporary with the hall and was completed in around 1636. The hall remained the seat of the Crewe family until 1936, when the land was sold to the Duchy of Lancaster.

Dating from the same period is Dorfold Hall and Moss Hall, with the former built by Sir Roger Wilbraham between 1616 and 1621 (see *Quirky Cheshire [Acton]* for the history of Dorfold Hall). As for Moss Hall (also known as Audlem Hall), this was built in 1616 by Hugh Massy, and was owned by his descendants until 1760 when it passed to William Massy's son-in-law, Robert Taylor. The house is now owned by the Vernon family. Meanwhile, nearby is Highfields at Buerton, a half-timbered manor house built in 1585 by

William Dod, and another house that not only hosted troops during the English Civil War, but also Prince Rupert himself who was said to have stopped at Highfields in May 1642, when his army of 10,000 was on its way north-east to the siege of Stockport.

We return now to the Cheshire magistrates who, of course, were largely drawn from the closed aristocratic circle just discussed, and they met and administered civil business and lesser criminal justice at the quarter sessions, held four times a year in 16th and 17th century Cheshire. These meetings were circulated around Cheshire so that Knutsford, Middlewich, Nantwich and Northwich became session towns as well as Chester. However, certainly in the first half of the 16th century, Chester still had unusual privileges. Its charter of 1507 meant that it was still legally a county in its own right, independent of Cheshire, and hence it had its own sheriff, while its courts continued to hold greater power than those of other English borough courts. As for other Cheshire boroughs, there was only Congleton (incorporated in 1584) and Macclesfield (1595) which had corporate and separate councils. Stockport had a mayor and aldermen, but its council didn't achieve corporate independence, as the manor courts of the local manorial lords, the Warrens of Poynton, held sway in the town. It was also a similar story in Altrincham where the real power rested with the Booths of Dunham Massey rather than with the mayoralty and the town's borough officials.

Given that Cheshire only had three corporate boroughs, and also retained into the 16th century its special autonomy thanks to still having palatinate status, the county did not send any representatives to Parliament until 1543. Thereafter, Cheshire elected two knights of the shire to Westminster, while Chester sent two burgesses; Congleton and Macclesfield remained unrepresented, with the former thought to be due to the borough's desire to be rid of its manorial lord, the Duchy of Lancaster – and hence they weren't granted a voice! Cheshire, therefore, only had a meagre four MPs in the mid-to-late 16th century.

> ## Quirk Alert: *The Ultimate Selflessness*
> *In the tiny village of Tushingham, near Malpas, all seven of the Dawson family were killed by the plague in 1625. Knowing that he was beyond help, and too heavy for the others to carry, the father – a big man – dug his own grave and lay down in it to die.*

This long row of white 17th century cottages at Prestbury includes a pub in the middle, The Admiral Rodney, which was originally a 17th century coaching inn.

The Lower Chequer at Sandbach was built in 1570 and was a 16th century coaching inn. The story goes that it was so-named because it used to have a chequer board to help uneducated customers count their money!

Ye Olde Black Bear at Sandbach dates from the 17th century.

Ye Olde Kings Arms, Congleton also dates from the 17th century. Legend has it that condemned prisoners were brought through tunnels to the cellar of the inn for their last drink!

Before launching into Cheshire's role in the English Civil War, it is worth summarising this hugely important historical event. Having ascended the throne in 1625 King Charles I believed in the Divine Right of Kings. However, this was a time when Parliament was beginning to assert greater control and to limit the royal prerogative. Nevertheless, Charles ploughed on with his unpopular religious policies, leading to costly intervention in Europe in 1627, a move which led to Charles dissolving Parliament which was opposed to his plans. Despite his desperate need for money, Charles refused to recall Parliament for another decade, and instead, resorted to a series of deeply unpopular taxes that gradually turned large parts of the country against him. Furthermore, Charles' religious policy led to rebellion in Scotland and the Bishops Wars of 1639-1640. Again without sufficient funds, Charles' forays into Scotland were another disaster and ultimately led to the Scots taking Newcastle and Charles having to pay Scotland war expenses.

Desperate for cash, Charles finally recalled Parliament in England in 1640 – an opportunity for Parliament to discuss grievances against the Crown and to oppose an English invasion of Scotland. True to

form, Charles took offence at this slight on his Divine Rule, promptly dissolved Parliament again and forged ahead with his attack on Scotland. This time, not only did he lose again, but the Scots promptly occupied Northumberland and Durham and Charles had to pay £850 a day to stop them from advancing further! So in November 1640, Charles had no choice but to recall Parliament again. Naturally, by now, Parliament was openly hostile to Charles, and with control slipping away, Charles withdrew to the Royalist stronghold of northern England.

The resulting English Civil War was fought in three distinct phases between the Parliamentarians (the Roundheads) and the Royalists (the Cavaliers). The first phase ran from 1642 to February 1646 when the King surrendered. Alas, Charles refused to accept Parliament's demand for a constitutional monarchy, and temporarily escaped captivity in November 1647, and hence the second phase of the war (1648-1649), but which again resulted in his capture, this time by Oliver Cromwell's now established New Model Army. This time, he was tried, convicted and executed for high treason on 30th January 1649. The monarchy was subsequently abolished and the Commonwealth of England established in its place. However, the third phase of the war took place between 1649 and 1651, when supporters of Charles II battled with Parliamentarians, and which ultimately resulted in Royalist defeat at the Battle of Worcester on 3rd September 1651.

Anyway, in the months before the English Civil War first broke out on 22nd August 1642, the Cheshire gentry were divided in their allegiances, and any opposition to the king was decidedly lukewarm. Indeed, a core of 40 Cheshire gentry strove hard to prevent the fracture of county society and sought to stem the gradually increasing disorder. However, even this group had divided loyalties and 16 eventually declared for the king and 25 for Parliament, although if you took the Cheshire gentry in total, around two thirds were Royalist. In the other third who declared for Parliament were most of the middle-ranking gentry as well as most of the active justices of the peace, including Sir William Brereton of Handforth, a staunch Parliamentarian and the most active of the pre-war Cheshire justices. Throughout the summer of 1642, both sides took to drilling trained bands of militia and there were armed confrontations in both Nantwich and Stockport, as local government began to disintegrate. When war eventually broke out in the Autumn of 1642, the Royalists held Chester and a number of important fortified manors

The White Bear at Knutsford dates from the 16th century and was a popular coaching inn. It was also a haunt of the notorious Highwayman Higgins!

Seventeenth-century cottages in Malpas.

Quirk Alert: *The Rector's Pulpit*
The Priest's House in Prestbury (shown below) was originally built in the 16th century although it was much altered in the 17th century. It eventually became a vicarage in the 17th century, the local Manor House in 1706, and later cottages and even a bank!

However, during the Commonwealth period of the mid-17th century, the rector – who had been ejected from his church over the road – used the platform on the right-hand side as his pulpit!

Much later during 20th century restoration, two cast-iron firebacks were found with the oldest dating to 1635 and including the arms of Charles I.

Quirk Alert: *The Final Leg*
Sir Arthur Aston of Catton Hall, near Frodsham, was declared by Charles I to be more feared by the enemy than any other man in his army. However, Sir Arthur met the most ignominious of ends, when fighting gallantly in Ireland in 1649 – for he is said to have been beaten to death…with his own wooden leg!

throughout the county, but the rest of the county's towns were soon held for Parliament – such as Congleton, Knutsford, Middlewich, Nantwich, Northwich and Stockport. By this stage Sir William Brereton had been appointed as the Parliamentary commander in Cheshire, but despite an overwhelming numerical advantage, the Parliamentarians could not initially muster the strength to take the well-defended stronghold of Chester; that came later when Brereton's forces were augmented by soldiers from outside of Cheshire.

Nantwich was claimed for Parliament in late January 1643 following a victory there over the local Royalists – a victory which resulted in the Royalists reinforcing Chester with troops from north Wales. Thereafter, Nantwich became the main Parliamentary base for attacking the Royalists in the northern Welsh borders. November 1643 was a significant month, as Brereton's forces took a number of Royalist strongholds a few miles south of Chester, including Holt and Wrexham, but then had to abandon them as a large

The Bears Head Inn at Brereton was built in 1625, but was originally known as The Boars Head. It was a popular posting house on the London to Liverpool turnpike road which resulted in a new wing being built in the 18th century along with new stables, in order to cope with demand.

The Bear's Paw at Frodsham dates from 1632 according to the lintel above the front door. It was originally called The Lion's Paw, named after the feature on the arms of local lords of the manor, the Savage family, but was switched to a bear in the 18th century when it was a popular coaching inn.

Royalist force landed at Chester from Ireland. In the wake of Brereton's retreat to Nantwich, much of western Cheshire was then taken for the king. As the Royalists asserted their control and moved further east, there followed one of the most shocking episodes of the English Civil War, on 26th December 1643, when sheltering locals were butchered at Barthomley church (see *Quirky Cheshire [Slaughter Hill]* for the detail of this grisly episode and the resulting revenge at Slaughter Hill). The Royalists then laid siege to Nantwich, but the town held out for a month until the siege was broken by the arrival of Sir Thomas Fairfax from Manchester on 25th January 1644. The Royalists were roundly routed and from this point onwards, virtually all of Cheshire, bar Chester, was under Parliamentarian control.

The Phoenix Tower is a much-restored medieval structure standing on, or close to, the site of the original Roman north-east tower in Chester. It is also known as the King Charles Tower, as this is where Charles I observed the defeat of his troops at Rowton Heath in September 1645.

Rowton Heath – within view of the city and its Royalist defenders. The Royalists were defeated, and those who fled for the safety of the city were systematically picked off by the Parliamentarian besiegers. The city eventually fell to Sir William Brereton and his forces in February 1646, while the first phase of the English Civil War ended in May 1646 when Charles I surrendered.

Cheshire wasn't particularly troubled by the second and third phases of the English Civil War, but the cost of the first phase was substantial. Unsurprisingly, the impact on Chester and Nantwich was severe, with both places enduring long sieges and hence suffering from widespread destruction. Elsewhere, three expeditions through the county by Prince Rupert had led to extensive destruction of property, much of it simply as revenge for the county being largely in Parliamentarian hands, while Parliament got its own back after the war by sequestering estates and properties from Royalist supporters, who had to pay large amounts of compensation to regain them. For example, it took the ousted Leghs until 1656 to re-acquire Adlington Hall following the payment of heavy fines for taking the Royalist side during the war. Smaller scale damage was inflicted in places like Stockport where a couple of minor skirmishes had taken place, but perhaps the largest impact was upon the ordinary people of Cheshire. Like most other English counties, common folk had been the victim of both sides commandeering "free quarter" during the war, and using that as an excuse to take

> **Quirk Alert:** *Night of the Long Knives*
> *The Slaughter Hill chapter on page 139 explains why that place is so-named. It also describes the Royalist atrocities which preceded it at Barthomley church on 26th December 1643, much of which was inflicted with knives. It is interesting, therefore, that when Sir Thomas Fairfax routed the Royalists who were besieging Nantwich in January 1644, amongst those captured were "120 Irish women with long knives"...*

The crucial turning point in the First English Civil War (1642-1646) occurred on 14th June 1645, this being the Battle of Naseby in Northamptonshire. Thereafter, Charles was on the run, and on 22nd September 1645 he retreated to Chester. As the city had been under siege by Parliamentarian forces for several months, Charles had to gain access to the city from the unguarded approach from Wales. The plan was for an accompanying Royalist force to attack the Parliamentarians from the rear, but this plan was thwarted by a large Parliamentary force which had been in hot pursuit of Charles up through the Welsh borders. A battle took place between these two factions on 24th September at whatever they wished. They also suffered from widescale crop destruction and then having to pay increased taxes to pay for the war – not to mention the huge losses of friends and family in the fighting. Finally, there were other costs, too – like the cost to age-old churches, vandalised by Parliamentarians in the name of Puritanism, with statues and screens smashed and altar rails removed because they didn't fit with the new ideology.

From 1654, England was placed under military rule and divided into regions under the control of a major-general. Cheshire was aligned with Lancashire and Staffordshire under Charles Worsley, who was ruthless towards Royalist sympathisers, even down to farmers and labourers. This may well have been a major factor in the uprising of 1659 in Cheshire by Royalist supporters, and which was led by a former Parliamentarian, Sir George Booth of Dunham Massey. Despite serving as MP for Cheshire from 1654, he became totally disillusioned with Parliament and began secret negotiations with Charles II in 1658, planning separate revolts in various counties for August 1659. However, the plot was exposed, but whereas other counties backed down, Booth made sure that Cheshire went ahead, and on 1st August, Royalist forces were mustered at Warrington and marched on Chester where they were admitted by the mayor and governor. Booth's forces also rapidly took control of most of the rest of Cheshire, south Lancashire, and north Wales, but without the support of any other county, they were doomed to failure, and were eventually defeated at the Battle of Winnington Bridge near Northwich. Booth himself escaped disguised as a woman, but was captured on 23rd August and imprisoned in the Tower of London. Surprisingly, though, Booth was soon liberated and returned to his seat in the Convention Parliament in 1660. He then became one of the key players in bringing about the Restoration of the English monarchy, and on the coronation of Charles II, he was created 1st Baron Delamer. The same year he was also appointed Custos Rotulorum of Cheshire.

At the turn of the 17th century, 60% of the value of larger farming estates was already invested in livestock, and as the century progressed, the now-familiar

This is another view of the Anglo-Saxon Greenway Cross looking north-westwards. By the early 17th century it had stood here for many centuries on this lonely trackway which led down from the western Peak District towards Macclesfield. However, in 1603 and 1646, it was used as a plague cross where the town dwellers of Macclesfield came to buy provisions from country dwellers. The sellers would place their goods near the cross along with a marked price, and then retire. The townsfolk would then approach the cross, select their goods, and pay the marked price by dropping their money into a basin or socket filled with water (and possibly vinegar, too), which was intended to remove all traces of infection.

pastoral landscape of southern and central Cheshire began to take shape. That said, 15-25% of south Cheshire's landscape still remained given over to arable farming until as late as the 1820s and the production of cereal crops remained an important part of the county's economy. Flax and hemp were grown throughout the county, except on the mid-Cheshire ridge and the Pennine slopes. These crops therefore supported a variety of textile trades producing linen, canvas and fustian, some of which were operating on a commercial scale as early as the 1590s. Nevertheless, the importance of cheese to the county economy had become critical by the late 17th century, with that well-known commentator of the day, Celia Fiennes, emphasising the point in 1695, while two decades later, Daniel Defoe remarked that "there is about four thousand ton of Cheshire cheese brought down the Trent every year". And indeed it was, from where it would then be shipped from Gainsborough or Hull to London. As the

The Old Hall Hotel at Sandbach was built in 1656 on the site of a previous manor house, and eventually became an 18th century coaching inn.

The Angel Hotel on King Street, Knutsford dates from the 18th century, but is more famous for its appearance in Elizabeth Gaskell's 19th century novel, Cranford.

cheese industry developed, so too did demand for cheese, particularly from the growing towns of south Lancashire and the West Midlands. Certainly from around 1700 onwards, the farms on the Mersey lowlands from Eastham to Ince, and in the north Wirral, began to produce increasing quantities of cheese for the increasing demand from Liverpool. A similar arrangement saw the cheese and butter-making industry around Altrincham ramp up its production for supply to Manchester, while a butter market was founded in the town in 1684 by Lord Delamere.

Bluecoat School in Chester, just beyond the north gate, was built in 1700 on the site of a former medieval hospital.

Quirk Alert: *Farmer's Wives and a Big Chest*

St Oswald's church at Lower Peover is home to a big oak chest which for many years housed parish records, vicars' robes, chalices and church documents. Local legend has it that if a girl wished to be a farmer's wife she must be able to lift the chest lid with one arm – thus demonstrating enough strength to be able to lift the famous Cheshire cheeses made in the area!

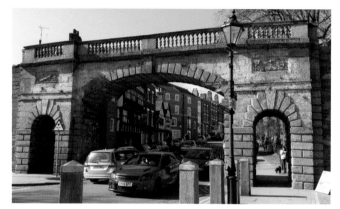

Bridgegate in Chester was constructed on the site of the former Roman south gate in 1782.

In the eastern part of the county, cattle were less important in the early 18th century, and sheep were still being reared in large numbers. Spinning and weaving took place on a small scale in the 17th and early 18th century, largely at home, with the Longdendale Valley home to a high proportion of farming families weaving on a commercial scale.

One of the most important enablers to the Agricultural Revolution in Cheshire was the issue of land enclosure, as this allowed farmers to invest in land that they owned. The grand majority of enclosures occurred between 1760 and 1836, but some parishes had already been either fully or partly enclosed during the 16th and 17th centuries. Typically, this would have involved the enclosure of common and arable pasture for personal use, which obviously removed such common land from the communal system and often provoked violent opposition from evicted tenants. It also had social consequences, leading to the depopulation of some parishes and an increase in vagrancy. For example, at Aldersey in the Dee valley, grants of land in 1546 referred to open unenclosed fields for farming, but by 1658, this land had been enclosed and converted to hedged fields. Essentially, people gave way to animals, and although the hamlet of Middle Aldersey survived until the 16th century, a survey of 1698 lists not a single dwelling in the pasturelands of the area. Eventually, even the unfenced grazing areas of the Pennine slopes were enclosed and turned into sheep farms, thus further reducing common land; in fact, by the mid-18th century, there was virtually no open common field left in Cheshire.

At the same time, agricultural reformers were introducing improved methods of farming, particularly in terms of land drainage. Better-quality grasses were introduced to produce richer pasture, such as those techniques used at Wythenshawe in the mid-17th century which involved deeper ploughing followed by a period of arable use along with manuring and further ploughing, which was then followed by the laying of good quality grass.

As well as agriculture, many other Cheshire industries developed between 1500 and 1700. This included a coal industry in the east of the county, based upon the coalfield which ran from just south of Stockport in a south-easterly direction towards Buxton. There was certainly a coal pit at Worth in Poynton by 1589, and these typically small Elizabethan collieries expanded throughout the 17th century to meet local industrial demand for coal – i.e. for the process of salt boiling, or for domestic use in the growing towns of the region. By 1700, the Poynton mines had reached depths of 60 feet or more, and had been joined by other mines such as those at Lyme Handley, Norbury and those in the upper Dane region.

Quirk Alert: *Eleven Boys in a Tree!*

According to Arthur Mee's The King's England, *there is a gnarled old oak at Arley, into which the local squire is said to have once squeezed eleven boys, paying them each a shilling a piece for the feat. Today, this seems wrong on so many different levels.*

In addition to coal, the late 17th century saw the development of quarries for building stone, such as those at Kerridge and Mow Cop, while the 1690s also saw the first evidence of small workings at Alderley Edge, and of copper mining in the Peckforton hills. The mid-17th century also saw the development of an ironworking industry which provided forged rods for nail and chain-making, with the first recorded forge appearing at Betley in 1646. By 1658, John Turner of Stafford had built a furnace and forge at Church Lawton, while two years later in 1660, a forge was built at Cranage near Holmes Chapel. The late 17th and early 18th century saw further forges and ironworks built at Disley, Street near Alsager, Vale Royal and Warmingham, and which produced goods such as salt-pans, frying pans and saw blades. Other more local iron products included nails for the nailers at Church Lawton (founded 1663), Macclesfield (1667) and Tushingham (1678), and locks for the locksmiths of Nantwich (1663). Interestingly, the iron industry actually declined in Cheshire between 1720 and 1730, with the Vale Royal furnace having been closed down by the famous ironmaster, Abraham Darby, in around 1716, and with others following, thereafter – such that county output in 1730 was half of its total of ten years earlier. The exception to this trend was the ironworks at Warmingham which, under the management of the Vernon family, expanded to become one of the largest ironworks in the country. Nevertheless, most of Cheshire's other ironworks had closed by 1785, mainly due to the competition from coalfield-based furnaces.

One Cheshire industry that could always be relied upon to thrive was the salt industry, particularly after the technological advances of the late 16th century allowed for a more efficient and cost-effective method of brine extraction. These methods included the use of Cheshire coal as a fuel for the evaporation process, as well as using iron rather than lead-based evaporation pans which could withstand the higher temperatures of the coal-based fires. Figures from 1682 show that around 21,000 bushels of salt per week were being produced, with around 58 per cent of that total coming from Northwich and the remainder shared roughly

equally between Middlewich and Nantwich. However, in 1670, during explorations around mid-Cheshire for coal (so that the Cheshire salt and coal workings could be co-aligned), a trial boring at Marbury near Northwich revealed beds of rock salt. Mining quickly followed, and by the early 18th century it was more economical to raise rock salt and refine it near the coalfield than to import coal for the refining of brine – something which obviously hit the owners of the brine pits rather hard.

Despite this fortunate discovery and the technological advances in extraction, transport of the product remained difficult. Much was transported overland to Frodsham Bridge and then by sea to Ireland, south Wales and northern Europe, or across the Mersey to Dungeon near Hale where England's first salt refinery was built, fuelled by nearby Widnes coal.

The high cost of the initial overland part of the journey led to a revival of plans to make the River Weaver navigable from Frodsham down to Nantwich, and an Act of Parliament was secured to do so in 1721. Over the following twelve years, the river was improved as far upstream as Winsford Bridge, but plans to extend the Weaver Navigation to Nantwich,

A view inside one of today's modern salt silos at Middlewich, but which gives some perspective (man vs. salt pile) on the amount of salt that was available to the thriving 17th and 18th century salt industry in Cheshire.

Whereas the previous photo showed a salt "pile" at Middlewich, here's a salt "mountain" at the same site!

And here's another rock salt mountain just north of Winsford. The salt industry exploded at Winsford in the mid-18th century after the 1721 Act of Parliament which made the River Weaver navigable from Frodsham down to Winsford.

The Grade I listed Dunham Massey Hall was initially built in 1616 by Sir George Booth, although it was re-modelled in the 18th century.

Also Grade I listed at Dunham Massey are the stables and carriage hall which date from 1721.

and to Middlewich via the River Dane were never realised. As a result, Nantwich and Middlewich saw a decline in salt production due to the additional transportation costs. Conversely, Northwich thrived, and also took advantage of the cheaper import of south Lancashire coal up the Weaver, while Winsford also began to develop as a centre for the salt extraction industry, too. By 1744, the Weaver Navigation was carrying 30,000 tons of salt down from Winsford and Northwich.

Leather goods were another important industry in Cheshire during this period, with glove-making an important part of Nantwich's economy. However, Chester was the focal point for leather-working and included cordwainers, glovers, hatters, saddlers, shoemakers and tanners. Meanwhile, Cheshire centres for the textile industry were over in the east of the county in towns such as Macclesfield, but even in 1700, this was only on a small scale compared with what was just around the corner. Nevertheless, cloth from East Cheshire was certainly an established product and small-scale industry as early as the beginning of the 17th century with Manchester merchants commonly selling what was known as "Stockport cloth" to the London market. In the 17th century, though, it would have been coarse woollen cloth produced in fulling mills such as those at Congleton, Macclesfield and Rainow, while by

the early 18th century, Sale and Ashton-on-Mersey were famed for their production of "girthweb", a coarse fabric used for saddle-girths; indeed, over 25 per cent of adult men in this locality worked in this trade between 1706 and 1730.

As well as textiles, Macclesfield was also a centre for button-making in the early 17th century, for which it gained an international reputation. This meant that the button merchants already had a sophisticated network of trading which they were able to tap into once silk began to be produced in Macclesfield in the mid-17th century, an industry which soon spread to Congleton, Rainow and Stockport. In particular, Macclesfield was renowned for ribbons and narrow-silks, while Congleton gained a reputation for lace-making.

Although the great explosion of canals didn't occur until the late 18th century, there were other schemes that pre-dated them in Cheshire, such as the Weaver Navigation improvements already mentioned in the 1720s. Even earlier than that, a scheme in the 1690s had dredged the tidal stretch of the River Mersey from Runcorn to Warrington, while an extension upstream to Manchester known as the Mersey and Irwell Navigation was authorised in 1720, finally unlocking the vast Manchester commercial potential to Britain's waterways.

Similar problems of silting and shallowness had hampered Chester's potential as a port, and the Dee Navigation was therefore also improved in the 1690s, and by 1698, Francis Gell, a London merchant, had built a new wharf at Chester. Even this water-course became victim of the shifting sands though, and in the 1730s, a completely new channel was cut through the sandbanks on the Welsh side of the Dee from Chester and beyond. Unfortunately, this latest venture ended up damaging the access to Chester's port at Parkgate, the main disembarkation point for Ireland, but conversely, it enabled the reclamation of the estuary above Shotton – which came in handy three centuries later when the 20th century steelworks were built there! The general problem with the shallowness of the River Dee, though, meant that Chester was always going to lose out to Liverpool as the main port of the north-west, particularly once the Industrial Revolution got under way; ships became

Quirk Alert: *Mean Spirit*

Parson Gastrell was an 18th century vicar of Frodsham for thirty-two years from 1740 to 1772, but he also bought Shakespeare's New Place in Stratford-upon-Avon in 1756. However, he apparently hated people peering over his Stratford wall to see the mulberry tree that Shakespeare had planted – and so he committed the heinous crime of cutting it down, and then selling it as firewood! Unsurprisingly, he became the most unpopular resident of Stratford, made worse when he quarrelled with the town about his taxes. His reaction to this: he pulled down Shakespeare's house to spite the Stratford corporation! Needless to say, he was hounded out of town.

Tatton New Hall, built in 1716 for the Egerton family.

This is the hunting tower at Lyme Park, built in 1737 on the site of an older structure built around 1580.

larger, industry exploded in south Lancashire...and the Dee probably quite happily took a step back!

Nevertheless, Chester still maintained its place as an important trading and commercial centre, and retained a wide range of specialised fairs and markets; for example, by 1700, there were four annual horse fairs. Chester also continued to trade overseas, especially with Ireland, as well as with France and Spain, with Chester being a major outlet for Cheshire, Lancashire and Yorkshire cloth, as well as its own extensive leather-ware products. Coal, lead and lead-ore also went outbound, while imports included dried fruits, glass, soap, spices and sugar, with wine the main import from France. To put this trade in perspective, though, in 1634, Chester paid £120 in export duties, while Bristol paid £424 in 1631 and Plymouth and Cornwall paid £798. More significantly, in the same year (1634), Chester's £120 still dwarfed Liverpool's £18!

During the early 17th century, the Puritan movement gained ground in Cheshire, and in Chester, the altar rails and other high Anglican symbols were removed from

Quirk Alert: *Midsomer Bidston?*
The list of former vicars at St Oswald's church in Bidston reveals that there were nine vicars here, in nine consecutive years of the 18th century! But not why...

most churches in the city, while the cathedral walls were whitewashed and its stained glass destroyed. However, the Church of England was restored in 1660, and Bishop Hall oversaw the ejection of over one hundred clergy with nonconformist leanings, so that between 1660 and 1663, three quarters of all Cheshire churches had new incumbents! Of course, the ejected ministers simply infused the congregations of dissenters, which became particularly active in the east of the county. When the Toleration Act was passed in May 1689, allowing freedom of worship to nonconformists, 92 meeting houses were licensed in Cheshire and by 1700, that number had risen to almost 250, with the strongest centres at Knutsford, Macclesfield and Nantwich. By 1771, there were 2909 Methodists in Cheshire, a number which had climbed to 6123 by 1808, while in the 1790s, Macclesfield was thought to be the town with the highest percentage of Methodists in England.

In terms of politics, the wealthy (and Tory) Grosvenor family had something of a monopoly on Chester and hence Cheshire politics from the early 18th century to the late 19th century; indeed at least one Grosvenor was an MP for Chester in every Parliament from 1715 to 1874. Meanwhile at Congleton, a bitter split between Tories and Whigs was sustained for decades. Matters came to a head in 1714 when the Tories, loyal supporters of the High Church and sympathisers with the Jacobite cause, forbade the ringing of the Congleton church bells to celebrate the

The Jenkin or Saltersford Chapel, 3 miles east of Rainow, was built in 1733 by local subscription, and must be one of the remotest in England.

St Mary's church at Rostherne largely dates from its mid-18th century rebuild.

This packhorse bridge at Hockenhull Platts, dates from the 18th century, and is one of three Grade II listed bridges here across the River Gowy.

The Packhorse Bridge over the River Dane at Three Shires Head, where Cheshire, Derbyshire and Staffordshire all meet. The spot was also a well-known meeting point for illegal prize-fighting, where the protagonists and crowd could hot-foot it over the county border when challenged by officials of other counties.

accession of George I. Both Whigs and dissenters weren't having that, though, and promptly stormed the church and rang them anyway – at which point a riot ensued, culminating with a Tory mob ransacking the nonconformist meeting house and burning the pews on a bonfire.

Prior to the 18th century, the responsibility for maintaining roads had rested with under-funded local parishes, and so the Cheshire road network was in a poor state of health. Road travel was particularly difficult across the uplands of eastern Cheshire, especially in winter. The solution to this problem was the introduction of turnpike trusts – bodies set up by Acts of Parliament with powers to collect tolls in order to maintain principal highways, and which were generally run by groups of local trustees. Cheshire's first turnpike road was introduced in 1705 and included the short stretch of the Chester to Whitchurch road between Barnhill and Hatton Heath.

The next road to be improved and run by a trust in Cheshire didn't happen until 1724 when the route from Manchester to Buxton, via Stockport, was turnpiked. Other early turnpikes in Cheshire included the route up through Longdendale from Manchester to Barnsley (1728), Lawton to Cranage (1731) and Woore to Chester

(1744). Thereafter, turnpike trusts came thick and fast, and longer stretches of road were turnpiked meaning that Cheshire had a road network that linked all of its main towns and villages by the early 19th century. But perhaps the most ambitious scheme came a little later, in 1821, when the section from Macclesfield to Buxton was turnpiked and which included the infamous section between Macclesfield and the Cat and Fiddle Inn, which climbs some 1,250 feet. Interestingly, the 1821 turnpike replaced a 1730 predecessor, which had just gone up and downhill in a reasonably straight line. However, the horse-drawn carriages of the 19th century preferred gentler gradients, and hence the new turnpike was constructed as a series of long bends which gently wended their way up to Cat and Fiddle and Shining Tor, and similarly down the other side.

The early 19th century also saw a network of turnpikes developed around Stockport to connect this fast-growing textile region, while another important early 19th century turnpike, linked Birkenhead with Hoylake and West Kirby; interestingly, this latter turnpike was intended more for commuters than goods. Meanwhile, the last turnpike in Cheshire was the road from Hooton to Queensferry, constructed in 1838. In total some 582 miles of road in Cheshire were turnpiked between 1705 and 1835.

Quirk Alert: *The Alderley Wizard*
According to a late 18th century legend, a farmer from Mobberley was walking along Alderley Edge, taking a white mare to sell at Macclesfield market, when an old man in grey and flowing garments stopped him, offering the farmer a sum for his horse. The farmer refused, anticipating greater profit in Macclesfield, but returned empty-handed. On his return journey, the old man appeared again, repeating his offer, which this time was accepted. The farmer followed the old man told to a place known locally as Stormy Point, where the old man raised a wand and uttered a spell. Immediately, the rocks opened, revealing a pair of huge iron gates which led into a cavern – where the farmer observed countless men and white horses, all asleep. The old man paid the farmer the agreed sum, took his horse, and explained that the sleeping men and horses would one day awaken when England was next in mortal danger!

Cheshire's Industrial Revolution

The Industrial Revolution began in England in the late 18th century, with the arrival of water-powered cotton mills, the birth of factories and mass production of goods, all of which utterly transformed the landscape of eastern Cheshire. However, the transport of bulk product would not have been possible without the development of brand new canals, which exploded all over England in the late 18th century – and which largely started with the Bridgewater Canal, partly in Cheshire.

Of course, it wasn't just the textile and coal industries in the north-east of the county that benefitted; the salt industry in the centre of the county and the agricultural industry throughout the county did so too. But an even more compelling reason for developing Cheshire's waterways was due to its location between the growing giants of Liverpool and Manchester. The early proposals for waterway development centred on Cheshire's main rivers – the Mersey, the Dee and the Weaver – as well as linking these waterways to the Severn and the Trent, slightly further afield. However, these rivers already had navigation trustees, who tended to be driven by self-interest, therefore the canal engineers opted for routes which bypassed the existing navigations.

The Bridgewater Canal was Cheshire's first, and the Act of Parliament for its construction was passed in 1759. The requirement for the canal was driven by Francis Egerton, 3rd Duke of Bridgewater, to transport coal from his mines at Worsley in Lancashire, to Manchester, and the canal first opened between Worsley and Manchester (so purely in Lancashire) in 1761. The engineer for this project was the great James Brindley and, having completed the first part of the Bridgewater Canal, attention then turned to linking the canal at Manchester to Runcorn in Cheshire. This was covered by the Bridgewater Canal Extension Act of 1762 – despite opposition from the Mersey and Irwell Navigation Company. A junction was created at Trafford Park and

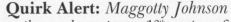

Quirk Alert: *Maggotty Johnson*

Gawsworth was home to an 18th century Samuel Johnson (1691-1773) – although this one was an eccentric fiddler, dancer, stilt-walker, dramatist and writer who was eighteen years the senior of the more-famous Lichfield-born Dr Johnson! The former's greatest work was an opera, Hurlothrumbo *(1729), in which he played the leading role of Lord Flame, fiddling, dancing and, of course, walking on stilts! Although highly unusual, the opera ran in London's Haymarket for over a month – an unusual success for the period. He wrote three other plays, not as successful, and retired to Gawsworth where he was known variously as Flame, Fiddler Johnson…or Maggotty (not explained)! He died in 1773 at New Hall, and was buried in a small wood nearby; still known as Maggotty Wood, it is reputedly haunted by his stilt-walking ghost!*

which became known as Waters Meeting, and the extension headed south-westwards via Stretford, Sale, Altrincham, Lymm and finally to Runcorn.

One of Brindley's biggest challenges was the western terminus, as Runcorn basin was almost 90 feet (27m) above the Mersey. Consequently, a flight of ten locks were built to connect the two, and which became known as "the wonder of their time". The final connection to the Mersey was made on 1st January 1773,

NORTH EASTERN CHESHIRE CANALS

Marple Aqueduct (above left and right) was built between 1795 and 1799 to carry the Peak Forest Canal over the River Goyt at Marple.

Above left: *The Macclesfield Canal at Marple. The canal was constructed between 1826 and 1831, and linked the Peak Forest Canal at Marple, to the Trent and Mersey Canal on the south Cheshire border with Staffordshire.* Above right: *The Macclesfield Canal at Oakgrove.*

enabling the Duke's coal to be sent from the Lancashire coalfields to Liverpool at minimum cost. The duke also built Runcorn Dock alongside the Mersey, as well as several warehouses. Other challenges included the circumnavigation of Norton Priory, as Sir Richard Brooke demanded that the canal should not pass through his lands, as he was concerned that boatmen might poach his game and wildfowl! The Act therefore had to be modified to include clauses stating that the canal should not come within 1066ft (325m) of his house, and a requirement for no quays, buildings, hedges or fences to obstruct the view, and no vessels to be moored within 3281ft (1,000m) of the house, other than during construction!

Quirk Alert: *The Montpelier of the North*

The Montpelier of the North was, in fact, Runcorn – this between the years 1790 and 1840 when the town was a health spa and people use to flock to the place for its air and waters!

CENTRAL AND WESTERN CHESHIRE CANALS

Significantly, the Bridgewater Canal also included a junction with the Trent and Mersey Canal at Preston Brook – this following the passing of the Trent and Mersey Canal Act of 1766. This new canal link therefore enabled the duke's coal to be shipped to the Midlands markets as well. The first part of the new extension was opened in 1767, while the entire project wasn't completed until March 1776, four years after Brindley's death. The Bridgewater Canal was also extended in 1807 to take it around the Runcorn headland, thus giving it access to deeper water in the Mersey.

One of the main effects of the Bridgewater Canal was that trade on the Weaver Navigation dropped dramatically after 1777. The trustees therefore responded by improving the river and seeking a connection with the Trent and Mersey Canal. The most suitable point to effect this junction was at Anderton, just north of Northwich. Initially, in 1799, this was provided via an inclined plane between the canal and the river and, once complete, this resulted in increased traffic on the waterway.

Meanwhile in Chester, commercial and civic interests combined to propose a new link to the Trent and Mersey Canal, originally at Middlewich. However, the

The Trent and Mersey Canal heads into this tunnel at Barnton which stretches for 572 yards (523m) and is only wide enough for one narrowboat. It was built in 1775 to take the canal through a spur above the Weaver valley.

The Trent and Mersey Canal at Middlewich. The path to the left goes up over the bridge which links the Trent and Mersey Canal to the Shropshire Union Canal Middlewich Branch, via the Wardle Canal.

The Shropshire Union Canal at Brassey Green.

Barbridge Junction, where the Shropshire Union Canal heads northwards (to the left), and where the branch known as the Shropshire Union Canal (Middlewich Branch) heads off in a north-easterly direction towards Middlewich.

Trent and Mersey Canal Company were not keen, and hence the canal was constructed to Nantwich, instead. The first stretch of the canal, from Chester to Huxley, was opened in 1775, with the remainder to Nantwich opening in 1779. Unfortunately, the River Dee Company were also uncooperative, effectively blocking through-traffic to the Dee, and hence the expected salt traffic didn't materialise. The Cheshire Canal therefore became uneconomic, and part of it was closed in 1787, when Beeston staircase locks collapsed, and there was no money for repairs. However, salvation came in the form of the Ellesmere Canal, which intended to link the Mersey with the Severn. It was opened in 1790 and by 1797, it provided a link from Chester to the Mersey at Ellesmere Port – where the canal soon lent its name to the community that grew up there in the 1790s. The Ellesmere Canal also included a route into south-west Cheshire from Wales, linking with the Chester Canal just north of Nantwich in 1805. This enabled limestone and slate to be transported to Cheshire and beyond from the Welsh hills along with iron from foundries in the Ruabon area, and all of a sudden, the canal became viable. The two companies then merged in 1813, becoming the Ellesmere and Chester Canal. When the Birmingham and Liverpool Junction Canal was proposed in 1826, which would provide a link from Nantwich to Wolverhampton and the Birmingham canal system, the Ellesmere and Chester Canal Company saw an opportunity to finally build that branch to Middlewich and hence connect on to Manchester and the Potteries, too. As a result, the Middlewich Branch opened in 1833, and the Junction Canal opened in 1835.

At the opposite end of the county, the Ashton Canal was authorised by an Act of Parliament in 1792, linking Manchester with Dukinfield and hence tapping into the coalfields of the Oldham, Denton and Ashton under Lyne areas, as well as serving the textile industries of the Tame Valley. An extension to link the Ashton Canal to the Bridgewater Canal was completed in 1800. Meanwhile, the Peak Forest Canal was authorised by an Act of Parliament in 1794, and was completed in 1800, linking the limestone works in north-west Derbyshire with the Ashton Canal and thus Manchester as well as Liverpool via the Bridgewater Canal. The canal included the construction of an impressive flight of sixteen locks at Marple, as well as a stunning aqueduct. Finally, the Macclesfield Canal linked the Peak Forest Canal in the north-east of Cheshire, to the Trent and Mersey Canal in south Cheshire, stretching from Marple in the north-east, passing through Bollington, Macclesfield and Congleton, before joining the Trent and Mersey at Hall Green on the Cheshire border with Staffordshire. The Act of Parliament for the construction of the Macclesfield Canal was passed in 1826 and the canal opened in 1831. Of course, being a latecomer to the canal scene, the Macclesfield Canal almost immediately found itself up against the emerging railways, and therefore only enjoyed modest prosperity in the 1830s.

Aldford Iron Bridge was built across the River Dee in 1824, linking Aldford with Eaton Hall. The bridge was designed by Thomas Telford and built by William Hazledine for the 1st Marquis of Westminster.

Runcorn Railway Bridge was built over the River Mersey between 1864 and 1868 to link Runcorn and Widnes. It was built by the London and North Western Railway (LNWR). From this angle, the span of the railway bridge is partly obscured by the 20th century road bridge, but the piers and arches belong to the 19th century bridge.

The arrival of the railways in the 1830s and 1840s obviously put an end to much of the freight traffic on Cheshire's waterways, but some of them managed to hold their own. This was certainly the case for the Trent and Mersey and the Macclesfield Canal, as they were bought by the North Staffordshire Railway in 1845 and 1847, respectively, and were used as railway feeders to compete with its rival railway company, the London & North Western Railway. This was only a stay of execution, though, and by the mid-1870s, canal traffic was in decline. Meanwhile, over in the west of the county, the Ellesmere & Chester Canal amalgamated with the Birmingham and Liverpool Junction Canal to become the Shropshire Union Canal, although the waterway was leased by the London & North Western Railway from 1849.

Of course, railways, tramroads and waggonways all existed before the 1830s, throughout Cheshire, albeit mainly serving quarries and mines. For example, there were waggonways serving the Poynton collieries by 1793, while in the south-east of the county, a colliery line was built from the pits in the Biddulph and Mow Cop area of north Staffordshire, to Congleton. Contemporary with this was a tramroad that linked the quarries on Helsby Hill with the River Mersey at Ince. However, the first major railway route *across* Cheshire was authorised in 1833 when the Grand Junction Railway planned its line from Birmingham to Warrington, where it would connect with the Warrington & Newton Railway and thence onto the Liverpool & Manchester Railway. The latter railway was, of course, the first public transport system on land which did not use animal traction power, and had been opened three years earlier in September 1830. The route through Cheshire opened in 1837 and, as it ran on a south-to-north trajectory, it became logical to build branch lines heading in a north-westerly direction to Liverpool and north-easterly to Manchester. The location selected by the railway developers for this hub was, of course, at Crewe, and having done this, the GJR then commenced building their main workshops at Crewe, thus changing the industrial dynamic of the place forever. Interestingly, the construction of the Manchester branch line was actually in the balance, as the decision on the route to be chosen was in the hands of prominent Mancunian industrialists. Some favoured a line heading due south towards Stoke and then on to Tamworth and Rugby, but in the end the route from Stockport to Crewe was selected, and was completed in 1842. The route included an impressive viaduct at Stockport, which is considered to be one of the greatest triumphs of Victorian railway engineering, and which

was completed in December 1840. As for the route north-west from Crewe to Liverpool, this didn't materialise for another three decades, thanks to the natural barrier of the Mersey – and hence trains still went via Warrington until the 1870s; it was 1864 before work began on the route from Weaver Junction through Runcorn and over the Mersey to Widnes via the railway bridge, and then west into Liverpool.

Back to 1840, though, and the next main route to be laid down by the GJR was from Crewe to Chester, a line that would eventually be part of that which carried traffic from London to Holyhead. At the same time, the Chester & Birkenhead Railway laid down track between these two towns, thus connecting the Wirral to the railway network, and offering another route to Liverpool via the Mersey ferry. However, the GJR initially refused to offer any connections to the Birkenhead line at their Chester station, in order to preserve their longer route to Liverpool via Warrington!

By July 1846, the Grand Junction Railway had merged with the London and Birmingham Railway and the Manchester and Birmingham Railway, to form the new London and North Western Railway (LNWR), and thereafter, the LNWR became the dominant railway company in Cheshire. Happily, in 1860, the LNWR assumed joint ownership of the Chester & Birkenhead Railway, and finally allowed connections at Chester to

The Grade II listed Hovis Mill at Macclesfield was built in 1830, and was the original home of Hovis bread from 1886, made from the grain milled here. However, production had been moved to Manchester by 1914.

Clarence Mill was built in Bollington in 1834 for the Swindells family, but today is home to many luxury apartments.

Surviving garret houses in Paradise Street, Macclesfield.

Salford Mill, an early 19th century silk mill in Congleton.

the Birkenhead Railway! As for the co-owner, this was the Great Western Railway, who were keen to capture some of the Merseyside freight traffic. The co-owners hence ran the Birkenhead Joint Lines, which included another route from Chester to Warrington.

Meanwhile, by 1863, the Midland Railway reached Manchester from St Pancras and became a challenger to the LNWR's dominance of Cheshire territory. As for the far south of Cheshire, this area benefitted from the North Staffordshire Railway (NSR), a maze of branches woven around the Potteries, and which operated an additional branch to Sandbach, thus tapping into the salt traffic. The NSR also owned the Macclesfield-Congleton-Stoke section of the alternative main line from Manchester to the south, operating through services with the LNWR. Finally, in the far north-eastern corner of Cheshire, the Great Central Railway operated the route between Manchester and Sheffield, along with a few local lines in that area.

Also improving in the 19th century were ferry crossings from Liverpool to the Wirral, including to Tranmere (1817), Birkenhead (1819) and Woodside (1822), while turnpike roads across the peninsula provided faster road links to the ferry ports. This development made it possible for Liverpudlian merchants and businessmen to work in the city and live in rural peace on the Wirral. Developing along similar lines was Altrincham, with respectable housing springing up in the 19th century, homes to Manchester businessmen who could now live out in the country and take the train into work.

As well as the huge strides forward in terms of transport brought by first the canals and then the railways, the other major feature of the Industrial Revolution was the mass migrations from the countryside to the burgeoning towns, and from the agricultural industry, to the textile industry, particular in east and north-east Cheshire. However, the birth of the silk industry in Cheshire pre-dates the canal revolution, for it was in the 1720s that the mechanised Italian process of silk-throwing was smuggled into England – by a gentleman called John Lombe, of Derby, who paid for his espionage with his life when poisoned by a mystery female assassin – who also happened to be Italian! However, the secret was out, and over the next twenty years several factories were established in Cheshire, with the earliest established at the water-powered

Macclesfield Town Hall was built in 1824.

Peckforton Castle was built by John Tollemache between 1841 and 1850 in the image of a medieval castle. Tollemache was the largest landowner in Cheshire in 1871 – not on account of his girth, but on account of the 25,380 acres of land that he owned!

Logwood Mill in Stockport in 1732, by John Guardivaglio. Indeed, at that time, Logwood Mill was one of the first three silk-throwing mills in the country, and was built on the site of a logwood mill that ground logwood to create dyestuffs. Twelve years later the Carr Brook was dammed to support a new mill, while another followed at the confluence of the Carr Brook and the River Mersey. By 1760, there were 2000 silk-throwing workers at these three sites in Stockport.

However, the Cheshire town most famous for silk manufacture is Macclesfield, and it was here in 1744 that Charles Roe built the Royal Button Mill. A third important Cheshire silk mill was erected at Congleton in 1753 and became known as the Old Mill which used an internal water wheel to power Italian silk throwing

---

Quirk Alert: *William Buckley*

William Buckley of Macclesfield, was 6ft 6in tall, and was one of a small group of men who mutinied at Gibraltar during the Napoleonic Wars, intent on murdering their commanding officer – who was none-other than Prince Edward, Duke of Kent and Strathearn – the future father of Queen Victoria! Of course, the mutiny failed, three ringleaders were shot, and Buckley was transported to Australia. There he escaped into the bush, where he eventually came across a spear of a buried local chieftain. On later beholding the giant Buckley, holding the revered spear, the natives concurred that this was their dead chief come back to life again. Buckley therefore learned their language and for 32 years was their chief – until one day, he finally met a white colonist. Thereafter, he returned to civilisation, was pardoned and pensioned and lived until age 76 in Hobart, Tasmania.

machines. By 1771, Old Mill was employing 600 workers. Meanwhile, Macclesfield had seven major silk-throwing firms by 1765, while east Cheshire had around one third of the total silk mill capacity in England. Sadly, none of these three historic Cheshire silk mills survive today.

As well as the factories powered by water, silk was also woven on hand looms in the home, and these garret houses – with upper lofts purpose-built for hand looms – are still a distinctive feature of Macclesfield and Congleton today, with around 300 surviving in Macclesfield alone. The industry continued to grow into the early 19th century, but in 1824, the government lifted the duty on the import of raw silk, and the price of the product fell rapidly. At the same time, technology advancements resulted in the gradual mechanisation of silk weaving.

The late 18th century saw the cotton industry explode in England, and water-powered cotton mills spring up in the north-east of Cheshire along the fast-flowing Etherow, Goyt and Tame. Some of these early cotton masters had previously worked in the silk trade and they brought their technical experience into the cotton industry with Stockport a well-recognised centre for technical innovation in this field. Indeed, the industry expanded rapidly after the first steam-powered mill opened in Stockport in 1791, and this resulted in a great influx of people into the town in the late 18th century to work in these new mills. The town itself therefore expanded rapidly to the extent that by 1800, Stockport had overtaken Chester as the largest town in the county, while by 1811, Stockport was second only to Manchester as a centre of the spinning industry.

Stockport also pioneered the steam loom which resulted in the town becoming a focus of mechanised weaving between 1815 and 1830. However, a number of major industrial disputes hit Stockport in the 1830s, which resulted in the break-up of the family firms who had driven the growth, industrialisation and prosperity of the town since the 1780s, and Stockport began to fall behind other areas in terms of both innovation and output. This decline coincided with the general depression years of 1840 and 1853, while worse was to come during the American Civil War of 1861-1865, which triggered the so-called "Cotton Famine" in England. At this time, the cotton industry employed over a third of the town's workforce, and it was a similar ratio in other towns of north-east Cheshire, but many workers were laid off and by January 1862, the number of paupers in the Stockport union workhouse had increased from 180 to 499. The industry then enjoyed a revival in Stockport during the 1880s, when private owners combined as large public limited companies to invest in new technology and buildings. As a result, Stockport saw two of the largest mills in the region built, Stockport Ring Mill No. 2 in 1906 and Broadstone No. 2 in 1907; by 1914, Stockport was ranked the sixth largest spinning centre in the country. The cotton industry then hit its peak in 1920, and thanks to the continued innovation in the

Quirk Alert: *Bonny Brid*

The cotton workers of Manchester and East Cheshire suffered greatly from the Cotton Famine during the American Civil War (1861-65), times which are poignantly captured by poet Samuel Laycock whose family had moved from West Yorkshire to Stalybridge in 1837. His Famine Songs *and poems were published in the mid-1860s, and include this wonderful verse to a new-born baby boy:*

Tha'rt welcome, little bonny brid,
But shouldn't ha' come just when tha did;
Toimes are bad.
We're short o' pobbie for eawr Joe,
But that, of course, tha didn't know,
Did ta lad?

town, it didn't suffer to the same extent that others did during the depression of the 1920s and 1930s.

Further north-east in Cheshire, Dukinfield, Hyde and Stalybridge were also hot-beds of the cotton industry, with Stalybridge's first mill built as early as 1776. The key accelerant to the three towns came in 1806, though, when the Ashton family introduced the power-loom at Hyde. The benevolent Ashtons also ensured that many of their employees became the freehold owners of their mill cottages. The three towns also earned a reputation for specialising in high quality printed cloths, with Hyde becoming famous for felt hats, leather dressing and glove-making. However, like Stockport, the towns were hard hit by the American Civil War, during which time their respective populations fell, and in 1885, Hyde was dealt a devastating blow when the Hibbert weaving mills were closed. Fortunes then improved again in 1890 when the Ashton family built the first steel-framed mill at Bayley, then in 1904, they introduced the extremely productive Northop automatic loom. As a result, the number of

The Grosvenor Museum building in Chester was built between 1865 and 1866 to house the collections of the Chester Archaeological Society, and the Chester Society of Natural Science, Literature and Art.

looms in Hyde mills increased by almost 50 per cent between 1904 and 1921, with Hyde recognised as the 12th largest weaving centre in the region in 1904, but the fourth largest between 1934 and 1963. That said, output capacity actually peaked at Hyde in 1916, as it did in Dukinfield; Stalybridge peaked in 1912.

The textile industry and working class political agitation were also closely linked during these times. In Macclesfield, the weavers rioted because of the scarcity of food in both 1757 and 1762, and there was widespread Cheshire unrest from 1795 onwards, thanks to shortages caused by the Revolutionary Wars. The late 18th century saw rioting in Chester, Congleton, Nantwich, Northwich and Stockport, while the year 1800 also saw riots in rural areas such as Bunbury. Then in 1812, there was even fiercer rioting in north-east Cheshire, at Bredbury, Macclesfield, Stalybridge and Stockport, where people were close to starving to death. The end of the Napoleonic Wars in 1815 then exacerbated the problem, and chronic unemployment and famine ensued as soldiers came home to no jobs, while the introduction of the Corn Laws resulted in domestic grain prices being kept artificially high. North-east Cheshire was the site of numerous meetings in 1817 and 1818, while a crowd of around 20,000 people gathered in Stockport in 1819 for a political meeting.

All of this worker discontent then exploded at St Peters' Field in Manchester on 16th August 1819. The Manchester Patriotic Union, a group agitating for Parliamentary reform, organised a demonstration to be addressed by the well-known radical orator Henry Hunt. However, shortly after the meeting began, local magistrates deployed the local militia to arrest Hunt and other radical leaders, and then to disperse the crowd. Their method was appalling. Cavalry actually charged into the crowd with sabres drawn, and in the resulting melee, 15 people were killed and around 700 people injured, many seriously. The massacre was given the name Peterloo as an ironic comparison to the Battle of Waterloo, which had taken place four years earlier. Despite national outrage, though, the government reac-

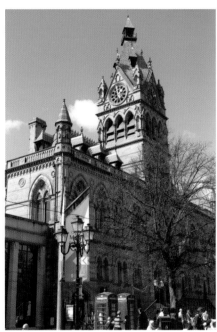

Top: *The Gothic Congleton Town Hall was opened in July 1866.* Above: *Chester Town Hall was built by William Henry Lynn and was opened in 1867. It took the place of the former Exchange building which burnt down in 1862.*

tion was to pass what became known as the Six Acts, aimed at suppressing any meetings that were propounding radical reform.

Throughout the Industrial Revolution, Nantwich became a centre for shoemaking and for the leather trade, and was already exporting shoes to London by 1795. However, the town became most famous for the "Nantwich Boot" during the 19th century, favoured by mill workers for its durability. However, Nantwich suffered from an employment crisis that was contemporary with the Cotton Famine, although this issue was first caused by mechanisation between 1858 and 1865 when the owners of the boot factories introduced riveting and sewing machines. Then, when the depression hit the cotton trade between 1861 and 1865, there was less demand for their product and the industry never recovered in Nantwich, as it found itself unable to compete with other English footwear centres. So where there were 33 manufacturers and 31 individual shoemakers in 1859, by 1890, there were only 7 and 15, respectively, while the industry had vanished in Nantwich completely by the 1920s.

In terms of 19th century engineering, Cheshire was not a hotbed. There were some small firms, such as the Hydraulic Engineering Co. at Chester. Founded in the 1820s, the company became one of the pioneers of hydraulic power equipment for docks, goods depots, power stations and industrial processing. Meanwhile, at Sandbach, Foden's began manufacturing commercial vehicles in 1850, such as traction engines and threshing machines, while they diversified into steam lorries from 1897.

Coal continued to be mined throughout Cheshire during the 19th century, but not on the scale elsewhere. However, it is worth mentioning that new reserves of coal were discovered on the Wirral in the late 1750s, and Ness colliery became one of the largest in Cheshire – mainly supplying coal to Chester and to Ireland via the quay that was built there in the 1760s. Surprisingly, there were also six collieries established by 1810 in the Wildboarclough and Wincle areas, although their remoteness meant that distribution was an issue.

> **Quirk Alert:** *The Ultimate Philanthropist*
> *Cotton mill owners of the 18ᵗʰ and 19ᵗʰ centuries are commonly seen as philanthropists, but spare a thought for Laurence Earnshaw of Mottram. A clockmaker, he made musical and optical instruments, but he also created a cotton-spinning machine in the mid-18ᵗʰ century. However, he destroyed it, lest it take away the work of poor men!*

Meanwhile, the already established east Cheshire coalfields expanded rapidly during the Industrial Revolution, with the collieries at Poynton and Norbury substantially helped by the deployment of steam pumps from 1750 onwards to effect appropriate drainage of the pits. In 1795, around 27,000 tons of coal was extracted from the Poynton pits. Deeper reserves were then exploited after 1810 while the colliery was served by a railway from 1845, all of which helped increase output to 243,000 tons by 1859. By 1897, the county as a whole was only producing 730,000 tons of which a third came from Poynton Colliery, with the rest being mined at Adlington, Lyme Handley and Ness, as well as the pits in the Upper Dane area. The decline of mining in Cheshire occurred many decades earlier than it did elsewhere in Britain, a fact suitably represented by the mere 280,000 tons that were mined in 1915, with Poynton responsible for two thirds of that total. By 1935, the last pit at Poynton had been closed.

Quarrying continued throughout the 19ᵗʰ century, with the largest, at Danebower, surviving until the 1950s. Elsewhere, new quarries were developed in the early 19ᵗʰ century at Kerridge, at Helsby, and at Storeton on the Wirral, with output including paving stones, kerbstones and large building stones. Copper ore continued to be mined at Alderley Edge, with the optimum point occurring between 1857 and 1877 when around 250,000 tons of ore was extracted, while copper was still mined sporadically in the Peckforton hills, too.

> **Quirk Alert:** *Little Fanny Bush*
> *So, not a character from a Jilly Cooper novel, but according to Arthur Mee's Cheshire volume of* The King's England, *she was "one of a party of Bush people on exhibition in a travelling show". The poor lady in question was performing in Hyde when she died from tuberculosis, and her grave (certainly in the 1930s) was located in the churchyard of St George's at Hyde.*

Of course, salt mining continued in central Cheshire on an industrial scale, with businessmen from south Lancashire investing heavily in the product as well as funding waterway improvements for exports. Salt production increased from 15,000 tons in 1732 to 150,000 tons in 1800, an increase assisted by the discovery of deeper beds of salt in 1779. Indeed, these lower beds at a depth of 175ft were up to 12ft thick and of exceptional quality, meaning that deep mines were sunk from 1781 in the Weaver Valley between Winsford and Northwich. In fact, Winsford eventually overtook Northwich by the 1840s to become the most important centre for salt production; conversely, at Middlewich, output steadily dwindled while salt production at Nantwich ceased in 1856. Nevertheless, by the 1870s, Cheshire salt was being exported in vast quantities to overseas markets, particularly India, and exceeded a million tons per year. Cheshire was responsible for 80 per cent of British output in 1887, and accounted for around one third of the tonnage shipped out of Liverpool.

One negative impact of the salt industry in central Cheshire is widescale subsidence. On occasions, the subsidence has been fatal, such as that in 1838 when seven men drowned when Ashton's Mine at Witton disappeared into its own workings, with the inrush of water overwhelming the miners and pit ponies before they could reach the surface. Another salt works that vanished into a large hole in 1928 was the Adelaide Mine at Marston, while over 40 houses in Marston were lost in the 1890s alone. Then we have Northwich. As Arthur Mee describes, "here and there the streets have a crazy look, some houses leaning forward and others propped up on crutches". Bearing in mind he is writing in the 1930s, he goes on to explain that "sixty years ago,

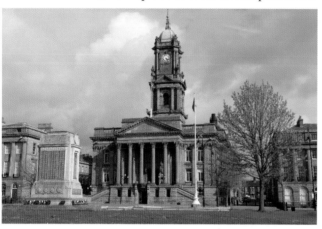

Top: *Birkenhead Town Hall was built between 1883 and 1887.*
Above: *Sandbach Town Hall was opened in 1889.*

the High Street was moved six inches, and another three at the beginning of this century" and "other parts of the town, such as the Bull Ring, are still going down, and the Brunner Library is moving at a rate of half an inch a year", while he also mentions a poor horse and cart that once disappeared into a Northwich sink-hole. Other subsidence has proven less severe but hugely damaging to property, which is why many of the buildings in Northwich are now designed such that they can be jacked up if necessary. Meanwhile, the Sandbach flashes appeared in the mid-19th century and are still expanding; Moston Long Flash, for example, is a narrow but still-growing lake which now stretches for over a mile, while between Wimboldsley and Winsford, the River Weaver widens into Bottoms Flash, another mile-long lake and up to half a mile wide all caused by 19th century subsidence. Incredibly, the salt companies actually refused to accept any liability for the subsidence and subsequent destruction of property, and when in 1873, a compensation arrangement was propounded by the Board of Trade, counter-lobbying by the salt companies saw the proposed bill rejected in 1881. Thankfully, the Brine Pumping (Compensation of Subsidence) Act was passed in 1891, and a wide number of households in central Cheshire became eligible for compensation.

THE AMAZING PORT SUNLIGHT

Here are six photographs taken in the amazing place that is Port Sunlight on the Wirral, surely England's finest surviving "garden village". It was created by William Hesketh Lever (later the first Lord Leverhulme) in 1888 for his workers at Lever Brothers Soap Works. There are wide avenues, spacious greens, beautiful flower beds, stunning monuments, as well as the Lady Lever Art Gallery (shown in first two photos). What also hits you is the sheer diversity of architecture; the architects must have had a ball! The montage above doesn't do it justice and these are just six photos out of 177 that I took.

One famous brand that was developed in Cheshire in the early 19th century was seeded in 1803 when John Johnson opened a small soapworks in Runcorn. It was this business which eventually developed into Johnson Brothers' soap, and by 1832, the company was the largest soap manufacturing company in the country by some distance; of the 2750 tons produced in Britain, 36 per cent came from Runcorn. However, the largest soap firm of all, Levers, also opened a factory on the Wirral on the shore south of Bromborough where they manufactured Sunlight soap. By 1897, the firm employed 2200 people and was producing 2400 tons of soap each week, while by 1914, Port Sunlight (as the place was now known) produced 60 per cent of the entire UK's soap output. Arthur Mee piles up superlatives for Port Sunlight in *The King's England (Cheshire)*, claiming it to be "one of the most astounding industrial and social spectacles in the world", and "cleanliness is next to godliness and Port Sunlight cleans half the world". He also states that by his day (the 1930s), the company employed 70,000 people around the world working in 250 factories or on millions of acres of plantations.

Runcorn also became a focal point for the chemical industry in the 19th century, producing alkalis, glass, soda, vitriol and paints, and was subject to major growth in the 1880s. The arrival of the Manchester Ship Canal helped, as did the building of the pipeline from Llyn Vyrnwy in mid-Wales to Liverpool, which fed the chemical plants with the pure water that they required in abundance. Meanwhile, in 1874, Ludwig Mond, in partnership with John Brunner, began manufacturing pure soda at his new works in Winnington, which gradually developed into one of the largest complexes of chemical plants in Europe.

The shipbuilding industry first took off in Birkenhead in 1824 when William Laird opened an ironworks and shipyard on the Wallasey Pool, with the first vessel completed four years later in 1828. Laird moved the works to a site on the south side of the town in 1857, and which became known as the Cammell Laird yard, with the move a necessity because the size of ships were increasing all the time and the Wallasey Pool could no longer accommodate them. Laird also leased a large area of land in the 1840s which resulted in the creation of the Morpeth and Egerton Docks which were opened in 1847. This site was sold to the Liverpool Corporation in 1855, and in 1857 the Mersey Docks and Harbours Act brought the Liverpool and Birkenhead docks and waterfronts together under the same ownership.

It was inevitable that a large town would grow up around William Laird's docks, and so he engaged an architect, James Gillespie, to design a town of a spacious nature and thus attempt to avoid the insanitary problems in other Victorian towns. The new Birkenhead was therefore centred on Hamilton Square and was laid out as a grid with wide streets, while the town became one of England's first to lay out a public park. In 1844-1845, the Birkenhead Dock Company also built for its workers the first flats in England in the form

The works of Brunner Mond (now owned by Tata Chemicals Europe) at Winnington, Northwich. The company was formed here in 1873 by John Brunner and Ludwig Mond who initially manufactured soda ash before growing into one of the largest chemical complexes in Europe.

of four blocks. Other industrialists built housing for their workers, too, such as those built in the 1820s in Parr Street and Crown Street West in Macclesfield, for the workers at Crompton Road mill, while at Buglawton in Congleton, 48 cottages were owned in 1840 by John Johnson, the owner of Throstles Nest silk mill. Meanwhile, a number of mill villages were built in east Cheshire, the most famous being Styal, built from 1790 by Samuel Greg (see *Quirky Cheshire [Styal]* for more). From the 1820s, Compstall was also laid out by the Andrew family, with rows of cottages, a church, a Sunday school (1839) and a library and reading room (1860s). Finally, it is worth mentioning that 18th and 19th century industrialism saw the birth of the first true new town in Cheshire, this being Ellesmere Port at the end of the Manchester Ship Canal.

> **Quirk Alert:** *Utopian Etiquette*
> *At Lowerhouse in Bollington, Samuel Greg Junior took over Lowerhouse Mill in 1832 and founded a utopian community. Here, workers were not only supplied with their model cottages, but were also given lessons in natural history and singing, whilst they were also schooled in social etiquette!*

The Cheshire settlement that saw the biggest impact in terms of population growth was Crewe. In 1837, on the eve of the arrival of the railways, the village of Church Coppenhall had around 200 inhabitants. However, not only was this location selected as a major railway junction point, but large industrial complexes were laid down here, and a sizeable town sprang up almost overnight to accommodate all of those workers. Crewe therefore grew to a town of around 4570 people by 1847, and 17,800 by 1871. The London and North Western Railway also provided housing, schools, churches and public buildings for their employees, with the quality of housing well above the standard of the day, and with every house equipped with a gas supply and a nightsoil collection!

As for Chester, the town became one of the earliest provincial centres to develop a printing and publishing trade, while the town also had bowling greens and a racecourse. The town also had municipal baths and washouses by the 1850s, as did Stockport; indeed, Stockport had developed as a centre for the book and printing trades, too, with Macclesfield not far behind. Stockport also had a theatre as early as 1763, as well as horse racing, as did Knutsford, Nantwich, Northwich and Tarporley.

In terms of sanitation, though, not all towns were as lucky as the mill villages, the new towns, and Crewe. Industrialisation throughout the 19th century brought about huge population increases in many of Cheshire's towns, and one of the effects of this was that people lived in squalor, with disease and epidemics rife. A report into public health in Macclesfield in 1849 recorded that the streets were covered in engine ashes which became a "perfect morass" in wet weather, while the streets were unsewered and thus open sewage ran down the channels at either side of the footpath. And at Stockport, as late as 1876 (long after sanitary and public health reforms had been passed), railway workers' houses near the station were reported to be "surrounded with swamps of sludge, slops and other offensive matters, resulting from a want of drainage and privy accommodation", and that "women and children were obliged to navigate their way on planks, blocks of wood and old doors".

By contrast, though, the Birkenhead Improvement Commissioners secured an Act of Parliament as early as 1843 to compel owners to provide privies for their workers, while the town council was one of the first to ban the construction of back-to-back housing – with one medical officer citing this as the key reason for the falling death rate in the town during the late 19th century. Similarly, William Hesketh Lever's Port Sunlight, founded at Bromborough for his factory workers in 1888 provided probably the ultimate in residential attractiveness along with a full complement of facilities; the workers' houses being suitably interspaced while the houses themselves were also spacious, each containing a scullery, pantry and what

was a novelty back then – a bathroom! Lever believed that a workforce that is content is more productive and efficient. For this reason, he also subsidised the rent, incurring a short-term loss in the belief that he would reap longer-term reward.

The overall population of Cheshire increased by 74 per cent in the first thirty years of the 19th century, and by another 51 per cent between 1831 and 1861, by which time more than half the population were town-dwellers, previously unthinkable for such an agriculturally-biased county. Some significant population increases are demonstrated in the following table:

#	Town	From	To	From	To	%Diff
1	Birkenhead	1821	1851	319	31,000	9618%
2	Crewe	1837	1871	200	17,800	8800%
3	Dukinfield	1821	1851	1,700	26,400	1453%
4	Runcorn	1801	1851	1,379	8,049	484%
5	Wallasey	1871	1911	15,000	78,500	423%
6	Stockport	1754	1801	3,100	14,800	377%
7	Macclesfield	1801	1851	13,300	54,000	306%
8	Ellesmere Port	1901	1911	4,082	10,366	154%
9	Altrincham	1800	1845	7,000	17,000	143%
10	Nantwich	1801	1861	3,500	6,250	79%
11	Chester	1750	1851	16,000	26,000	63%

In contrast to the poverty and squalor suffered by the many, at the other end of the social scale were rich industrialists and city businessmen. To the south of Altrincham, a carefully designed suburb was laid out after 1850, with opulent mansions set in extensive grounds along tree-lined roads. These houses soon became occupied by architects, cotton magnates, physicians, solicitors and members of the stock exchange, making this suburb the wealthiest part of Cheshire by the end of the 19th century. Nearby Hale also evolved into a wealthy commuter settlement, while a similar scenario unfolded at Wilmslow and Alderley Edge, thanks to the railway from Crewe to Stockport. However, here, although Wilmslow developed into a sizeable town, Alderley Edge remained fairly small and maintained its air of exclusivity. Commuter railways didn't work quite so well on the Wirral, though, and the Hoylake Railway which opened from Birkenhead in 1866 saw so little traffic that it was bankrupt by 1870. The later Wirral Railway Company had a little more success after 1883, operating a short network linking West Kirby, New Brighton, Seacombe and Birkenhead Park, and benefitted significantly when the Mersey Railway opened the first tunnel between Liverpool Central, Tranmere and Birkenhead Park.

Across Cheshire, agriculture remained an important industry, and in the rural south-west of the county, forty per cent of adult males were still involved in agriculture in 1841. Dairy farming continued to dominate and in the first half of the 19th century, most of the milk

Quirk Alert: *Joule's Rules*

James Prescott Joule (1818-1889) conducted many of his heat-related experiments at his Sale home, which ultimately led to the law of conservation of energy, which led to the development of the first law of thermodynamics; hence the SI derived unit of energy, the joule, named after him. He also co-worked with Lord Kelvin to develop the Kelvin scale, while Joule's First Law describes the concept of magnetostriction. However, just prior to his death, he humbly stated: "I believe I have done two or three little things, but nothing to make a fuss about."

Quirk Alert: *Bottom's Up*
In 1877, the five Longdendale Reservoirs built in what is now north-west Derbyshire, were part of Cheshire in the Longdendale Valley. These five reservoirs made up the largest expanse of inland man-made water in the world at that time. From top-down, they are Woodhead, Torside, Rhodeswood, Valehouse and Bottoms (shown right).

produced was used to create cheese, the majority of which went to London – which by 1823 was estimated at around 10,000 tons per annum. Thereafter, it was Lancashire that became the chief consumer. By 1900, cheese fairs were being held in rotation at Chester, Nantwich and Whitchurch, although cheese had been overtaken by milk as the main dairy product by this stage. Thanks to the ease of transport due to canals and railways, liquid milk was being produced on farms along the Bridgewater Canal around Altrincham and Dunham Massey from 1845 and transported into Manchester, while farmers in Seacombe and Wallasey were supplying Liverpool. Indeed, after 1860, the emergence of fast early milk trains to city centre depots meant that fresh milk was rapidly available for consumption. Many former cheese farmers switched to milk production, such as those with herds grazing the Frodsham and Helsby marshes. Meanwhile, in north Cheshire, thanks to their proximity to the growing conurbations, market gardening, fruit farming and potato growing began to flourish, while market gardens on the Wirral supplied Liverpool.

Throughout the Industrial Revolution, the shape of local and national politics was developing, too. Cheshire had been grossly under-represented in Parliament, but that was ended by the 1832 Reform Act. Two county constituencies were created, each returning two MPs, and Macclesfield and Stockport were made new parliamentary boroughs with two members each. These new seats added to the two at Chester meant that Cheshire was now returning ten MPs, and this number gradually increased as the century progressed. As for local government, this also underwent reform, commencing with the Municipal Corporations Act of 1835 which reformed the existing Cheshire boroughs of Chester, Congleton, Macclesfield and Stockport. The 1835 Act also opened the doors for other towns to apply for borough status, and in Cheshire that status was granted to Stalybridge (1857), Birkenhead and Crewe (both 1877), Hyde (1881) and Dukinfield (1899).

Modern local government was then introduced following the Local Government Act 1888. This was the Act which introduced county councils and county boroughs in England and Wales, alongside administrative counties based on the boundaries of their historic county counterparts. Just to be clear, though, the Local Government Act 1888 did *not* abolish or alter the historic counties and went to great lengths to distinguish between historic and administrative counties,

making it clear that the two were distinct entities and that the former still existed. In terms of impact upon Cheshire, the Act introduced the democratically elected Cheshire County Council, superseding the previous system of administration by the county justices. Also created as county boroughs at this time were Birkenhead, Chester and Stockport, making them completely independent of Cheshire County Council, but with equal powers to administer their own areas. Wallasey was later granted county borough status in 1910. Meanwhile, local authorities continued to take on more responsibility, something started in 1848 following the passing of the Public Health Act. By the start of the 20th century, these authorities could be as small as Compstall (only 875 people), but were obviously more appropriate for those large urban areas that hadn't acquired county borough status, including Cheadle and Gatley (population in 1891 of 8252), Hazel Grove and Bramhall (9791) and West Kirby with Hoylake (6545); Ellesmere Port & Whitby became an urban district in 1902 (population 4082). Of course, existing county boroughs were expanding all the time and looking to annex territory on their outskirts – such as Stockport annexing Reddish in 1901.

During the 19th century, parts of Cheshire became a holiday destination for the first time, such as New Brighton. This seaside resort on the north-eastern tip of the Wirral peninsula was originally created as a new town in 1832 by James Atherton, a Liverpool property speculator. It had a full range of public amenities, including a billiard room, a post office, a reading room, and numerous villas nicely spaced out. Thanks to the transport improvements, though, the place became a magnet for day-trippers from Liverpool during the 1880s. In order to tap into that market, plans were drawn up in 1896 to build the New Brighton Tower – a rival to the Blackpool Tower which had been erected two years earlier. Completed in 1900, the New Brighton Tower stood at a height of 621 feet, eclipsing its more northerly rival by 100 feet; in fact, it was at that time the highest structure in the United Kingdom, plus it boasted one of the largest ballrooms in the world. However, it never acquired the popularity of Blackpool's tower, was vilified by a large group of local residents, and was hence demolished in 1920 – but check it out on Google: there are lots of old photographs.

Finally for the Industrial Revolution, we will end where we began – with canals. Earlier, we mentioned the incline plane at Anderton that linked the Weaver

Navigation with the Trent and Mersey Canal. In 1875, the incline plane was replaced by the world's first boat lift. The Anderton Boat Lift used two huge water tanks (or caissons) with sealable doors, and which functioned as counter-balances to transport the boats up and down the 50ft (15m) difference between the two watercourses. The construction could transport up to sixteen boats an hour between the two waterways, with each passage lasting around eight minutes. Initially, the lift was only working at 5% of its capacity, with 1876 recording 31,294 tons. However, in the 1890s when pottery started shipping up the navigation, from the Potteries to the Mersey, the boat lift started to pay its way – and in 1895, 129,187 tons were lifted, while 1906 saw this number increase to 192,181 tons.

The Anderton Boat Lift was built in 1875 to transport boats from the Weaver Navigation down to the Trent and Mersey Canal at Anderton. In 1976 it was designated as a Scheduled Monument.

Finally, the 36 mile-long (58km) Manchester Ship Canal was driven by Manchester businessmen looking to break the Liverpool shipping monopoly (and the "excessive" charges imposed by Liverpool docks) and make Manchester an international port by providing a route into the city for ocean-going vessels. The scheme was first presented to Parliament as a bill in 1882 but, unsurprisingly, faced fierce opposition from Liverpool; it therefore took until 1885 to acquire the necessary Act of Parliament. Construction began in 1887, and it took six years to build, costing £15 million. When the canal opened in January 1894 it was the largest river navigation canal in the world, and soon enabled Manchester to become Britain's third busiest port, despite the city being about 40 miles (64 km) from the sea! The canal generally follows the original routes of the rivers Mersey and Irwell, with several sets of locks lifting vessels about 60 feet (18m) up to Manchester. At Ellesmere Port, new rail-served warehousing and storage depots were built by the Shropshire Union Canal at the interchange with the ship canal, and trade here increased rapidly, especially with regard to iron, pig-iron and china clay destined for the Potteries up the Manchester Ship Canal and then down the Trent and Mersey Canal.

From the Late Victorians to the Present Day

As Cheshire moved into the 20th century, a clear distinction of its industries had developed between the north-east – with its older textiles and coal-mining industries – and the north-west – with its vast and newer industries strung out along the south shore of the Mersey, and given a huge shot in the arm by the emergence of the Manchester Ship Canal in 1894. Ellesmere Port was Cheshire's fastest-growing industrial town, while the marshes to the east of the town were drained by German prisoners of war during World War I, opening the way for this area to develop into the vast complex of oil refineries and petrochemical plants that exist at Stanlow today. Indeed, by 1980, the Shell refinery located there was the largest in the UK, although its hey-day had passed by this point, as the Manchester Ship Canal, although deep, was not deep enough to accommodate the increasing size of the modern super-tanker. As a result, all oil had to be brought to the site by pipeline from deepwater terminals. Ellesmere Port also became the location of Bowaters' newsprint and paper mills (1930-1934) while Vauxhall established their massive car plant here in 1958, too.

Also expanding rapidly in north Cheshire after World War II was the petrochemicals industry, with vast new refineries built at Partington in the early 1950s and at Carrington in 1970 (both now in Trafford, Greater Manchester), while existing plants at Runcorn and Eastham were expanded. These industries were dominated in the mid-to-late 20th century by ICI, which as well as acquiring many manufacturing plants and companies also took over the salt-producing companies, too. As for the salt industry in the 20th century, it continued to flourish. By 1900, the most efficient extraction method was to pump brine to the surface, and most rock-salt mines had closed by the 1960s – although the Meadowbank Mine just north of Winsford is still going strong today.

In north-east Cheshire, though, the textile and silk industries declined throughout the 20th century, as the development of artificial fibres resulted in a drop in demand for silk and cotton, and very few east Cheshire firms survive today. Meanwhile, at Crewe, railway engineering continued to flourish. In 1923, the London, Midland and Scottish Railway (LMSR) built a small steelworks at Crewe and re-equipped the railway works, resulting in almost 2000 locomotives being built at Crewe between 1923 and 1948. Fortunately, for Crewe, as railway engineering declined after World War II, the town still had the aero-engine factory to employee the town's workers, and which had been built here by Rolls-Royce in 1938.

At Birkenhead, shipbuilding continued to thrive for the first seventy years of the 20th century, but since then it has gone the same way as Britain's other great shipbuilding hotspots. Cammell Laird eventually closed in 1993.

Returning to the early 20th century, this period saw a revolution on the roads, which started with motor buses, trolley buses and trams. By the 1920s, major improvements had been made to the roads of Cheshire, while bypasses were constructed to avoid busy town and village centres. In 1934, the corporations of Liverpool, Birkenhead and Wallasey jointly opened the first road tunnel under the Mersey, although this soon became heavily congested. A little further south in 1936, another major route was opened between Shotwick and Helsby to serve Stanlow Refinery and the other industrial complexes on the former marshland, whilst also offering a quicker route into North Wales from Manchester.

Of course, the main thoroughfare through Cheshire arrived in the late 1950s when work began on the M6. The Stafford to Preston section was eventually completed in 1965, taking the motorway through Cheshire from just south of Alsager to just north-west of Lymm, and hence creating a new east/west Cheshire divide. The 1970s then saw the emergence of the M56, running across northern Cheshire from east to west, again linking Manchester with North Wales, while those ex-Cheshire areas that went to Greater Manchester in 1972 eventually became served by the M60, and then in 1978, the M67 which links with the M60 at Denton and heads eastwards via Dukinfield and Hyde towards the Longdendale Valley. However, the M60 took forty years to complete and eventually formed an amalgamation of former motorways and roads, including the former M63/Stockport section which was formerly in Cheshire. Finally, in 1972, the M53 was constructed to link the M56 at Ellesmere Port to Wallasey at the northern edge of the Wirral and continuing on as the A59 through the Kingsway tunnel to Liverpool.

When it was first constructed in 1935, Manchester Airport was located in Cheshire, roughly half way between Wilmslow and Altrincham. A temporary airfield at Ringway had been opened by Manchester Corporation in 1928, and was the first municipal aerodrome in the country. In 1935 it was reconstructed as a permanent airfield with scheduled flights commencing on 25th June 1938. The site was initially known as Ringway Airport after the nearest village, and during World War II it was known as RAF Ringway, where it was used as a base for the Royal Air Force. The airport then expanded rapidly with the Manchester to New York service commencing in 1953, making Ringway only the second intercontinental airport in Britain. The re-name to Manchester International occurred in 1975, by which stage the airport was no longer in Cheshire, and by the 1990s, it had two terminals and was the world's 20th busiest airport. Now, with three passenger terminals, a goods terminal and two runways, Manchester Airport has flights to around 225 destinations, and the airport covers an area of 560 hectares (1400 acres), while in 2016, the airport handled 25.6 million passengers.

The Eastgate Clock in Chester was made in 1897 to commemorate Queen Victoria's Diamond Jubilee. It is said to be the second-most photographed clock in Britain after Big Ben.

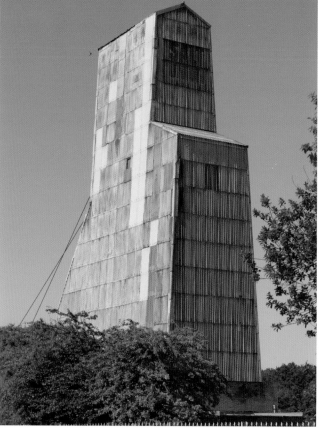

Part of the Meadowbank Mine, alongside the River Weaver just north of Winsford, and Britain's largest rock salt mine. The mine supplies a large percentage of the salt used for de-icing our roads.

during the mid-20th century – for example, all five stations on the line between Crewe and Chester! Conversely, every station between Crewe and Manchester, *did* survive. Again, during the Beeching Axe of the mid-1960s, Cheshire got off fairly lightly, although there were protests at the closure of the Woodhead route to Sheffield, as well as West Kirby to Hooton (on the Wirral) in 1968 and Macclesfield to Rose Hill, Marple, in 1970. In the early 1990s, Manchester's Metrolink tram network became the first modern street-running rail system in the UK, radiating out into former Cheshire territory, while the Merseyrail electrified network, incorporated the Wirral lines from 1977, and by 1994 had been extended to Ellesmere Port and Chester.

The road revolution obviously meant that the majority of Cheshire's waterways became defunct, with the exception of the Manchester Ship Canal and the Weaver Navigation. Similarly, rail traffic became less prevalent, although Cheshire didn't suffer to the same extent as other counties owing to the large volumes of industrial traffic and the fact that many of Cheshire's railways were important through-routes. However, some infrequently used lines were closed as early as the 1930s, while many stations on surviving lines were closed

OLD MEETS "NEW"

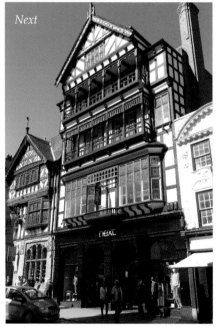

As you head westwards along Foregate Street and Eastgate in Chester, you will find the above well-known 20th and 21st century retailers, Boots, WH Smith and Next. However, not all is as it seems, as many of Chester's apparent Tudor buildings were re-built in sympathetic style starting in the 19th century. Of the three retailers above, only the left-hand side of the Boots store is old (dated to 1597); the right-hand side was built in 1914, and was also the Nag's Head until the 1980s! Meanwhile, the WH Smith building frontage dates from the early 19th century, although everything behind that is dated 1986, which is when the entire building other than the frontage was re-built. Interestingly, the shop sign of a newsboy was first created by the artist Fred Taylor in the early 20th century, and the one used by the Chester store is one of the few remaining original signs. Finally, the Next building dates from 1892 when the original was replaced by Charles A. Ewing for Messrs Dickson.

Urban development intensified throughout the 20th century. Between 1921 and 1951, the population of Manchester's "Cheshire suburbs" grew rapidly including Altrincham (by 55%), Bredbury & Romiley (75%), Cheadle & Gatley (185%), Hazel Grove and Bramhall (100%), Sale (79%) and Wilmslow (88%). Similarly on the Wirral, Merseyide's "Cheshire suburbs" saw Hoylake's population increase by 63%, Ellesmere Port's by 98%, Bebington's by 115%, and Heswall's by a whopping 193%. Conversely, the former textile towns of Dukinfield, Hyde and Stalybridge saw their population peak at the start of the 1920s, as did Northwich, while Birkenhead peaked in the 1930s; the remaining industrial towns of Cheshire did continue to grow, population-wise, but at slower rates, including Congleton (15%), Crewe (9%), Macclesfield (4%) and Winsford (13%).

The most dramatic interwar urban development in Cheshire territory, though, occurred on a site outside of Manchester's immediate territory at Wythenshawe. A large housing estate had already been built here during the 1920s, and in 1931, the territory was formally moved from Cheshire to the county borough of Manchester when Parliament authorised the annexation of Wythenshawe. The transition to Manchester was far from smooth, though, and took several years due to the opposition of Cheshire County Council and Bucklow Rural District Council. However, once the annexation was complete, development was rapid. By 1939, over 8000 houses had been built and the population of Wythenshawe increased from around 6,000 to 40,000, an increase of 667%. It also became the largest housing estate in Europe at that time.

Of course, the urbanisation of Cheshire continued apace after World War II, fired by the enormous growth in car-based commuting and the decentralisation from cities. As a result, the demand for council housing increased steadily, while the number of houses built for private ownership increased exponentially. Examples of significant population growth between 1951 and 1971 are Cheadle & Gatley (92%), Hazel Grove (101%), Marple (81%) and the Wirral (54%), while broad swathes of territory throughout north-east Cheshire and the Wirral became contiguously urbanised. In tandem with this decentralisation was the clearance from old town centres of Victorian slums along with urban renewal, something that was attacked in places like Birkenhead, Chester, Macclesfield and Stockport. As a result, the 1960s and 1970s saw the appearance of peripheral estates, such as Brinnington in Stockport, and of high-rise blocks in town centres.

As for new towns, pre-war Wythenshawe had continued to grow to a population size of 100,000, but sadly lacked essential amenities. New "new towns" would therefore learn from this deficiency, with one such project planned for Mobberley – but which had to be abandoned in the end, not due to local resistance, but to local subsidence! In the end the Manchester Corporation and Cheshire County Council agreed on

The observatory at Jodrell Bank was established in 1945 by Sir Bernard Lovell, a radio astronomer at the University of Manchester. Shown here is the Lovell Telescope. When constructed in 1957, it was the largest steerable dish radio telescope in the world with a diameter of 250ft (76.2 m). Today, it is the third-largest, having been passed by the Green Bank telescope in West Virginia, and the Effelsberg telescope in Germany.

an overspill policy, such as that introduced at Knutsford in the 1960s with the development of estates on its eastern side, and which saw the town's population increase by 46%; Liverpool made similar agreements with Ellesmere Port. An alternative plan for new towns came later with the idea of building around an existing core, and in 1964, Runcorn New Town was earmarked for a population increase from 29,000 to 100,000, by taking in some of the Merseyside overspill; a similar plan was put into action for Warrington, too. The most interesting plans for dealing with overspill, however, were for a planned convergence of Macclesfield with Congleton which would have created a new city of over 200,000 people, while another idea floated was for a new "Weaver City", to be created by the merging of Northwich and Crewe into a city of almost 500,000 people.

As for the boundaries of Cheshire, they were due to change drastically in 1974, but there were a number of boundary changes before then. For example, in 1931, Manchester annexed the townships of Baguley, Northenden and Northen Etchells in order to expand Wythenshawe, and in 1936, the ancient parish of Taxal (including the Cheshire half of Whaley Bridge) was transferred to Derbyshire, with the townships of Mellor and Ludworth going in the opposite direction. However, this was small fry compared to what was to come, and which had been building throughout the middle of the 20th century. County boundaries had been under review for some time during the 1950s and the 1960s, mainly with a view to restructuring the local government of England's largest conurbations, and 1966 saw the commencement of the Royal Commission on Local Government. This culminated in the infamous Redcliffe-Maud Report which, amongst many other drastic countrywide proposals, had actually proposed the complete abolition of Cheshire. A new county known as SELNEC (South East Lancashire/North East

Historic Counties – Pre-1974

Redcliffe-Maud Proposals - 1969

Ceremonial Counties – 1974-2017

Cheshire) would have stretched right down into Cheshire as far as the towns of Northwich (to the south-west) and Macclesfield (to the south-east), whilst Merseyside would have stretched down as far as north Shropshire, thus swallowing up the entire western part of Cheshire, including the towns of Neston, Ellesmere Port and Chester and many dozens of villages, too. The remainder of the county to the south-east, would have gone to a new county called Stoke and North Staffordshire, and would have included the Cheshire towns of Alsager, Congleton, Crewe, Nantwich and Sandbach.

Thankfully, in 1970, the incoming Conservatives rejected the Redcliffe-Maud Report and its subsequent Labour-issued White Paper, and created their own White Paper instead. The subsequent Local Government Act 1972 was then based upon the Conservatives' 1971 White Paper proposals, which were considerably less incursive than its Labour predecessor, but still drastically changed the shape of the county. Gone was most of the Wirral peninsula to the new metropolitan county of Merseyside, while great swathes of north-eastern Cheshire were gobbled up by the new metropolitan county of Greater Manchester. The furthest tip of historic Cheshire in the Longdendale Valley was now cut off from the rest of Cheshire and hence went to Derbyshire as part of that county's High Peak district. Conversely, Cheshire actually *gained* large parts of former Lancashire along its mid-northern border, including the towns of Warrington and Widnes. At the same time, the *administrative* county of Cheshire was abolished along with its county boroughs, and those parts that weren't lost to Merseyside, Greater Manchester and Derbyshire, went on to form the non-metropolitan county of Cheshire along with the additionally gained territory from Lancashire. Indeed, Cheshire no longer bordered Lancashire at all, as it had done for almost a thousand years prior to 1st April 1974, whilst poor old Lancashire actually suffered even more territorial butchery than Cheshire.

Naturally, some areas were unhappy being moved out of Cheshire into a brand new metropolitan county, and some towns actually succeeded in their resistance, including Neston in its fight to stay out of Merseyside, and Wilmslow, Poynton and Disley to stay out of Greater Manchester.

The new non-metropolitan county of Cheshire was initially comprised of eight non-metropolitan districts, which slotted exactly into the four modern unitary authorities shown in blue text on the map left. Halton and Warrington had exactly the same boundaries, but between 1974 and 2009, Cheshire West and Chester was comprised of the three non-metropolitan districts of Chester, Ellesmere Port & Neston and Vale Royal, while Cheshire East was comprised of Crewe & Nantwich to the south, Congleton adjoining to the north-east, and Macclesfield covering the northern section. What the map left also allows you to see, is how modern

Historic & Modern Cheshire Combined

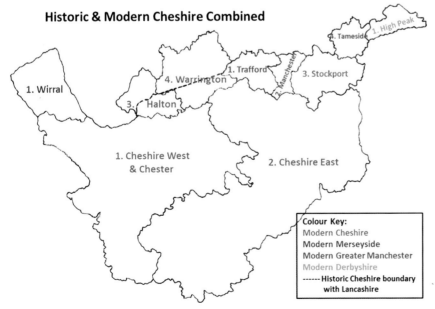

Colour Key:
Modern Cheshire
Modern Merseyside
Modern Greater Manchester
Modern Derbyshire
------ Historic Cheshire boundary with Lancashire

Cheshire (blue text) compared to old Cheshire – which is everything on the map except the Halton and Warrington territory north of the dotted line, which historically belonged to Lancashire. Put another way, everything in purple, red and green text was ceded to Merseyside, Greater Manchester and Derbyshire, respectively.

Since 1974, though, there have been two further local government changes *within* the county. Firstly in 1998, Halton and Warrington became unitary authorities, and then in 2009, Cheshire's remaining six non-metropolitan districts were merged into the two new unitary authorities, Cheshire West & Chester and Cheshire East, each absorbing three former non-metropolitan districts apiece, as outlined above.

As for the county-wide emergency services, they remained unaffected by the 1998 and 2009 changes, with the Cheshire Police Authority and Cheshire Fire Authority consisting of members of the four current councils. Of course, despite the splitting of Cheshire into four unitary authorities and thus disbanding the former Cheshire County Council, the county of Cheshire still retains the offices of Lord Lieutenant and High Sheriff for ceremonial purposes under the Lieutenancies Act 1997, and thus Cheshire is still an English ceremonial county.

In 1951, the Peak District National Park became Britain's first, and included two large parts of Cheshire: the Longdendale Valley to the north and the uplands to the east of Macclesfield. National Park status therefore limited commercial and residential development within these areas, while the other helpful measure in stemming relentless urbanisation was the enforcement of greenbelt areas from the 1970s onwards – and in Cheshire, the Manchester greenbelt area formed a giant hemisphere from Mossley in the north-east to Lymm in the west. A greenbelt was also enforced between Chester, Ellesmere Port and Neston, and which has probably ensured that the entirety of the Wirral peninsula *isn't* urbanised by now, while the enforcement of a greenbelt area to the north of the Potteries has prevented that area coalescing with Alsager and Congleton.

Finally, many of Cheshire's canals are today used for leisure, and the Cheshire Ring, in particular, is very popular. The circuit includes sections of six canals in and around Cheshire and Greater Manchester, these being the Ashton Canal, Peak Forest Canal,

Today, Chester is a huge tourist hotspot and here we see on the left a beautiful old motor bus outside Chester Cathedral that transports tourists around the city sights. Meanwhile, on the right is the bandstand on the banks of the River Dee where pleasure cruises on the river can be boarded. In the background is the suspension bridge which was built over the Dee in 1923.

This is the second Mersey bridge from Runcorn to Widnes under construction in the spring of 2017. Known as the Mersey Gateway, it opened in Autumn 2017 and will relieve some of the 80,000 vehicles which typically use the Silver Jubilee road bridge every weekday, ten times the number it was designed for!

Macclesfield Canal, Trent and Mersey Canal, Bridgewater Canal and Rochdale Canal. As for the Manchester Ship Canal, usage declined in the latter part of the 20th century. This was caused by changes to shipping methods while the growth of containerisation during the 1970s and 1980s meant that many ships were now too big to use the canal and traffic declined, resulting in the closure of the terminal docks at Salford. By 2011 traffic had decreased to less than half of its value in 1958. The canal is now privately owned by Peel Ports, whose plans include redevelopment, expansion, and an increase in shipping from 8000 containers a year to 100,000 by 2030, as part of their Atlantic Gateway project.

Quirk Alert: *Sacred Mersey*

The Mersey is considered sacred by British Hindus, and worshipped in a similar way to the River Ganges. Festival of Immersion ceremonies are held annually on the river, in which clay figures representing the Hindu Lord Ganesha, the elephant deity riding a mouse, are submerged in the river from a ferry boat while followers throw flowers, pictures and coins into the river.

BEAUTIFUL TATTON PARK

Left: *The Rose Garden.* Right: *The Choragic Monument, designed by William Cole of Chester in 1820 to commemorate Wilbraham Egerton's tour of Europe. It is based on the ancient Athenian monument celebrating Lysicrates, the famous leader of the Greek Chorus.*

Left: *The Japanese Garden.* Right: *Another angle on the Japanese Garden showing the bridge and the pagoda (part-hidden).*

Left: *The formal gardens in front of Tatton New Hall.* Right: *Looking back towards Tatton New Hall.*

Some Quirky Cheshire Stats

To complete the Conventional Cheshire section, here are some unique and quirky Cheshire statistics. For starters, in 1844-1845, the Birkenhead Dock Company built for its workers the first flats in England, while the town also saw the launch of one of the first iron vessels in the world, the steel paddle boat that took Livingstone up the Zambezi, and other world-famous ships such as the *Alabama* and the SS *Birkenhead*. The town was also the location of the first tram service in the world in 1860, founded by American, George Train!

In the 1930s, Stockport had the largest non-denominational Sunday school in the world while at 750ft (229m) above sea-level, Ridge Hall Farm at Sutton is one of the highest moated properties in Britain.

Ecclesiastically, Chester Cathedral has one of the oldest fonts in the world, thought to have been fashioned in Italy, around 1300 years ago, while Shocklach St Mary's church has a rare seven-sided font and Nantwich an octagonal tower. Chester Cathedral also has one of England's smallest cathedral naves, but conversely, one of the largest transepts (the 78ft south transept). Meanwhile, Astbury's church is quirky for having two towers and a spire, while Boughton St Paul's has a chancel which faces south; Wallasey St Hilary's chancel faces west!

Still church-related, Barthomley's church is the only one in England dedicated to the 8th century prince, St Bartoline. Lower Peover's church has a curious wooden hand nailed to one wall of its chapel, while Macclesfield's St Michael's church must be the only church with a sedan chair donated by a former 18th century churchgoer! Meanwhile, Oughtrington's church is the only one with a spire containing 48 windows.

Swettenham St Peter's church has rare oval windows and unusual wooden pillars in the chancel, while Weston's church (in Runcorn) has a curious north aisle of four timber arches. Then at Farndon St Chad's church, the ancient custom of strewing the floor with rushes is still carried out every July, while the church must be one of only a handful to be home to an 18th century bassoon! Elsewhere, Hyde's St Thomas the Apostle church contains an east window with a rare portrait of Jesus without a beard, while Sandbach St Mary's is a rare example of a church with a walk-through tower.

In other news, Farndon's John Speed (1551-1629) is widely recognised as England's first historian, while Knutsford, the childhood home of Elizabeth Gaskell, became her Cranford. The 178ft clock tower at Eaton Hall is home to the oldest carillon in England, while the church gate at Rostherne is one of the oldest "automatic" doors in the world, courtesy of its weighted cord passing round a wheel at the top. Meanwhile, the twin villages of Hatton and Daresbury have a library in a telephone box and the only stained glass windows depicting characters from Alice in Wonderland!

Next, in the 1930s, the post office at Wildboarclough was the largest sub-post office in England – courtesy of being incorporated into a former mill. At Gawsworth, there are traces of one of the finest tilting grounds in England, while Kettleshulme was for many centuries home to one of very few candlewick mills in the country. Finally, at Parkgate, the 335 foot-long swimming pool was England's largest in the 1930s, while Tarporley's Utkinton Hall is one of only two to have been built around an oak tree!

Hatton's library.   *Nantwich's octagonal tower.*   *Oughtrington's 48 spire windows.*   *Sandbach's walkthrough tower.*

Part of the stained glass window at Daresbury church, which depicts scenes from Alice in Wonderland, thus commemorating Lewis Carroll who was born in the village in 1832.

This is the view northwards from the top of the Saddle of Kerridge including the Grade II listed structure known as White Nancy. The structure was created in 1817 by John Gaskell Junior of North End Farm to commemorate the Battle of Waterloo (1815), and is named after the stout horse that hauled the building material up the Saddle of Kerridge. It has also been painted over the years to commemorate many things; in 2012 a Jubilee crown, and later the five Olympic rings, a large red remembrance poppy and, in 2015, for the 200th anniversary of Waterloo. Meanwhile, during the 1980s she was commonly painted at Christmas as a Christmas pudding!

Lyme Park in north-east Cheshire. The house and grounds now belong to the National Trust and are a very popular visitor attraction.

Quintessentially Quirky – Appleton Thorn

NAME (STATUS):	**APPLETON THORN** (Village)
POPULATION:	6416
DISTRICT:	Warrington
EARLIEST RECORD:	*Apletune*, 1086 (Domesday Book)
MEANING:	Farmstead where apples grow or apple orchard
DERIVATION:	From the Old English word *æppel-tūn*, meaning "farmstead where apples grow"

The *Quintessentially Quirky* chapter focuses on a place in the county that encapsulates English tradition and eccentricity. For Cheshire, it was a close call between Appleton's "Bawming the Thorn" and Lymm's Easter Monday duck race, but Appleton wins out on account of the history of the custom...

The Thorn Inn, Appleton Thorn.

The church of St Cross at Appleton Thorn.

Quirk Alert: *Bawming the Thorn*

The custom known as *Bawming the Thorn* originally took place annually, on 29th June, at Appleton Thorn, for many centuries, whereby children would dance and sing around trees that were bedecked with ribbons and coloured paper. Integral to the custom was a cutting from the Glastonbury Thorn, which was said to have originated from the staff of Joseph of Arimathea, he who laid Jesus to rest. The cutting was allegedly brought to Appleton Thorn by Adam de Dutton, a knight of the Crusaders and lord of Appleton. Having taken a pilgrimage to Glastonbury Abbey, he returned with the cutting to plant in Appleton as thanksgiving for his safe return from the Crusades. An offshoot of the Glastonbury Thorn has been sustained in Appleton Thorn ever since. Meanwhile, other theories suggest that this was actually a pagan fertility rite, similar to dancing around the maypole!

Anyway, by the 19th century, the custom had been interwoven into the village's "walking day", whereby children from Appleton Thorn Primary School walked through the village and held sports and games at the school. The ceremony

View of St Cross from the other side. To the right is the thorn tree, decorated with ribbons and ready for the 2017 ceremony.

The ceremony starts with a brass band leading the parade off round the village of Appleton Thorn.

stopped in the 1930s, but was revived by the school headmaster in the early 1970s, since when "Bawming the Thorn" occurs on the third Saturday of June, and hence the nearest Saturday to Midsummer's Day.

Today, Bawming the Thorn involves local schoolchildren dancing around a hawthorn tree in the centre of the village, singing verses to the tune of Bonnie Dundee, with the following repeated chorus:

Up with fresh garlands this Midsummer morn,
Up with red ribbons on Appleton Thorn.
Come lasses and lads to the Thorn Tree today
To Bawm it and shout as ye Bawm it "Hurray"!

As for the word "Bawming", it means to decorate – and during the ceremony the thorn tree is decorated with ribbons and garlands.

Right: *For the 2017 parade, the line-up included Celtic and medieval characters…*
Below: *…and the children, of course (note the tribute of flowers they are holding)…*

…plus the odd bird of prey…and Viking!

With the thorn tree already bawmed with ribbons, the children of Appleton Thorn deposit their tributes of flowers and ribbons and prepare…

…to dance, while the local choir and all gathered around sing the songs, including the verse printed above.

Quirky Cheshire

Introducing the Shire-Ode

A Shire-Ode tells the story – in rhyming verse – of fictitious, eccentric inhabitants of the county in question. However, in so doing, it also incorporates into the flow of the verse, many place-names that can be found within that county – places which then go on to form a county almanac, of sorts. Each place appears in roughly alphabetical order, although some of the smaller places are batched up into trios known as a "Three's Up" or appear in the final "Best of the Rest" section. The location of all of the places is pinpointed on the map following the Shire-Ode.

As for the *Cheshire* Shire-Ode, this tells the tale of *The Witches of Keckwick* and how the Higher Wych, Middlewich and Lower Wych, come under attack from the evil Northwich…

Cheshire Shire-Ode: The Witches of Keckwick

This tale of three witches is certain to chill -
Victoria Park, **Hazel Grove** and **Rose Hill**
They each live in **Keckwick**, on apt-named **Broomhill**
Approached through a **Whitegate**, by **Woodside** mill.

But these three old girls, though a motley **Crewe**
Are really white witches; they're good, through and through
No, the threat's from the north, where the **Northwich** dwells
On **Slaughter Hill**, where she casts evil spells.

A traditional dark witch, with huge **Wharton** chin
A tall, black **Hatton** and sly gap-toothed grin
She **Picton Mere** mortals who wandered nearby
Didn't matter how **Manley**, for this witch had guile.

For the victims, some cooking-pot rumours are rife
For **Warmingham** up before cruel **Hackingknife**
They say that they're buried in **Flowery Field**
Or **The Marsh**, or **The Valley** or in **Woodlands** they're
sealed.

They say she gave **Cobbs** to one poor naive gang
Who'd **Eaton** them all, 'fore they sussed the odd **Tang**
Then **Heaviley** sedated, she cast her cruel spell
Turned them all into **Roaches**, or so folk do tell.

And let's not forget her partners in sin
Her pit-bull called **Ashley** and moggie called **Bryn**
One evil, one wily; a formidable pair
And they've caused endless **Hassall** to travellers round
there.

As time passed, the Northwich got less **Sound** of mind
Her spells **Boughton** madness – of the envious kind
It was not in her **Styal** to make do; she craved **Moore**
Like control over Broomhill and settling old scores.

So back to our three, and the bottom of the hill
Where the **Lower Wych** lives – that being Rose Hill
She looks like Miss **Marple**; her home's a pet-hive
With her **Westy** called **Sydney** and a budgie called **Clive**.

Half-way up Broomhill, lives witch number two
Hazel Grove is the **Middlewich**, who loves doggies, too
Her soft mongrel, **Tarvin**, he sleeps with her cat
Or does so till **Elton** goes looking for rats.

At the top of the hill, lives witch number three
Victoria Park, the **Higher Wych**, you see
Though she sports a **Broadbottom**, she dresses to kill
That's why she's still known as the **Bell o' th' Hill**.

So the scene is now set – it's good against bad
Or **Godley** v. wicked; sane against mad
For the Northwich did strike, beneath the **Noonsun**
When she set fire to Rose's **Woodhouses** for fun.

Now Sydney escaped, but for Clive, Rose did **Greave**
He'd gone for a **Burton** in those flames, she believed
Distraught, Rose fled up the hill at full tilt
Since Tori and Hazel had **Brickhouses** built.

Arriving at Hazel's with Sydney in tow
The shocked witches viewed **Reddish** hue from below
But twas no time to dwell, **Midway** up that hill
For their enemy now had the scent for a kill.

With nowhere to **Hyde**, to Tori's they fled
With Tarvin and Elton and Sydney ahead
There they huddled like sheep in a **Fold**, feeling grim
For on top of this world, they were out on a **Lymm**.

Then the sound of **Gravel** underfoot they did hear
And the Northwich with **Long Green** wand did appear
"The **Lowerhouse** has gone, now it's your turn to pay"
(Though not by the fire spell which worked once per day).

So the Northwich sent Bryn in to **Stoak** up the heat
He entered by cat-flap, all brash and up-beat
But though Elton was **Littler** than Bryn, he could fight
And he sent the puss packing with one well-aimed bite.

Bryn's withdrawal brought hope and instilled renewed grit
Sparked **Dunkirk** spirit; now to **Acton** it
A **Little Moor** subtlety; time to outflank;
Time to invest in the **Gallantry Bank**.

First, Tarvin and Sydney fixed Ashley real good
They sneaked out and mugged him and made him eat **Mudd**
The Northwich was fuming, behind **Row-of-trees**
Where she planned her next spell – not to burn, but to freeze.

CHESHIRE: UNUSUAL & QUIRKY

So, **Over** she walked; raised up **Lyme Green** wand
Cast ice and **Hale** spell, to freeze Tori's pond
But the chance never happened to cast it once more
For three witches on **Brushes** did **Sale** out the door.

They **Rushton** the Northwich, and circled around
With **Broomedge** they bashed her, till she fell to the ground

It is said she then vanished, disappeared without trace
And she now dines with **Saighton** in a shadowy place.

That said, there's a place that some folk do espouse
Between **Yew Tree** and **Cherry Tree** outside Tori's house
Where a **Broken Cross** stands, dark, brooding and chill
They say there she lies – 'neath the **Cross o' th' Hill**.

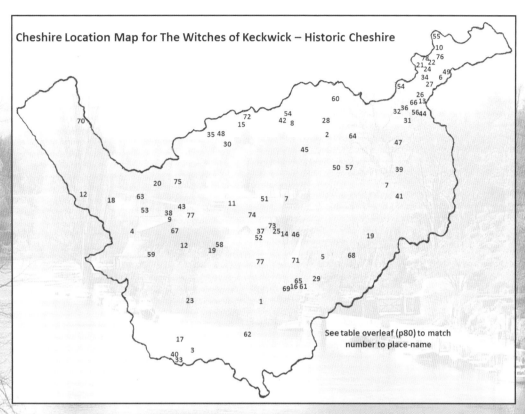

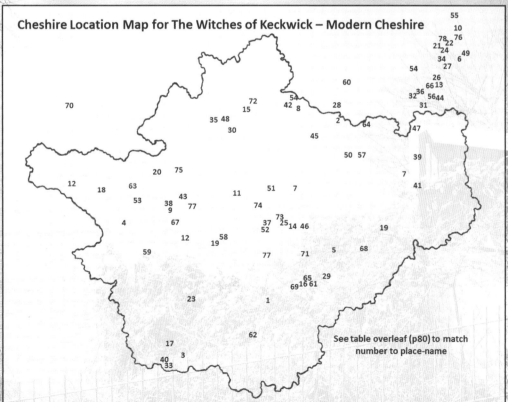

PLACE-NAME TABLE FOR THE WITCHES OF KECKWICK

1	Acton	2	Ashley	3	Bell o' th' Hill	4	Boughton
5	Brickhouses	6	Broadbottom	7	Broken Cross[1]	8	Broomedge
9	Broomhill	10	Brushes	11	Bryn	12	Burton[1]
13	Cherry Tree	14	Clive	15	Cobbs	16	Crewe
17	Cross o' th' Hill	18	Dunkirk	19	Eaton[1]	20	Elton
21	Flowery Field	22	Fold	23	Gallantry Bank	24	Godley
25	Gravel	26	Greave	27	Hackingknife	28	Hale
29	Hassall	30	Hatton	31	Hazel Grove	32	Heaviley
33	Higher Wych	34	Hyde	35	Keckwick	36	Little Moor
37	Littler	38	Long Green	39	Lowerhouse	40	Lower Wych
41	Lyme Green	42	Lymm	43	Manley	44	Marple
45	Mere	46	Middlewich	47	Midway	48	Moore
49	Mudd	50	Noonsun	51	Northwich	52	Over
53	Picton	54	Reddish[1]	55	Roaches	56	Rose Hill
57	Row-of-trees	58	Rushton	59	Saighton	60	Sale
61	Slaughter Hill	62	Sound	63	Stoak	64	Styal
65	Sydney	66	Tang	67	Tarvin	68	The Marsh
69	The Valley	70	Victoria Park	71	Warmingham	72	Westy
73	Wharton	74	Whitegate	75	Woodhouses	76	Woodlands
77	Woodside[1]	78	Yew Tree				

[1] Appears twice in Cheshire.

Here is a rather perfect cottage to complement the Shire-Ode, The Witches of Keckwick. To me, this would be perfect for the Lower Wych, Rose Hill; it's not too hard to imagine a Miss Marple-like character living here along with her Westy called Sydney and her budgie called Clive! Back in the real world, though, this beautiful cottage can be found in Crewe Green, just east of Crewe. It is also within half a mile of Sydney, to the west – although Slaughter Hill (home of the evil Northwich) lies half a mile to the east…

The Witches of Keckwick –
A Cheshire Shire-Ode Almanac

NAME (STATUS):	**ACTON** (Village)
POPULATION:	404
DISTRICT:	Cheshire East
EARLIEST RECORD:	*Acatone*, 1086 (Domesday Book)
MEANING:	Farmstead or village where oak-trees grow
DERIVATION:	From the Old English words *āc* (oak-tree) and *tūn* (farmstead or village)

The former Star Inn at Acton, now a private residence.

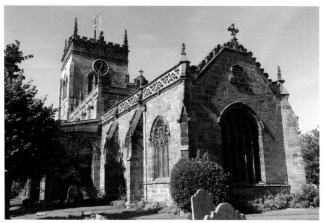

St Mary's church, Acton.

Acton Church: St Mary's

The Grade I listed St Mary's church is the owner of the oldest tower in Cheshire, built in around 1180 – although it was largely rebuilt in 1757 after its upper reaches collapsed during a storm. The original tower had been 100ft (30m) high, but the rebuilt tower was only 80ft (24m) high. There was a predecessor church here before 1180, though, as Domesday Book records one that was served by two priests, after which the church and its lands were given to Combermere Abbey at its foundation in 1133. However, St Mary's remained the main parish church for a large area to the west of Nantwich, with subsidiary churches including the much larger St Mary's church at Nantwich which remained a chapel of ease to Acton until the 17th century.

As for today's church, the tower arches leading into the nave are 13th century, as are the piers of the nave arcades, while the north aisle was built in the late 14th century and the south aisle and chancel were built in the early 15th century; Arthur Mee suggests that the font is "older than Domesday Book". The church was restored in the 17th and 18th centuries, and again in 1897–98 which included a rebuild of the north wall of the north aisle and the clerestory.

One unusual feature of the church interior is the retention of the old stone seating around the sides, while there are also some ancient carved stones dating back to the Norman era in the south aisle. The architectural historian Alec Clifton-Taylor includes St Mary's church in his list of best English parish churches.

Acton Historic Trivia: Dorfold Hall

Ancient field systems have been identified in the parish, while at the time of Domesday Book (1086), the township of Acton was one of the wealthiest in the Nantwich Hundred; indeed the 1066 valuation of Acton was the same sum as Nantwich itself (£10), thanks to its manor, mill and one of the largest areas of meadow in Cheshire at that time. During these times, the forests in the parish were also valuable as the wood yielded from them was used as fuel for salt production in neighbouring Nantwich. However, by the end of the 16th century, the area had been largely deforested and animal husbandry and cereal production had become more common.

In 1602, the Dorfold Estate was acquired by Sir Roger Wilbraham, a prominent lawyer who served as Solicitor-General for Ireland under Elizabeth I and also held positions at court under James I. It was Sir Roger who had the current Dorfold Hall built on the site of the earlier hall between 1616 and 1621 for his younger brother and heir, Ralph Wilbraham. Three centuries later, the Grade I listed hall was considered by Nikolaus Pevsner to be one of the two finest Jacobean houses in Cheshire.

Twenty years after Dorfold Hall was built, Acton village saw a number of sieges, with the parish church serving as a base for Royalist operations during the siege of Nantwich, while the Battle of Nantwich in 1644 also took place close to the village. A century later in 1754, the Dorfold estate was sold to Nantwich lawyer James Tomkinson, although it passed back to the Wilbraham family in 1861, following its inheritance by Anne Tollemache, the wife of Wilbraham Spencer Tollemache, and High Sheriff of Cheshire in 1865. The grounds of the hall had been remodelled a few years before (1861-1862), by William Andrews Nesfield and included the construction of several buildings including a Grade II listed gateway, while also Grade II listed is the late 18th century icehouse and the late 17th century Dairy House, as is the adjacent red-brick farm building which is known as Madam's Farm.

In the early 1770s, the Chester to Nantwich branch of what later became known as the Shropshire Union Canal was built, just north of the parish at Basin End. However, the more southerly Nantwich to Birmingham section wasn't completed until 1835, and the Tomkinson family objections were so loud that a half-mile embankment was constructed along with an aqueduct to avoid the canal passing through Dorfold Park!

During World War II, Dorfold Hall was home to a number of Liverpool refugees, although by November 1940, the hall had been handed over to American soldiers. Meanwhile, today, Dorfold Hall plays annual host to the Nantwich and South Cheshire Show, a single-day agricultural show with trade stalls and ring displays organised by the Nantwich Agricultural Society and which draws up to 30,000 visitors.

Acton Quirk Alert: The Largest Cheese Exhibition and Marble Wickets

The previously-mentioned Nantwich and South Cheshire Show at Dorfold Hall, includes the Nantwich International Cheese Awards, established in 1897 and is thought to be the largest cheese exhibition in Europe, usually attracting in excess of 2000 entries from dozens of countries.

Acton is also the final resting place of Albert Hornby (1847 – 1925), the first man (of only two) to captain his country at both cricket and rugby, while he also played football for Blackburn Rovers. However, he is perhaps best remembered as the England cricket captain whose side lost the 1882 Test match which gave rise to the Ashes and, more happily, thanks to his immortalisation in one of the best known of all cricket poems, *At Lord's*, by Francis Thompson. The grave of A. N. Hornby, in St Mary's churchyard, is marked with marble wickets, bails, bat and ball.

Main picture: *View from St Mary's churchyard onto the main road through Acton. To the left of the photograph is a sundial, which was mounted in the 17th century at the top of this 12ft Grade II listed former medieval cross.* Inset: *The gatehouse to Dorfold Hall. The Hall was built by the Wilbraham family between 1616 and 1621.*

NAME (STATUS):	**ASHLEY** (Village)
POPULATION:	323
DISTRICT:	Cheshire East
EARLIEST RECORD:	*Ascelie*, 1086 (Domesday Book)
MEANING:	Ash-tree wood or clearing
DERIVATION:	From the Old English words *æsc* (ash-tree) and *lēah* (wood, woodland clearing or glade)

The Greyhound Inn was built in the late 19th century when it was known as the Orrell Arms. It was later re-named to honour Lord Egerton's favourite breed of dog!

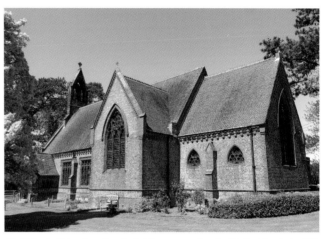

St Elizabeth's church at Ashley was also built in the late 19th century (1880).

Ashley Church: St Elizabeth's

The Grade II listed St Elizabeth's church at Ashley was built in 1880 as a chapel of ease to St Mary's church at nearby Bowdon, although it became a parish in its own right the following year. The church was designed by Wilbraham Egerton, who later became the 1st Earl Egerton. Today, its benefice is combined with that of St Peter's at Hale.

Ashley Historic Trivia: Ashley Hall

Ashley is located on Cheshire's northern border with Greater Manchester, close to Tatton Park. The place includes the Grade II listed Ashley Hall, which dates from the late 16th century, with 18th and 19th century additions. In 1715, the house was the location for a meeting of local gentry to decide whether to support the Stuarts or the Hanoverians, eventually deciding upon the latter. Also Grade II listed are the gate piers to the forecourt of the building, a carriage house in the forecourt, the kitchen garden wall, and the stable block.

Finally, Ashley Hall Showground is comprised of over 50 acres on the Tatton Estate, and its shows – such as Traction Engine Rallies and Steam Fairs – attract a wide range of visitors.

Ashley railway station was founded by the Cheshire Lines Committee in the late 19th century, but since 2010, it has been a "request stop" only.

This stunning house is located across the road from The Greyhound Inn.

Three's-Up!

	BELL O' TH' HILL	BROKEN CROSS	BROOMEDGE
STATUS:	Hamlet	Suburb * 2	Village
DISTRICT:	Cheshire West	Cheshire East; Cheshire West	Warrington
MEANING:	Unknown	Probably the location of a former preaching or market cross	Edge where broom grows, from the Old English words *brōm* and *ecg*

Three's Up Trivia!

Bell o' th' Hill is a tiny hamlet in south-west Cheshire that comprises a handful of houses, a farm, and the pub known as the Blue Bell Inn, with the latter dating to around 1650 when John Davis was landlord; the pub website lists all of his successors up to present day! Meanwhile, there are only two places called **Broken Cross** in the British Isles, and they are both located in Cheshire! The larger is located in the north-western quadrant of Macclesfield, while the other is situated a couple of miles east of Northwich. The Macclesfield suburb is home to the Broken Cross Methodist Church and a Broken Cross Club (private members), as well as Macclesfield's General Hospital. Meanwhile, the Northwich Broken Cross is home to a pub called The Old Broken Cross Inn. Finally, **Broomedge** is a hamlet a mile east of Lymm, and consists of residential housing, two attractive pubs and the Broomedge Farm Cottages, the latter having been formed from a former 18th century dairy parlour. One cottage is called "The Dairy", while the other is known as "The Shippon", which derives from the Old English word *shippon*, meaning a barn or cowshed.

The Blue Bell Inn at Bell o' th' Hill, which dates back to 1650.

The Bulls Head at Broken Cross (Macclesfield), on the road called Broken Cross.

The Old Broken Cross Inn at the Northwich Broken Cross and which is situated alongside the Trent and Mersey Canal.

Broomedge is home to two attractive pubs, the Jolly Thresher (above), while a little further east along the A56 is The Wheatsheaf (top right).

NAME (STATUS):	**BROADBOTTOM** (Village)
POPULATION:	4389
DISTRICT:	Tameside, Greater Manchester
EARLIEST RECORD:	*Brodebotham*, 1286
MEANING:	Broad valley bottom
DERIVATION:	From the Old English words *brād* (broad or spacious) and *bothm* (broad river valley or valley bottom)

Broadbottom Geographic and Historic Trivia

The former Cheshire village of Broadbottom is separated from Derbyshire only by the River Etherow. Given the village location alongside the river, mills have always flourished here, including a water-powered corn mill back in the 14th century, while Moss Mill was a woollen mill in the 18th century and a cotton mill in the 19th century. Another former Broadbottom mill is Hodge Printworks which started out as a woollen mill in 1798 but converted to a dyeworks in 1805; indeed some pieces of the dyed cloth are still on display in the Victoria and Albert Museum, thus indicating its importance and quality. Meanwhile, Broad Mills was a collection of mills that included a calico printing mill, which was run by the Sidebottom family who happened to live in the Summerbottom area of Broadbottom! By the 1840s, their mill was running 25,000 spindles and 1500 looms, and by 1860, they were employing 1200 people on-site. The mill remained active until 1934 and then suffered from a devastating fire in 1940. It was eventually demolished in 1949. Today, just one mill (textile) remains.

Broadbottom Quirk Alert: Wizard's Milestone

Over the years, Broadbottom railway station has been re-named to Mottram (1845), Mottram with Broadbottom (1884), and then in 1954 it reverted to just "Broadbottom", but with the suffix "for Mottram and Charlesworth". However, probably of more interest to Harry Potter fans' is the fact that the station is situated between milestones 9 ¾ and 10! Now, form an orderly queue, children…

The Grade II listed Broadbottom Viaduct over the River Etherow dates from 1842. The viaduct is 137ft (42m) high and 169 yards (155m) long.

The church of St Mary Magdalene at Broadbottom was built in 1890. Since 2008, it has become known as the Magdalene Centre.

Former mill cottages on Old Row, Broadbottom.

The war memorial in the centre of Broadbottom.

More cottages towards the top of the hill in Broadbottom.

NAME (STATUS):	**BOUGHTON** (Suburb)
POPULATION:	5444
DISTRICT:	Cheshire West and Chester
EARLIEST RECORD:	*Bocstone*, 1086 (Domesday Book)
MEANING:	Most English Boughton's mean farmstead of either a man called Bucca, or where bucks (male deer or he-goats) are kept. This one, however, may mean "bluestone" or "beech-tree on stony ground".
DERIVATION:	From either the Old English personal name, *Bucca*, or the Old English word *bucca* (male deer or he-goat), plus the Old English word *tūn* (farmstead or village). An alternative of "bluestone" would probably refer to a long-since vanished blue boundary stone,[1] while another potential derivation is from the Old English words *bōc* (beech-tree) and *stān* (stone).
FAMOUS RESIDENTS:	John Douglas (1830-1911), architect; Thomas Hughes (1822-1896), author of *Tom Brown's Schooldays*; Ian Blair (b.1953), former Commissioner of Police of the Metropolis

The Grade II listed Ye Gardener's Arms, Boughton.

Boughton Geographic Trivia

Boughton is a largely residential area immediately to the east of Chester town centre, most of which forms part of an unparished area – while this entire unparished area was once part of the county borough of Chester between 1889 and 1974. However, the adjoining areas of Boughton Heath and Vicars Cross lie within the separate *civil* parish of Great Boughton, which is outside the boundaries of the city of Chester.

Boughton Church: St Paul's

St Paul's church is a striking Grade II listed building which was built in 1875 to the design of Chester architect, John Douglas; indeed, Nikolaus Pevsner stated that he regarded St Paul's as "the boldest of Douglas' church designs" while he also comments that the strength of the interior is thanks to its timber-work which includes a splendid timber-framed ceiling. The 1875 church was largely a rebuild of an earlier church built here in 1830 by William Cole the Younger, and the later church was extended with a south aisle in 1902 while the spire was added in 1905. Built in red brick with timber framing, the plan includes a combined nave and chancel of four bays plus an apsidal bay, a south aisle, a west porch and a broach spire at the west end.

Boughton Historic Trivia: George Marsh and the Boughton Shot Tower

Located alongside the important Roman city of *Deva*, it isn't surprising that Boughton has been the site of Roman discoveries, including numerous cremation urns suggesting Roman burial sites here. However, the most significant discovery was a Roman altar standing almost four feet high. It was discovered in a field by workmen in 1821, alas only after it had been damaged by a workers' pick axe. The altar also marked the position of a wellhead which was used to supply water to *Deva* via a pipeline. Part of the aqueduct was also found during the construction of the Grosvenor Park Lodge.

This building was built by Chester architect John Douglas in 1900 on the site of the ancient Boughton chapel which was demolished during the English Civil War.

St Paul's church at Boughton was built in 1875, also by John Douglas.

As for the altar, this was dedicated to "the Nymphs and fountains of the Twentieth Legion" (*Legio XX Valeria Victrix*)", with this inscription appearing on both sides. The altar was purchased privately by the Duke of Westminster and is now in the private grounds of Eaton Hall. As for the pipeline, it may have stayed in use after

Left: *The Boughton Shot Tower;* Centre left: *Obelisk in St Giles' cemetery at Boughton, and a memorial to George Marsh (1515-1555), the only person martyred in Cheshire during the reign of Mary I (1553-1558);* Centre right: *Ye Olde Wheatsheaf;* Right: *Boughton's Victorian water fountain.*

the Romans departed Britain, but by medieval times it was definitely in use by St Werburgh's Abbey in Chester – so the monks either restored the original or rebuilt a new system.

During the early 12th century, a leper hospital was founded at Boughton on the site of today's St Giles' cemetery, and was endowed by successive Earls of Chester. A small village grew up around the hospital and its chapel and became known as Spital Boughton, with the "Spital" part of the name deriving from the word "hospital". The site remained in constant use until 1643, when it became a victim of the Siege of Chester during the English Civil War, as defence of the city required the demolition of buildings outside the city walls. Then in 1644, the Royalists suffered heavy losses during a sortie into Boughton with many of the fallen buried here – as, too, were victims of the various plagues which ravaged the city in the 16th and 17th centuries.

Someone else whose ashes were interred here a century earlier, was Protestant martyr George Marsh, a preacher from Bolton who was burned at the stake on Gallows Hill on 24th April 1555. Condemned to his fate by the Bishop of Chester, he was actually the only person martyred in Cheshire under Mary I. It is also recorded that a barrel of tar was set above his head to drip on him as he burned. The last burial at St Giles' cemetery took place in 1854, while in 1898, Nessie Brown erected an obelisk in St Giles' cemetery to George Marsh.

The Grade II listed Boughton Shot Tower was built by Walkers, Parker & Co. in 1799. Standing at a height of 168ft (41.2m), the tower is located beside the Shropshire Union Canal and formed part of the now-disused Chester Leadworks. It is the oldest of the UK's three remaining shot towers, used to make lead shots for use in guns, and probably the oldest such structure still standing in the world. The method had been pioneered by William Watts in the 1780s and worked by pouring molten lead through a pierced copper plate or sieve at the top of the tower; during the fall, the droplets would form perfect spheres thanks to the surface tension. The spherical drops were then cooled in a vat of water at the base of the tower. Of course,

Britain was in the middle of the Napoleonic Wars at this time, and so the tower was a key supplier of lead shot for muskets. Incredibly, although many more sophisticated methods have been developed since, the Boughton Shot Tower was still in use as late as 2001, and the interior still retains a spiral staircase and melting pots. It was in 2001 that the leadworks closed and most of the buildings were demolished three years later, with the exception of the shot tower.

Boughton Quirk Alert: Relocation

In the 20th century the Peacock Inn was relocated from the north side of Christleton Road, where the Peacock Garage now stands, to the south side of the road at the junction with Heath Lane. This was simply to allow for the parking of cars!

This memorial in St Giles' cemetery at Boughton, records the history of the former leper hospital which had been set up on this spot by the Earls of Chester in the early 12th century.

View of the River Dee, taken from the A51 in Boughton.

Three's-Up!

	BRUSHES	CLIVE	CROSS O' TH' HILL
STATUS:	Housing estate, Valley, Reservoir	Former township	Hamlet
DISTRICT:	Tameside, Greater Manchester	Cheshire West and Chester	Cheshire West and Chester
EARLIEST RECORD:	*Brushes*, 1929	*Clive*, 1086 (Domesday Book)	Unknown

Walkerwood Reservoir, the western-most of the four reservoirs in the Brushes Valley.

Brushes Reservoir is the next reservoir along. Brushes Road then takes you up to Lower and Higher Swineshaw Reservoirs and then on to the Pennine Moors.

Three's Up Trivia!

Brushes is a housing estate on the eastern edge of Stalybridge, and is actually the second oldest former council estate in Tameside, having been built in two phases between 1929 and 1939. However, the Brushes Estate also lends its name to a road, a reservoir and a valley, with Brushes Road stretching out from the Brushes locality of Stalybridge all the way out to Walkerwood Reservoir and Brushes Reservoir, and then beyond to Lower Swineshaw Reservoir and Higher Swineshaw Reservoir. The valley in which the four reservoirs are located is also known as Brushes Valley, and eventually heads up into the Pennine Moors, while the area to the west of the first reservoir (Walkerwood) is known as Lower Brushes, and forms the main part of Stalybridge Country Park. Lower Brushes is comprised of a number of important habitats, including the wooded valley floor which is home to a variety of woodland birds; the grassland supports numerous insects and mammals, while the wetlands and ponds are home to dragonflies in summer as well as a variety of wetland birds.

Next up, **Clive** is a former township on the eastern outskirts of the town and civil parish of Winsford, while Clive Green is located a mile south-east of Clive. Clive was actually designated a civil parish in its own right in

1866, but this was abolished in 1936 and both Clive and Clive Green found the majority of their area (482 acres) aligned to Winsford and a small eastern part (less than one acre) to Stanthorne. Clive's population was 102 in 1851, 155 in 1851 and 147 in 1901, while the 482 acres moved to Winsford in 1936 had a population of 178 in 1931. Today much of the former Clive township has been replaced by the large Winsford Industrial Estate.

Finally, **Cross o' th' Hill** is a tiny hamlet between Malpas and No Man's Heath, while the latter is also home to Cross o' th' Hill Road.

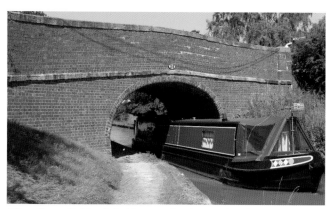

Clive Green Bridge is bridge number 24 on the Shropshire Union Canal and carries Clive Green Lane over the waterway.

NAME (STATUS):	**BURTON** (Village * 2)
POPULATION:	Burton (Tarvin): 50 Burton (Neston): c.150
DISTRICT:	Both Cheshire West and Chester
EARLIEST RECORD:	Burton (Neston): *Burtone*, 1086 (Domesday Book)
MEANING:	Fortified farmstead or farmstead near a fortification
DERIVATION:	From the Old English word *burh-tūn* (fortified farmstead or farmstead near or belonged to a fortification)
FAMOUS RESIDENTS:	Thomas Wilson (1663–1755), Bishop of Sodor and Man; John Peel (1939-2004) Radio 1 Disc Jockey

Burton Geographic Trivia: Two Burton's

There are two Burtons in Cheshire, one around six miles south-east of Chester and the other around six miles north-west of the county town; the former is sometimes known as Burton-by-Tarvin while the latter is simply known as "Burton", but thanks to its proximity to Neston, we will refer to it as Burton (Neston).

Of the two, Burton-by-Tarvin was actually a civil parish in its own right before 1st April 2015, despite having neither a parish council, nor a parish meeting, with services and amenities controlled by Cheshire West and Chester Council. However, since 01/04/2015, the former Burton civil parish has been merged with Duddon parish to create a new and larger Duddon civil parish. Meanwhile, the River Gowy passes a mile to the south of Burton-by-Tarvin, while the Eddisbury Way passes through the centre of the village – this being a 16.5 mile (26.6km) footpath running from Frodsham to Higher Burwardsley.

The other Burton is located at the southern end of the Wirral peninsula, and has recently been included in the much larger ward of Little Neston and Burton. This particular Burton has also become a much sought-after place to live in recent years, thanks to its picture post-card looks (it is home to more than 25 listed buildings) and proximity to Liverpool and Chester. Indeed, in 2001, Burton was ranked eighth in a UK market research survey by the Sunday Times Rich List of so-called "super-rich" communities, with millionaires comprising 16% of the population in its postal district. Finally, Burton Mere Wetlands, an RSPB reserve, lies on the southern outskirts of Burton (Neston).

Burton Church: St Nicholas's

The Grade II listed St Nicholas' church was built in 1721, although the Massey Chapel dates from 1380, while the chancel was rebuilt in 1870. However, two Norman scalloped capitals were unearthed in the churchyard, suggesting an even older predecessor to the 14th century church; these are currently on display in the porch. The church itself consists of a west tower, a four-bay nave which is continuous with a two-bay chancel, a north aisle, and a vestry to the northeast of the aisle. At the east end of the aisle is the Massey chapel. Built into one of the internal walls of the tower is a 13th century coffin lid which is decorated with a foliated cross, while one of the

Massey memorials is in marble and dates from 1579; the other is in alabaster and dated 1794. Further memorials are to the Congreave family. Meanwhile, the churchyard is home to a group of 18 chest tombs, a red 18th century Grade II listed sandstone sundial, and a group of eight Grade II listed raised grave slabs. Finally, a glass-topped case contains a volume of the prayers and meditations of Bishop Wilson, who was born in the village and went on to become the Bishop of Sodor and Man for a remarkable 58 years, from 1697 until 1755. A stone commemorating the Wilson family can also be found in the wall at the north end of the church.

Burton Historic Trivia: Burton Hall vs. Burton Manor

Burton-by-Tarvin includes the Grade I listed Burton Hall while the grounds of the hall contain a Grade II

St Nicholas's church, Burton (Neston) was built in 1721 from red sandstone.

Bishop Wilson's Cottage at Burton (Neston), home and birthplace of Thomas Wilson (1633-1755), who later became Bishop of Sodor and Man.

The village of Burton, near to Neston, was ranked 8th in the Sunday Times' UK Rich List of 2001.

Barn End Cottage, another beautiful home in the Burton near to Neston.

listed garden wall and gateway. Dating from the early 17th century, Burton Hall was built by John Werden to a square plan in brick with buff sandstone dressings, and has three storeys with a symmetrical three-bay front. The hall was extended in the 19th century, fell into disrepair by the late 20th century, but has undergone considerable restoration more recently.

Meanwhile, the other Burton near to Neston is home to the Grade II listed Burton Manor, built around 1805 for Richard Congreve and remodelled in 1904 by Sir Charles Nicholson for Henry Neville Gladstone, son of William Ewart Gladstone. An orangery was added in 1910. The garden was also designed in the early 20th century by T. H. Mawson, and included a pool, lawns, and terraces with views over extensive parkland. In the late 20th century, the house became a residential adult education college, operated by Liverpool City Council, but closed in March 2011. Since then, the Friends of Burton Manor have formed and are dedicated to restoring the manor and its outlying buildings, such as the Grade II listed coach house, library, boundary walls, gate piers and ice house, with the latter also registered as a scheduled monument. Even the gardens are listed Grade II on the National Register of Historic Parks and Gardens.

The medieval village of Burton (Neston) was on the London to Birkenhead route, and also sat close to the embarkation point for the ferry to North Wales, so by the early 14th century, Burton was flourishing. However, as the River Dee began to silt up, shipping trade declined, and Burton's prosperity took a downturn, particularly when the course of the Dee was diverted in the 18th century. By 1889, though, Burton had a station known as Burton Point on the Borderlands Line, and it survives to this day, largely intact, despite being closed in 1955.

Burton Quirk Alert: Saint Elmo!
The aforementioned Thomas Wilson, Bishop of Sodor and Man for 58 years, once declared himself as "the poorest bishop in Europe", while 19th century cleric Dean Farrar, called him "the last survivor of the saints of the English church". He died on Man in 1755 and was buried in a coffin made from an elm he had planted!

The centre of the more southerly Cheshire Burton.

NAME (STATUS):	**CREWE** (Town)
POPULATION:	83,650
DISTRICT:	Cheshire East
EARLIEST RECORD:	*Creu*, 1086 (Domesday Book)
MEANING:	A fish trap or a weir
DERIVATION:	From the Celtic word *criu*

FAMOUS RESIDENTS: Carl Ashmore (b.1968), children's author; Frank Blunstone (b.1934), (BORN IN CREWE) footballer; Neil Brooks (b.1962), Olympic swimmer; William Cooper (1910-2002), novelist; David Gifford (b.1965), golfer; Jimmy MacDonald (1906-1991), voice actor; John Morris (b.1964), cricketer; Shanaze Reade (b.1988), BMX and track cycling champion; Adam Rickett (b.1978), actor

The Duke of Bridgewater, Wistaston Road, Crewe.

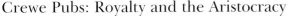

Ye Olde Manor Hotel on Nantwich Road, Crewe.

Crewe Pubs: Royalty and the Aristocracy

Crewe has 18 pubs, including from a royal perspective, the Imperial Hotel, Albert's Corner and The Brunswick, while from an aristocratic perspective there is the Earl of Chester, the Duke of Bridgewater and the Duke of Gloucester.

Crewe Church: Christ Church

The Grade II listed Christ Church at Crewe was built in 1843 by the Grand Junction Railway. The aisles were added in 1864, while a tower of yellow sandstone was added in 1877, having been designed by an engineer of the railway company, J.W. Stansby. The chancel was then added in 1898, and a chapel in 1906. However, between 1977 and 1979, the nave had to be demolished due to dry rot. Nevertheless, services continued to be held in the rest of the building until November 2013, when the church closed as a result of a dwindling congregation.

Crewe Historic Trivia: Railways, basically...

There is relatively little history to impart about Crewe until the magical year of 1837 – for this was the year that the first train passed through what was then just a small township. This was the Grand Junction Railway (GJR) from Birmingham to Warrington, and which initially linked to Liverpool and Manchester via the Warrington & Newton Railway. However, it was inevitable that both major cities would require a more direct branch line, and

it was at Crewe where this split first occurred. Work began in 1839 and was completed by 1842 for the Manchester branch line – and by this stage, the GJR had, quite reasonably, decided to build its main workshops at Crewe. The Liverpool branch line didn't materialise until 1864, though, due to the problem of how to traverse the Mersey estuary. Back to 1843, though, and by this stage Crewe not only had its station (built in fields near to Crewe Hall in 1837), but the growing locomotive workshops meant that the settlement had a significant railway colony that was growing fast. This led to GJR chief engineer, Joseph Locke, formally planning out an urban settlement, and a new town therefore grew up in the parishes of

Christ Church at Crewe was built in 1843 by the Grand Junction Railway.

Monks Coppenhall and Church Coppenhall, alongside the increasingly busy railway station. As a result, Church Coppenhall's population grew from only 200 in 1837, to 4,570 by 1847; by 1871 its population was 17,800. At the same time, the former adjacent township of Crewe was still essentially a village whose population in 1831 had been a mere 70.

The first locomotive built at the Crewe Works went into service in 1843, and by 1848, the works employed over 1,000 people, producing one locomotive a week. Meanwhile, by 1846, the GJR had merged with the London and Birmingham Railway and the Manchester and Birmingham Railway to form the London and North Western Railway (LNWR), and it was this latter company that proceeded to provide housing for its workers and their families – around 200 cottages – as well as schools, churches, public baths and other buildings for the inhabitants of Crewe. They even provided a doctor's surgery with a scheme of health insurance, while the housing was decidedly superior to most other Victorian industrial centres. This meant that even the lowest-ranked labourer cottages were serviced with gas, while the company operated a "nightsoil collection" to empty the privies. The LNWR also opened a cheese market in 1854 and a clothing factory for John Compton who provided the company uniforms, while McCorquodale of Liverpool set up a printing works.

By 1887, the still rapidly-expanding town had its own park, Queen's Park, laid out by engineer Francis Webb), on land donated by the LNWR. Having said that, one vicious rumour is that the LNWR's real motivation was business-related rather than philanthropic – which was to prevent the rival Great Western Railway building a station on the park site!

During the 20th century, Crewe's population growth rate slowed down to a mere 9% between the wars. However, by the start of World War II, Rolls-Royce also had a presence in Crewe, producing aircraft engines, and this made the town a target for German bombers along with its obvious strategic railway importance. The town was also in the flight path to Liverpool, a major target for Germany, and as a result, Crewe lost 35

civilians to bombing raids, with the worst occurring on 29th August 1940 when around 50 houses were destroyed, all close to the railway station.

The railway industry began to decline in Crewe towards the end of the 20th century, although there is still a presence in the town today. Crewe Works still perform train maintenance and inspection, although it has been owned by Bombardier Transportation since 2001. However, by 2005, there were fewer than 1,000 employees – bearing in mind that in its hey-day, the site employed over 20,000 people. Large parts of the former site have also been sold off, and the railway buildings replaced by a supermarket, leisure park, and a large health centre. Despite this, Crewe still boasts one of the largest railway stations in the North West, having 12 platforms, and remains a major interchange station. It also still has a direct service to London Euston, as well as to Birmingham, Cardiff, Chester, Derby, Edinburgh, Glasgow, Holyhead, Liverpool, Manchester, Stoke-on-Trent, Wrexham and many other towns. Finally, regarding Crewe's railway connection, the town is also being suggested as the site of a transport hub for the new HS2 line, when it arrives, and which should be completed by 2027 – perhaps thus preserving Crewe's position as *the* railway hub of the North-West.

As for other industries, there is still an electric locomotive maintenance depot to the north of the railway station, while to the west of the town there is the Bentley car factory. As well as Bentley's, the factory also used to produce Rolls-Royce cars, until the licence for the brand was transferred to BMW in 2003. This story dates back to just before World War II when the British Government required a location for a shadow factory to produce Rolls-Royce aero-engines. Thanks to its northwest location and superior road and rail links, Crewe was selected and construction of the factory started on a 60-acre potato field site in July 1938! Remarkably, it was only another five months before the first Rolls Royce Merlin aero-engine was completed there. By 1943, the factory employed 10,000 people, but after the war, Rolls-Royce engine production remained solely in Derby. However, at the same time, motor car produc-

The Lyceum Theatre in Crewe is the only Edwardian theatre remaining in the district of Cheshire East.

The Market Hall, Crewe, was built in 1854, and was purchased by the town council in 1869.

This beautifully restored signal box is one of three that can be found at the Crewe Heritage Centre which is located in the old LMS railway yard in the centre of Crewe. The site is also home to an extensive miniature railway as well as a number of historic trains.

Part of the original Crewe railway station, alongside the 21st century version. The station is still the main railway hub of the North West.

tion switched to Crewe, and the first car rolled off the production line in 1946 – a Bentley Mark VI. This model went on to become the most successful Bentley ever manufactured, with Crewe producing more than 5000.

The Rolls-Royce Motor Car division was eventually sold to Vickers plc in 1980, and by 1985, Bentley sales had overtaken Rolls Royce sales for the first time since car production moved to Crewe. Then in 1998, Vickers sold its car division, including the Bentley brand and the Crewe factory, to Volkswagen, although the Rolls-Royce brand went back to Rolls-Royce. However, BMW eventually bought the Rolls-Royce brand name from Rolls-Royce and, by 2003, the Bentley brand from Volkswagen.

Crewe Quirk Alert: Riddles, Mars and Armpits

The town of Crewe was founded in the township of Monks Coppenhall which, with the township of Church Coppenhall, formed the ancient parish of Coppenhall. Meanwhile, the railway station was named after the *township* of Crewe – then part of the

ancient parish of Barthomley. Eventually, the township of Crewe became a civil parish in its own right also named, rather confusingly, as Crewe, but which then changed its name to Crewe Green in 1974 to avoid confusion with the adjacent town. As for the railway station, this remained part of the *civil parish* of Crewe, outside the boundary of what had become the municipal borough of Crewe (i.e. the town) until 1936. So what this means is that the *town* of Crewe has neither been part of, nor has it encompassed first the *township* of Crewe, the later *civil parish* of Crewe, and later still the civil parish of Crewe Green adjacent to it, even though these places were the direct origin of the name of the town via the railway station – and which was also not part of the town before 1936 (although it is now).

Confused? Well fear not, because a local riddle explains all: *The place which is Crewe is not Crewe, and the place which is not Crewe is Crewe!* Clear?

Finally, Crewe Crater on Mars is named after the town of Crewe, while author Bill Bryson rather unkindly described Crewe as "the armpit of Cheshire" in his 1995 book *Notes from a Small Island.*

The Crewe Arms Hotel was built in 1880, opposite Crewe Station.

The Royal Hotel is another Victorian railway hotel, built a little earlier in 1853 and further up Nantwich Road.

The centre of Crewe, with The Crown Inn, Crewe Municipal Building (built 1902-1905 by Henry T. Hare) and the Market Hall. Also, perched on top of the weather-vane is a lovely representation of Stephenson's Rocket!

The Grade I listed Crewe Hall was built between 1615 and 1636 for Sir Randolph Crewe.

NAME (STATUS):	**EATON** (Village * 2)
POPULATION:	484 – Cheshire West and Chester: (parish of Rushton);
	374 – Cheshire East (parish of Eaton)
DISTRICT:	Cheshire West and Chester; Cheshire East
EARLIEST RECORD:	Cheshire West: *Etone*, 1086 (Domesday Book); Eyton, 1240
	Cheshire East: *Yeiton*, c.1262
MEANING:	Cheshire West: Farmstead on a spur of land, or on dry ground in marsh, or on well-watered land
	Cheshire East: Farmstead or estate on a river
DERIVATION:	Cheshire West: From the Old English words *ēg* (island, land partly surrounded by water, dry ground in marsh, well-watered land, or promontory) and *tūn* (farmstead)
	Cheshire East: From the Old English words *ēa* (river) and *tūn* (farmstead)

Eaton Geographic Trivia: Two Eaton's

So there are two Eatons in Cheshire, which are located less than 20 miles apart on a very similar line of latitude, with the more westerly Eaton lying four miles south-west of Winsford and the more easterly Eaton situated a mile north-east of Congleton.

Eaton Churches: St Thomas's (Cheshire West) and Christ Church (Cheshire East)

Both Eaton churches are relatively modern builds, with St Thomas's at the more westerly Eaton built in 1896, and Christ Church at the more easterly Eaton built between 1856 and 1858, having been designed by Raffles Brown. The latter is also Grade II listed. Given their youth, there is relatively little history to impart, although the westerly Eaton was refitted in 1936 with a new marble floor to the sanctuary, along with a new reredos, pulpit, stalls and chancel screen, while a new organ chamber was created at this time too. Meanwhile, the most notable feature of Christ Church is the external stair turret at the junction between tower and nave on the south side of the church.

Eaton Historic Trivia: Eaton Hall

Neither Eaton Hall nor the Eaton Estate is close to either village of Eaton. The estate is located a couple of miles south of Chester and covers the villages of Aldford, Eccleston and Saighton, as well as parts of Chester city centre and Handbridge. The estate dates back to the early 1440s and has been the home of the Grosvenor family ever since, and who have also been the Dukes of Westminster since 1874. Today they live at Eaton Hall, built between 1971 and 1973 by John Dennys, brother-in-law to the Duchess. Meanwhile, Eaton Park covers over 800 acres of which 88 acres are formal gardens and home to numerous listed buildings such as the 19th century chapel and the golden gates. The hall is also home to a diverse carriage collection, as well as the Eaton Railway, the latter having been built for the 1st Duke of Westminster by Sir Arthur Percival

Heywood, who had pioneered the 15 inch gauge railway. The new railway exported coal mined on the estate and also transported visitors to Eaton, including members of the Royal Family. Alas, the railway was taken up and sold in 1947 during the period when the previous Eaton Hall was leased to the War Department. However, in 1996 a replica engine, *Katie*, was acquired and the Eaton railway was reinstated. Now *Katie* and the railway provide pleasure and amusement for guests and visitors at the Garden Open Days.

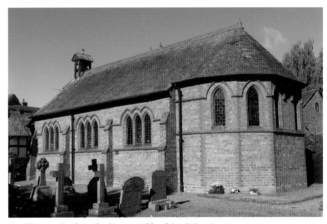
St Thomas's church, Eaton (Cheshire West).

Christ Church, Eaton (Cheshire East).

Quirk Alert: 65 Gardeners and the Hall of Eaton

When the title of Duke of Westminster was bestowed upon the Grosvenor family in 1874, it was the last of the non-royal dukedoms to be created. This was also at around the time that Eaton Gardens required 65 gardeners!

Despite Eaton Hall not being in Eaton (see *Historic Trivia*), the Eaton in Cheshire West does have a building called the Hall of Eaton! Also known as the Jessie Hughes Hall, it was opened on 26th September 1926, thanks to the efforts of the rector's wife of neighbouring Tarporley, Jessie Hughes. Alas, the Hall of Eaton fell into disrepair in the 21st century, and was rebuilt in 2008. Following a local ballot, it retained the name Jessie Hughes Village Hall and was also joint winner of the Cheshire Pride Community Project Award in 2008.

The Plough Inn at Eaton (Cheshire East), parts of which date back to the 17th century.

The first of a series of stunning houses in Eaton (Cheshire West)…

This sandstone cross in the centre of Eaton (Cheshire West) dates from the late 16th or early 17th century.

NAME (STATUS):	**ELTON** (Village)
POPULATION:	3586
DISTRICT:	Cheshire West and Chester
EARLIEST RECORD:	*Eltone*, 1086 (Domesday Book)
MEANING:	Farmstead where eels are caught
DERIVATION:	From the Old English words *æl* (eel) and *tūn* (farmstead)

Elton Pub: The Wheelwright Arms

During building work carried out at the Wheelwright Arms in 2013, a sandstone well was discovered underneath the old kitchen, and which is believed to be hundreds of years old. Out of respect for its age, not only was the well left untouched, but it was worked into the bar as a feature, with a glass cover placed over the top and appropriate lighting installed to enhance the overall effect. Customers can now therefore peer down the 55ft well, which is around one and a half metres in diameter. Given that the pub is around 300 years old it is probably a fair guess that the well is that old too.

The Wheelwright Arms at Elton, home to a mystery 55ft well discovered in 2013.

Elton Church: St James the Great

Elton has a church hall and a Methodist church, but its parish church is in the adjoining village of Ince and is dedicated to St James the Great. The current Grade II listed sandstone church dates from the medieval period, but it was preceded by a Norman chapel on the same spot. The only survivors from the medieval church, though, are the lower half of the tower and part of the chancel, both of which date from 1485 to 1493, with the latter still including some of its original 14th and 15th century glass in the chancel windows. The five-bay nave, north aisle and porch were rebuilt in 1854 by Edward Hodkinson when he also raised the tower by two courses. Meanwhile, inside the church, you will find a sanctuary chair dating from 1634 and a two-tier candelabrum dated 1724.

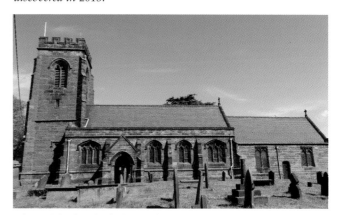

The parish church of Elton is located in adjoining Ince and is dedicated to St James the Great.

Elton Historic Trivia: Stanlow Refinery

Immediately west of Elton is Stanlow Refinery, an oil refinery currently owned by Essar Energy. The site dates back to 1924, when a small bitumen plant was established. By the 1940s, the site had expanded to such an extent that Stanlow and Thornton railway station was opened to ferry workers to and from the site. By the 1970s, an oil infrastructure was in place, with a pipeline from Amlwch on Anglesey pumping crude oil to Stanlow and which was then pumped ashore from tankers moored at deep-water pontoons. However, this pipeline closed in the early 1980s, and was replaced by today's infrastructure which sees crude oil delivered to the Tranmere Oil Terminal on the River Mersey, from where it is transferred via a 15 mile (24 km) pipeline to Stanlow. The crude oil is then refined at Stanlow and stored for delivery. However, despite being located in the North West, Stanlow serves much of England thanks to its link to the UK oil pipeline network, while other supplies are delivered by road.

During the fuel crisis of 2000, protests over government taxation on fuel actually began at Stanlow, while eleven years later a large fuel price protest was staged at Stanlow in May 2011, the aim being to shut down the refinery. Up until this point, the refinery had been owned for decades by Royal Dutch Shell, but a year earlier, the company had announced that they would be selling off some European refineries in order to concentrate on emerging markets in Asia and the Middle East. Indeed, there was even a possibility that Stanlow – Shell's last British refinery – would be shut down, but in the end, the company decided to put the site up for sale. Thankfully, the site was bought by Essar Energy for around £814 million.

As for today, the refinery employs around 800 people. It also occupies nearly 1,900 acres (7.7 km2) which is the seventh largest oil refinery in Europe, and it produces a staggering one-sixth of the United Kingdom's petrol. It currently produces up to 296,000 barrels of oil per day, which adds up to around 12 million tonnes of oil per year. Despite these huge figures, though, it is actually only the second largest refinery in the UK, as Fawley Refinery in Hampshire is larger. Finally, in addition to the oil, Stanlow is also a large producer for commodities such as diesel and jet fuel, with the latter delivered via a pipeline to Manchester Airport.

Also just to the north of Elton, the former Ince Power Station site, which was originally decommissioned in 1997, was re-developed in the mid-2000s into a large bottle production factory owned by Quinn Glass. This site contains two glass melting furnaces and 13 bottle production lines, and produces 1.2 billion bottles per year.

Elton Quirk Alert: Stanlow in Song

In 1980, the British synthpop band Orchestral Manoeuvres in the Dark featured a track about the Stanlow Refinery called "Stanlow" on their second album, *Organisation*. The song starts with the words: "Eternally, This field remains, Stanlow". Meanwhile, the band Jesu also featured a song entitled "Stanlow" on their 2007 album *Conqueror*, and which starts with these words:

All the ghosts that haunt us don't scare,
We're just too selfish to be that aware.

So no mention of oil – although the latter song does go on to talk about "ugly skylines", "rivers flow to grey buildings", and "sweet air bitter taste".

Above: *Stanlow Refinery is located immediately to the west of Elton, and is the seventh largest oil refinery in Europe.*

Left: *The centre of Elton.*

NAME (STATUS):	**FLOWERY FIELD** (Residential Area)
POPULATION:	c.3000
DISTRICT:	Tameside, Greater Manchester
EARLIEST RECORD:	Unknown
MEANING:	Presumably as it sounds!

The George and Dragon, Flowery Field, is probably the oldest pub in the area, dating back to at least 1756.

St Stephen's church, Flowery Field.

Flowery Field Pub: The George and Dragon

The George and Dragon is probably the oldest pub in the area, dating from at least 1756 when it became licensed premises. Its first two landlords served the locals for 70 years between them, James Harrison from 1756 to 1778, and Jonathan Smith the elder, from 1778 to 1826. The George and Dragon is also said to have been haunted since the 1950s by a chap known as Ferdinand, described as of average height with a long and bushy beard, along with appropriate Victorian side whiskers and a long frock coat.

Flowery Field Churches: Flowery Field Church and St Stephen's

An inscription on the church tower of Flowery Field church tells the story of its build and dedication, and mentions that the congregation is "bound by no Creeds or Confessions of Faith" – and indeed, today, the church is still a Free Christian Church and hence nondenominational. The church was dedicated by Thomas Ashton Junior of Hyde in 1878, the local cotton mill owner – although the history of the congregation goes back to the 1820s thanks to the famous Methodist preacher, Hugh Bourne, who had co-founded

Flowery Field church, built in 1878 by Thomas Ashton Junior.

Primitive Methodism in north Staffordshire in the early 19th century. Following Bourne's visits, the villagers held religious services in their cottages, and so impressed by this was Thomas Ashton Senior that he initially built "a school for all denominations" in 1830 at Spring Gardens, to provide the children of his workers with an education, while Sunday Services were held in the Schoolroom.

By the 1870s, the congregation resolved to have a church and minister of their own, and they requested the help of Thomas Ashton Junior in this endeavour. Something of a prudent philanthropist, Ashton Jnr tasked the congregation with raising £1000 – and this they did after a couple of years of endeavour – at which point, Ashton commenced to oversee the church build. He hired the architect Thomas Worthington and work commenced in 1876 and was completed in 1878. True to his word, Ashton Jnr then presented the new church leaders with the Trust Deeds along with the original sum of £1000. Prudent to the end, he asked that the money be invested and the interest used to augment the Minister's stipend.

Three's-Up!

	GALLANTRY BANK	GODLEY	GREAVE
STATUS:	Hamlet	Suburb	Suburb/Road
POPULATION:	278 (Bickerton Parish)	11,465 (Hyde Godley ward)	c.200
DISTRICT:	Cheshire East	Tameside, Greater Manchester	Stockport, Greater Manchester

Three's Up Trivia!

Gallantry Bank is a tiny hamlet just off the A534 between Bickerton and Bulkeley, and is part of the parish of Bickerton. Home to a cluster of houses, Gallantry Bank Cottage and Gallantry Bank Farm, the hamlet is also somewhat quirkily in Cheshire East, despite being close to Cheshire's western border with Wales!

Gallantry Bank was also home to a 19th century copper mine owned by the Egerton family of Oulton. The mine was first officially recorded in 1697, although it is fairly certain that copper has been mined at Gallantry Bank since the Bronze Age, and which was continued on a larger scale by the Romans. Today, a surviving chimney from the mine can be spotted from the A534, which in the 19th century was used by the boiler that served the pumping engine above the main engine shaft – this being the deepest at 156ft; the other five shafts ranged from 35ft deep to 135ft deep. It is believed that Shafts No. 4 and 5 were the oldest, and were worked until the beginning of the 19th century. However, by the mid-19th century, only Shaft No. 3 (110-120ft deep) was in use, but after the 1860s, the mine was abandoned.

Interestingly, a 1906 survey revealed that by widening and deepening the main shafts the mine could easily have yielded around 18,000 tons of copper which at that time would have delivered a net a profit of around £1.1m. However, the investment never took place and despite passing interest from mining companies, the next people to work the mine were three local men in the 1920s, who worked Shaft No. 3 using a bucket, rope and hand winch! Thereafter, the mines remained unworked and were finally sealed in the 1960s, while many of the buildings were demolished in the 1970s to accommodate the widening of the A534.

Next up, **Godley** is a suburb to the north-east of Hyde in Tameside, Greater Manchester. Despite now being part of the Manchester metropolis, it was recorded in the early 13th century as being the location of the earliest agriculture in the Tameside area. Six hundred years later, Godley Reservoir was constructed in 1851 and was a crucial part of the Longdendale Chain project that brought fresh water from the Peak District to Manchester via a chain of reservoirs and tunnels. All of this was made possible by the Manchester Corporation Waterworks Act of 1847 which saw the construction of the Woodhead, Hollingworth and Arnfield reservoirs as well as an aqueduct to channel drinking water from Arnfield and

View from Gallantry Bank towards Bulkeley Hill.

This chimney is part of the remains of a former copper mine that was worked at Gallantry Bank.

Hollingworth to the service reservoir at Godley – all under the supervision of civil engineer, John Frederick Bateman (1810-1889). The entire Longdendale Chain project ran from 1848 to 1877 and at that time, was the largest chain of reservoirs in the world. Having sourced the water from the River Etherow and stored it in the larger reservoirs to the east, the water then flowed through the 6-foot bore Mottram Tunnel to Godley. The tunnel runs through the ridge between the Etherow and Tame valley's and is 3,100 yards long (2,800m), running with a gradient of 5 feet per mile (95cm per km), and carrying up to 50 million gallons a day (230 Ml per day).

The tunnel was built between August 1848 and October 1850, and the Godley service reservoir built to receive and filter the water was completed in 1851. The water at Godley was filtered by passing it through straining frames made of oak and fine wires. It was then chlorinated to remove bacteria before it was allowed into Manchester's water distribution network. The 19th century system survived until the early 1960s, when additional treatment works were built at Arnfield and Godley. However, the latest development is the construction of a 3 MW, 45,500-square-metre floating solar farm on Godley Reservoir by United Utilities.

Sticking with Godley and 19th century industry, and it was during the 1880s that John Broomer developed an early form of margarine at Godley which was called Butterine. Broomer took over a former hat factory at the Olive Tree works, but the works were acquired by the Danish margarine manufacturer Otto Monsted in 1888. The factory was then sold to Maypole Dairies in 1902 and later used by Walls to manufacture ice cream and meat products.

Finally, **Greave** is a middle-class suburb on the north-eastern outskirts of Stockport, between Romiley and Woodley. It is also, quite strangely, the name of the main road through Greave. So, for example, the address of the pub on that road is: The Foresters Arms, 29 Greave, Greave! Although alternatively, it can be addressed as Romiley rather than Greave, as the road and place are part of the ward of Bredbury Green and Romiley.

Godley Viaduct.

St John the Baptist church at Godley was built in 1847, and includes this rather unusual turret affixed to the south-western corner of the tower.

Left and right: *Two views of Greave Fold, a charming little walkway of narrow paths and courts that winds away behind the Foresters Arms.*

Three's-Up!

	HACKINGKNIFE	HASSALL	HATTON
STATUS:	Hillside feature	Village and Parish	Village and Parish; Parish
POPULATION:	N/A	265	320 (Warrington); 198 (Cheshire W)
DISTRICT:	Tameside, G. Manc	Cheshire East	Warrington; Cheshire West
EARLIEST RECORD:	Not known	*Eteshale*, 1086 (Domesday Book); *Hatishale*, 13th century	*Hattone*, c.1230; *Etone*, 1086 (DB), *Hettun*, 1185
MEANING:	Not known	The witch's nook of land	Farmstead on a heath
DERIVATION:	Not known	From the Old English words *hægtesse* (witch or supernatural female) and *halh* (nook of land)	From the Old English words *hæth* (heath) and *tūn* (farmstead)

Hackingknife is the most prominent part of the hill known as Werneth Low, part of Werneth Low Country Park, and also the location of the Hyde War Memorial. It sits on the edge of the hill at around 800ft above sea level, with majestic views over much of Greater Manchester (*shown top left, looking westwards towards Manchester at sunset*), as well as further west towards the Welsh mountains, north towards the Lancashire moors and east towards the Pennine Hills. Also known as the Werneth Low Memorial, it was officially unveiled at Hackingknife on 25th June 1921, before a crowd of around 15,000 people. A year earlier, a public appeal had seen the Hyde War Memorial Committee raise around £14,000, of which £4,000 was spent on the purchase of Lower Higham Farm and all of its land, and a scheme launched to protect the land forever for the health and wellbeing of the community. This included the £2,000 construction of the imposing granite obelisk which was a memorial and lasting tribute to the 710 men from the area who gave their lives during World War I. The remaining money was also used to help the children of those who lost their lives, through scholarships and maintenance grants, and to convert nearby Aspland House (now demolished) into a maternity home.

The Hyde War Memorial on the part of Werneth Low known as Hackingknife.

Prior to the grand unveiling of the obelisk, the six wooden panels that bore the names of the town's dead were taken from Hyde town hall and placed around the base of the memorial. On the big day, the crowds were entertained by the Kingston Mills band who played patriotic airs, while a one-hour service followed with prayers led by the Rev. J.P. Richmond. The memorial was then unveiled by Mrs Evelyn Welch, who had been Mayoress of Hyde during the war, after which the Rev. H.E. Dowson of Hyde Chapel said the dedicatory prayer. The incumbent Mayor was then presented with the deeds to the land by the Chairman of the War Memorial Committee.

Several decades later, the World War II plate was unveiled on May 5th 1963, by the Mayor, Councillor John Grundy, and which commemorates 162 servicemen and women and 12 civilians. As for today, the land and farm are now held in trust by the Hyde War Memorial Trust, while the obelisk and surrounding land forms part of Werneth Low Country Park, which is administered by Tameside Metropolitan Borough and the Hyde War Memorial Trust. The country park was opened by HRH the Duke of Gloucester on 9th June 1980 and covers 80 hectares (200 acres) across the northern and western slopes of Werneth Low.

As for Werneth Low, the highest point is at 915ft (279m), around 100ft higher than Hackingknife. Historically, a flint knife and a Bronze Age stone mace head have been unearthed on Werneth Low, while during the Iron Age it was the location of a farmstead enclosed by a double ditch. There is also evidence of a Romano-British settlement on Werneth Low, with a sherd of 2nd

View north-eastwards from Hackingknife towards Mottram and the Longdendale Valley beyond.

St Philip's church at Hassall Green, and which is also known locally as the tin tabernacle.

century Roman pottery discovered, while there might have been a temporary Roman camp here too, as excavations have recovered a posthole dating to the Roman occupation of Britain. Much later, a Royal Observer Corps monitoring post was installed on Werneth Low from 1962 to 1968, which was intended to give warning of hostile aircraft and nuclear attacks on the country.

Next, **Hassall** is located around four miles northeast of Crewe while a mile or so further up Alsager Road is Hassall Green where you will find St Philip's church. Painted pink, it is actually a prefabricated building constructed in corrugated galvanised iron, and is hence known locally as the tin tabernacle. The building wasn't always in Hassall Green, though! It started out life in the early 1880s in Crewe Road, Alsager. However, in 1894, construction commenced in Alsager of a new stone church (St Mary Magdalene), and even before its completion in 1898, the tin tabernacle was sold for £150 and moved to Hassall Green in 1895. Despite its construction, though, St Philip's church has a three-bay nave, a short chancel and a north vestry, while the west gable is adorned with a bellcote surmounted by a slated broach spire.

As outlined on the previous page, the place-name Hassall means "the witch's nook of land", with the witch element deriving from the Old English word *hægtesse*. The word *hægtesse*, is one of the oldest English words for a supernatural female, and is also found in medieval West Germanic languages, too. In Britain, though, it eventually evolved into the Middle English word *hagge*, meaning a witch or an evil spirit, and then ultimately to today's modern English word, *hag*.

There are actually two **Hattons** in Cheshire. The most northerly is a village and parish in the south-western corner of the Warrington district, while the other is in Cheshire West and Chester, around four miles south-east of Chester. The latter village, however, is known as Hatton Heath, while the parish is called simply Hatton. The name of Hatton Heath is also slightly quirky in that the name "Hatton" means "farmstead on the heath", so presumably "Hatton Heath" means "farmstead on the heath…on the heath"!

The Hatton family coat of arms of a yellow chevron and three wheatsheaves on a blue background dates

The Grade II listed Hatton Arms at Hatton, Warrington. This 18th century building formerly incorporated a post office and a village store. Meanwhile, nearside is a Grade II listed K6 telephone kiosk – and which is now also the village library – this after BT offered the kiosk to the parish for the princely sum of £1!

back to the Norman Conquest and also includes the family motto: "To have a conscience free from guilt". Some of the first settlers in Virginia USA in 1613 were from the Hatton family.

Finally, the Hatton in Warrington is home to the Grade II listed Hatton Hall which dates from the 17th century, while the Hatton Hall in the Chester West & Cheshire parish dates from around 1830.

Hatton Hall (Warrington) dates from the 17th century according to the Hatton Village website.

NAME (STATUS):	**HALE** (Village)
POPULATION:	15,315
DISTRICT:	Trafford, Greater Manchester
EARLIEST RECORD:	*Halas*, 1094
MEANING:	Place at the nook or corner of land
DERIVATION:	From the Old English word *halh* (nook or corner of land)

The Cheshire Midland, Hale. A few yards further up Ashley Road is The Railway which is frequented by stars of Coronation Street.

The Bulls Head at nearby Hale Barns which adjoins Hale to the south-east. Hale Barns was originally the site of a medieval tithe barn owned by the manor of Hale.

Hale Geographic Trivia: All Change

Hale is yet another former Cheshire place that is now part of Greater Manchester, albeit only a mile from the border that was redefined on 1st April 1974, following the passing of the Local Government Act 1972. Hale is bounded to the south by the River Bollin, and since 1st April 1974, this has defined the border between Cheshire and Greater Manchester, while the village has been part of the Metropolitan Borough of Trafford along with Altrincham which it adjoins to the north and Bowden to the west.

Hale and Bowden, along with Hale Barns (to the south-east) are regarded as being the wealthiest areas in Greater Manchester; indeed Hale was recently named by the *Daily Telegraph* as the 12th most expensive place to live in Britain, with house prices 194% higher than those in surrounding areas, and having risen by a whopping 78%

between 2003 and 2008. Statistics also show that in 1931, 26.4% of Hale's population was middle class (compared with 14% nationally), but by 1971, this had increased to 56.3% (compared with 24% nationally).

Hale Church: St Peter's & Friends

St. Peter's church was built in 1892, but was preceded by Hale Chapel which was established in Hale Barns by Nonconformists in 1723 on what is now Chapel Lane. The Grade II listed Hale Chapel is therefore the earliest place of worship in either Hale or Hale Barns, and features an 18th century pulpit and 19th century stained glass. It underwent major alterations in around 1880.

Other religious houses in the area include a synagogue in Shay Lane founded by the Hale & District Hebrew Congregation in 1978, and what used to be St David's church on Grove Lane, but which was converted into a mosque in July 2003 by the Altrincham Muslim Association.

St Peter's church, Hale.

Hale Historic Trivia: The Masseys, The Tithe Barn and Royd House

Following the Norman Conquest, the manor of Hale was taken from the Saxon thegn, Ælfward, and given to the Norman nobleman, Hamo de Mascy (also known as Hamon de Massey). Hamo, who also gained several of the adjoining manors, was made a baron in 1071 by the Earl of Chester. What became known as the Masssey family retained control over Hale until the mid-14th century, when the last Lord of the Manor died without an heir.

A century later, a tithe barn was established in nearby Hale Barns to the south-east of Hale, and at this time, the value of the tithe taken from Hale was more than double that of any other township in the Bowdon parish. The formerly isolated hamlet of Hale Barns began to grow throughout the 16th century, and by 1616, the first written record of Hale Barns as a village appeared.

Moving into the 19th century, and a railway station was opened in Hale in May 1862 by the Cheshire Midland Railway (later the Cheshire Lines Committee), on its line from Altrincham to Knutsford. Initially named Peel Causeway station, it was re-named to Hale in 1902, by which stage Hale had been transformed from an agricultural settlement into a commuter village for middle class merchants working in Manchester.

The early 20th century also saw the building of the Grade I listed Royd House. Designed by architect Edgar Wood, it was built between 1914 and 1916 and is regarded as one of the best examples of early 20th century domestic architecture – a two-storey Y-shaped building with a concrete roof and a concave façade made out of Portland red stone and Lancashire brick.

Hale Quirk Alert:
What a Difference an "R" Makes

So, none of my Cheshire reference books have anything particularly quirky about Hale, so I had a quick surf of the internet, and found something on my first hit. Try putting in the words "Hale Greater Manchester quirky" into your search engine and see if you can find the same *faux-pas* that I did! It was a review about a certain high-class café in Hale and in amongst the opinions was an enthusiastic summary of the afternoon teas served there, which I think the lady meant to describe as "scrummy". Unfortunately, she missed out the "r"! Twice!

The Clock Tower, Hale.

Hale railway station was originally opened in May 1862 on the Altrincham to Knutsford line.

Two views of some of the fine buildings that grace Hale's attractive high street.

NAME (STATUS):	**HAZEL GROVE** (Suburb)
POPULATION:	15,265
DISTRICT:	Stockport, Greater Manchester
EARLIEST RECORD:	*Hesselgrove*, 1690
MEANING:	A hazel copse or grove
DERIVATION:	From the Old English words *hæsel* (hazel-tree) and *grāf* (copse or grove)

Hazel Grove: Etymological Trivia

So, the Oxford Dictionary of British Place-Names offers the above origin of Hazel Grove. However, research suggests that the *Hesselgrove* referred to above, relates to a small hamlet located to the east of today's settlement of Hazel Grove, towards High Lane. Meanwhile, the settlement that today is known as Hazel Grove was actually known as Bullock Smithy until 1836. Unsurprisingly, this name wasn't overly popular with the locals, and so the settlement was renamed Hazel Grove – either due to the large number of hazel trees in the area, or more likely because the settlement had grown to absorb the hamlet recorded as *Hesselgrove* in 1690.

Hazel Grove Church: Norbury Parish Church

Given that Hazel Grove (or rather Bullock Smithy) didn't develop until the 17th century, the place was never home to a Norman or medieval parish church – although a preaching cross is recorded here as early as 1005. However, a private chapel was built here for the local inhabitants of Norbury in 1485, and by the end of the 16th century, the chapel had become the focal point for Non-conformists of north-eastern Cheshire. However, following the Restoration of King Charles II in 1660, it became forbidden for ministers to preach without the Book of Common Prayer. This led to the minister of Norbury Chapel, John Jolie,

The Rising Sun, Hazel Grove, the first of a series of pubs in Hazel Grove running along the A6.

The pub known as Bullock Smithy – named after the place here that had its name changed to Hazel Grove in 1836.

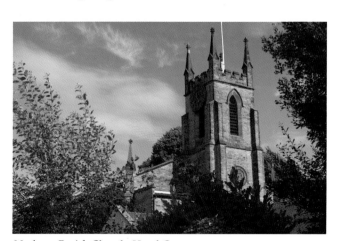

Norbury Parish Church, Hazel Grove.

Torkington Park, Hazel Grove.

The Civic Hall, Hazel Grove.

This viaduct cuts through the middle of Hazel Grove, and was built by the Midland Railway as part of the New Mills to Heaton Mersey line, which formed part of its main line between Manchester Central and London St Pancras.

being tried for Non-conformity, although the charges didn't stick as it was decided that Norbury Chapel was not a consecrated place.

A century further on, and John Wesley preached in Bullock Smithy in 1750, but described the village as "…one of the most famous villages in the county for all manner of wickedness." As for the chapel, that fared little better in the early 19th century when an inspector from Chester reported that it was '…a wretched building, little better than a stable'. In addition to the chapel's state of disrepair, the village population had grown to over 3,000 people by 1833, so it was decided that the area should finally have its own parish, with a new parish church located closer to the centre of the village. Norbury Church was consecrated on 2nd July 1834 by the Bishop of Chester, John Bird Sumner, and although it was still part of the Stockport parish at that time, the church became a parish church in its own right in 1843; a new chancel was added in 1925.

Hazel Grove Historic Trivia: Reinvention

Historically, "Hazel Grove" was comprised of three separate townships: Norbury (*Nordberie*, 1086), Torkington and Bosden-cum-Handforth. Then in 1560 Richard Bullock built a smithy on the corner of what is now Torkington Park, the building became known as the Bullock Smithy Inn, and then eventually the whole area became known as Bullock Smithy. The settlement was then re-named to Hazel Grove in 1836, as described earlier. However, Hazel Grove was still part of the civil parish of Norbury which became part of the Stockport Rural District of Cheshire from 1894 to 1900. Then from 1900 to 1974, Hazel Grove was part of the Hazel Grove and Bramhall civil parish and urban district before the latter was abolished on 1st April 1974, as part of the Local Government Act 1972, and Hazel Grove found itself part of the new metropolitan county of Greater Manchester, in the new Metropolitan Borough of Stockport.

Finally, Hazel Grove is home to the allegedly "world famous" Bamboo nightclub, and is also the birthplace of the journalist and presenter, Baroness Joan Bakewell DBE.

Looking south (left) and north (right) along Chester Road in Hazel Grove.

Three's-Up!

	HEAVILEY	LITTLER	LONG GREEN
STATUS:	Residential Area	Residential Area	Hamlet/Road
POPULATION:	1402	1463 (Winsford Verdin ward)	c.50
DISTRICT:	Stockport, G Manchester	Cheshire West & Chester	Cheshire West & Chester

Heaviley is another area of Stockport that was switched from Cheshire to the new Metropolitan County of Greater Manchester on April 1st 1974. It is home to the Grade II listed St George's church which although in the deanery of Stockport (Greater Manchester), still remains in the diocese of Chester and the archdeaconry of Macclesfield (both Cheshire). The church build commenced in 1893 and was consecrated on 25th February 1897. It was designed by Hubert Austin in the Perpendicular style, and comprises a six-bay nave with a clerestory, north and south aisles, north and south porches, a chancel and sanctuary with a Lady Chapel to the north, an organ chamber to the south, and a vestry to the southeast. The 112ft (34m) tower includes flying buttresses which connect to the spire which, in turn, rises to 236ft (72m). The east and west windows have seven lights, and the windows along the sides of the nave have four lights.

This splendid configuration has led to the *Buildings of England* series stating that it is "by far the grandest church of Stockport", while according to the church visitors' guide, the Rt Revd Geoffrey Fisher, former Archbishop of Canterbury, said that it is "the finest church built in England since the Reformation".

The church formed part of a group of buildings that also included the vicarage and schools, all of which were paid for by George Fearn, a local brewer – and which cost around £80,000 to build.

Opposite St George's church is Joseph Mott House. This timber-framed house dates from the late 16th century, although it was altered during both the 19th and 20th centuries, and indeed the timber is also 19th century. However, the parts of the house that still date from the 16th century were built when Heaviley was a rural hamlet known as Lockwood Fold, one of a group of "Folds" in north-eastern Cheshire and south-eastern Lancashire, including Fold (place #22 on the Shire-Ode map). Most of these places were named after their distinctive cluster of farm buildings and small workshops, with the latter used for domestic-scale manufacturing; in Lockwood Fold's case, this was for hat manufacturing.

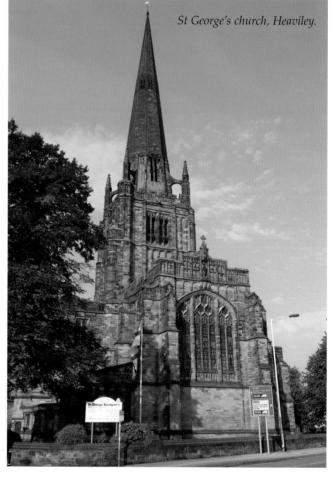

St George's church, Heaviley.

Joseph Mott House, Heaviley.

Next up, **Littler** is a residential area in the north-western part of the town of Winsford. Along Littler Lane – which ironically is in the neighbouring suburb of Over – is the Grade II listed Littler Grange, another former Tudor farmhouse and the best remaining half-timber building in Winsford. This impressive 16th century building was originally constructed with a thatched roof and a possible moat, while the wooden frame was in-filled with wattle and daub. Littler Grange was originally the home of the Bosier family of Agden, near Malpas, who had made their fortune from weaving. At a later stage, the building was converted into a sizeable dairy farm with numerous outbuildings including stables, pig sties, poultry sheds and a bull-pen as well as a large dairy, a granary store and a large orchard. Naturally, the farm produced Cheshire cheese and milk, while it also provided employment for the locals all the way up to its closure in the 1960's.

In terms of notable residents, Robert Bosier was incumbent in 1723, but was imprisoned for harbouring a Roman Catholic priest in Littler Grange. On his death in prison, Robert's sister, Elizabeth, inherited Littler Grange after which the property transferred to her husband Robert Atherton's family, the Whartons.

Robert and Elizabeth's son, Israel, later became one of the first trustees of the Weaver Navigation Company – although he had been declared bankrupt before his death in 1745.

It was around this time that Littler Grange was converted to a dairy farm, and by the mid-19th century it was being run by the Ravenscroft family – although that came to a tragic end in 1875. Thomas Ravenscroft had already died in 1870 and his wife, Ann, continued to run the farm. However, in 1875 she drowned when it was thought that she was collecting duck eggs from the nests round the farm pond, leaving her eight children as orphans. The Sherwin family eventually took over the running of the farm in the early 20th century, and continued to farm there until 1965 when Littler Grange became a private residence again. However, since 1999, Littler Grange has been a children's nursery, complete with sloping floors on part of the first floor!

Finally, **Long Green** is a hamlet half a mile north of Little Barrow and part of the same parish along with Great Barrow. It is also the name of a mile-long road along which the farms and houses of Long Green are stretched in linear fashion – one of which, Long Green Farmhouse, is Grade II listed and dates from c.1720.

Littler Grange on Littler Lane in Over, Winsford, part-dates from Tudor times.

This old barn is located opposite Littler Grange.

The Gate Inn, Littler.

The road of Long Green that lends its name to the linear hamlet that stretches out along its length.

NAME (STATUS): **HIGHER WYCH** (Hamlet)
LOWER WYCH (Hamlet)
POPULATION: 182 (Wigland parish)
DISTRICT: Cheshire West & Chester
EARLIEST RECORD: Unknown
MEANING: Place at the salt works
DERIVATION: From the Old English word *wīc*
(trading or industrial settlement
– i.e. salt works)

Higher Wych and Lower Wych Geographic and Historic Trivia

Higher Wych and its twin village of Lower Wych are both located alongside the Wych Brook, which marks the boundary between England and Wales for several miles in south-west Cheshire. The Wych Brook is a tributary of the River Dee and naturally, therefore, Higher Wych lies higher up the watercourse than Lower Wych does. Of course, both places derive their names (Old English *wīc*) from salt extraction, and indeed you can still see at Lower Wych today, a brine pit of about seven metres in diameter. The reason the salt-works were established in this particular area, is because the middle section of the Wych Brook (between Lower Wych and Dymocks Mill) is the narrowest and deepest part, where it lies over the Triassic rocks of

the Cheshire Plain. These include naturally occurring salt beds, and which were thus exploited at the Higher and Lower Wych salt-works until the late 19th century – although not on the scale seen a little further north in Nantwich, Northwich and Middlewich, where the deposits are much larger.

Higher Wych and Lower Wych Church: Methodist Chapels

Higher Wych is also home to a Methodist church which was built in 1879 and is located alongside the Wych Brook. However, a Methodist group had worshipped in various homes in and around Higher Wych since 1814. Meanwhile, Lower Wych is also home to a former Methodist chapel known as Valley Chapel – but which is no longer in use as a place of worship.

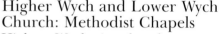

Above: *This fountain in Higher Wych was erected by villagers in 1877.*

Left: *This stunning house can be found towards the top of the road out of Lower Wych.*

Right: *Higher Wych Road as it heads out of Higher Wych.*

View across the Wych Brook towards Higher Wych, with Higher Wych Methodist chapel on the far right.

What is known as Valley Chapel in Lower Wych.

The Wych Brook at Higher Wych.

Looking up the "main" road through Lower Wych.

Three's-Up!

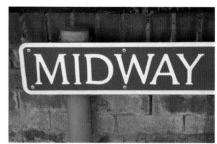

	LOWERHOUSE	**LYME GREEN**	**MIDWAY**
STATUS:	Residential Area	Village	Residential Area
POPULATION:	1214	1585	1104
DISTRICT:	Cheshire East	Cheshire East	Cheshire East

Looking down Moss Brow towards Lowerhouse Mill which was built in 1818 by the Antrobus family. However, it was Samuel Greg who first deployed it as a cotton mill in 1832.

Looking up Moss Brow from its junction with Long Row – the latter comprising 19 stone cottages built to house mill workers in the early 19th century.

Lowerhouse is located at the north-western edge of Bollington and features some lovely old mill cottages, thanks to Bollington being a major centre for the cotton industry in the 19th and 20th centuries. The nearest mill, and workplace of the majority of the inhabitants of these early 19th century mill cottages, is Lowerhouse Mill which can be found on Albert Road at the end of Moss Brow. Lowerhouse Mill was built in 1818 by the Antrobus family, but they never actually deployed the mill themselves. Instead, it was bought by Samuel Greg Jr, who opened it as a cotton mill in 1832. Indeed, almost the entire Lowerhouse community was created in the early 19th century by Samuel Greg, who as well as the mill, bought 53 of the houses and cottages for his workers from the estate of Philip Antrobus. Greg then developed the community further between 1832 and 1846, by building a school, a library, and land for allotments – and therefore as well as the area becoming known as Lowerhouse, it also earned the name of Goldenthal or Happy Valley. Indeed, it is also thought that the community inspired

The Methodist church at the top of Moss Brow.

Elizabeth Gaskell's industrial novels of *Mary Barton* (1848) and *North and South* (1855).

As for Samuel Greg Jnr (1804-1876), he would be remembered as an important 19th century industrialist and philanthropist. He was born in Manchester, the son of Samuel Greg Snr, who had built Quarry Bank Mill at Styal. Greg Jr soon became interested in the *consequences* of wealth (rather than the *creation* of wealth), and he used Lowerhouse Mill as a basis for social experimentation. He published his ideas on the model factory village in 1840 and later founded further educational and social institutions in Bollington. Later in life, he became president of the Society for the Diffusion of Useful Knowledge, while he also wrote the hymn *Stay, Master, Stay*, based on the story of the Transfiguration of Jesus. As for Lowerhouse Mill, it survives today and is still home to a number of businesses.

Lyme Green is a village just south of Macclesfield and is home to the Grade II listed Lyme Green Hall which was built in 1845. Alongside the hall is what is known as Lyme Green

The Macclesfield Canal at Lyme Green.

Lyme Green Hall, originally built in 1845.

Settlement, which is run by an independent charity providing accommodation for men and women with spinal injuries and other disabilities. Its beginnings started towards the end of World War II, when the Committee of the British Red Cross and the Order of St John in Cheshire decided that specialised accommodation was required for War Pensioners whose spinal injuries confined them to wheelchairs. Lyme Green Hall was therefore purchased in 1945 and converted into accommodation for single War Pensioners which included a clinic and two hospital wards, each capable of looking after the needs of six men. Workshops were also included to enable the residents (or Settlers, as they became known) to perform clock and boot repairs, thus giving them both occupational therapy and a trade – although it was actually a condition of residency that the men had to work in the workshops, receiving board and lodging in exchange. Electricity meter servicing was later added to the portfolio of services, as was the servicing of speedometers for police cars and gauges for use on steam machinery.

In addition to the Hall, 29 two and three-bedroom bungalows were built on the adjoining land and became available for occupation in 1948. As part of the development, the organisation had the support of the Ministry of Pensions, and also worked closely with the Spinal Unit of Stoke Mandeville Hospital where pioneering work on paraplegia was being carried out. From a leisure perspective, recreational facilities with a lounge, games room and library were also provided. The hall was eventually sold in 1976 and by the 1990s, the workshops had become inviable, too, and were also closed, as was the recreational hall. Today, the Settlement still looks after people with disabilities and still gives priority to disabled ex-service men and women, and it is managed by a board of Trustees who are still nominated by the British Red Cross and the Order of St John.

Finally, **Midway** is an area at the southern end of Poynton which was revolutionised by the cotton industry in the late 18th century when there were three cotton manufacturers in the area, including John Barrett of Midway. The start of the 19th century saw a multitude of handloom weavers appear in the area, but the introduction of steam-operated machine looms forced most of them out of business by the 1820s, and by the time of the first detailed census in 1841, there was only one cotton

weaver mentioned – this being Adam Pearson, aged 65, of Midway. Later, there were at least two communal silk weaving workshops in Midway, which employed local girls. The first had been established by Henry Horrabin in the 1850s, an experienced master fustian cutter who had strong links with Manchester merchants. By 1861, his Midway workshop was employing 26 girls in what had previously been the Methodist meeting room, but which became available in 1851 when a new chapel was built. Furthermore, the 1861 census lists a certain Hamlet Hadfield as a silk agent lodging in Midway and who later appears in Manchester directories as a silk and bandana manufacturer – where the bandanas were white or yellow spotted handkerchiefs. Further 19th century censuses list other master fustian cutters in Midway.

By 1873, Horrabin's former fustian cutting workshop in Midway had been rented from Lord Vernon and adapted for hat trimming by Christy's of Stockport. The workshop employed around 30 women and girls, including some of the older girls from Lord Vernon's Girls School at nearby Poynton Green. A horse and cart left Stockport every morning with a variety of hats for Midway, and the girls would manually add lining and trimming to all sorts such as military hats, fez and topi. By 1881, the workshop employed 50 workers, while an 1892 copy of the *Hatters' Gazette* refers to it as a great boon to the young women of the village. The hat workshop remained in business into the 1920s, although it was virtually idle by 1925, as much of the hat finishing had moved to the greatly expanded premises in Stockport.

These handsome buildings can be found in the centre of Midway on the A523.

NAME (STATUS):	**HYDE** (Town)
POPULATION:	34,003
DISTRICT:	Tameside, Greater Manchester
EARLIEST RECORD:	*Hyde*, early 13th century
MEANING:	Estate assessed at one hide, an amount of land for the support of one free family and its dependents
DERIVATION:	From the Old English word *hīd* (hide of land, or amount of land for the support of one family and its dependents of up to 120 acres)

Hyde Church: St George's

The Grade II listed St George's church was built 1831-1832 by John Hyde Clark of Hyde Hall, to a Gothic Revival design by T.W. and C. Atkinson. It was built as a chapel of ease to St Mary's church at Stockport, but became the parish church of part of Hyde township in 1842. The chancel was added 1882-1883 and part of the interior was redesigned two years later, while the ring of eight bells were cast in 1920. The church lychgate dates from 1855 and is also Grade II listed, while it is also allegedly made out of timber from a former farmhouse. Meanwhile, at the southern end of Hyde in Gee Cross, there is also a stunning chapel; Arthur Mee describes this 19th century Unitarian chapel as "one of the most beautiful Nonconformist buildings in England".

Hyde Historic Trivia: Cotton, Disasters and Serial Killers

Even by the late 18th century, Hyde only amounted to a cluster of houses known as Red Pump Street, and which was only known as "Hyde" courtesy of being part of the estates of nearby Hyde Hall.

Hyde's population expanded rapidly throughout the 19th century due to the proliferation of cotton mills that had sprung up in the late 18th and early 19th centuries. Raw materials and produce were shipped in and out via the Peak Forest Canal, which linked Whaley Bridge to the Ashton Canal at Ashton-under-Lyne, mainly for the transportation of limestone from the Derbyshire quarries. However, also taking advantage of the canal was Hyde Colliery which had been opened at Hyde Hall and as well as exporting coal down the canal, the colliery also sent it *up* the canal to be used for firing the lime kilns at Bugsworth.

By the 1830s, there were 40 working mills in Hyde, with mill-owning families including the Hibbert, Horsfield and Sidebotham families. However, by far the largest and most philanthropic employer was the Ashton family who ran a combined spinning and weaving company, and had mills in both Newton and Flowery Field. It was the Ashton family who built the aforementioned Hyde Chapel at Gee Cross, and offered employment to so many locals. Throughout the uncertain years of the Cotton Panic, the Ashton family distributed free food to their workers. Nevertheless, his family's benevolence didn't help Thomas Ashton when he was murdered during the Chartist disturbances of

the 1840s, with the Cotton Tree Inn in Hyde a favourite meeting place of the Chartists.

Hyde Colliery was the location of a mining disaster on 18th January 1889 when an explosion killed 23 miners. The morning shift had started as normal at 05:30 am, with two hundred miners assisted by seven pit ponies. The explosion occurred underground at just after 9:00am in the Two Foot Seam where 43 men and boys and three

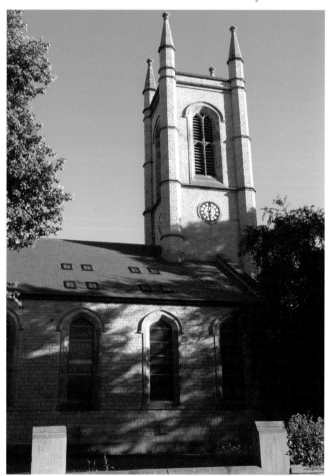

Above: *St George's church, Hyde, built during 1831 and 1832.*

Right: *The Grade II listed lychgate outside St George's church.*

LEFT: Captain Clark's Bridge on the Peak Forest Canal at Hyde which is named after the naval officer, John Clarke who lived at Wood End in the 19th century. It is here that the towpath changes sides, going up and over the canal and then curving down and round the other side (partially shown, right) and under the bridge. Its design meant that horses pulling barges could complete the whole manoeuvre without having to detach the towline.

ponies were working. The rescue teams worked throughout the day to retrieve the dead and injured, with the last of them brought out at 08:45 pm. Of those who survived, many suffered serious burns, mainly to their head and shoulders, but it was actually suffocation that led to the majority of the deaths.

The inquest was held at the Navigation Inn (now the Cheshire Ring), where accounts were given by some of the surviving miners. A recurring tale was of being blown off their feet by the explosion, which also took out the lights. They then had to somehow feel their way to the surface, despite being repeatedly driven back by contaminated air. One miner, William Gee, described how he made it to safety by following a current of air. The inquest was also told that the lights in question were naked candles, authorised by management because the pit showed few signs of gas and was also very well ventilated. The inquest therefore decided that there must have been a roof fall which caused a release of gas, and that the naked candles were the cause of the resulting explosion. The jury returned verdicts of accidental death for all 23 miners. Remarkably, all three ponies working in the Two Foot Seam survived. For the victims, a charity football match was played to raise money for their families. It was contested between Ardwick AFC (now Manchester City) and Newton Heath (now Manchester United), and was attended by 10,000 people.

In 1881, Hyde was incorporated as a municipal borough of Cheshire. This covered the parishes of Hyde, Godley and Newton, along with part of Compstall, while in 1936 the borough was extended following the annexation of the civil parish of Hattersley and part of the civil parish of Matley from Tintwistle Rural District. The whole of the municipal borough became part of the Metropolitan Borough of Tameside on 1st April 1974, thanks to the Local Government Act 1972; this was also when Hyde was moved from Cheshire into the new metropolitan county of Greater Manchester.

The Unitarian chapel at Gee Cross, Hyde.

Sticking with the 20th century, and Hyde was the location of the arrest of the notorious Moors Murderers, Myra Hindley and Ian Brady – this after police found the body of 17 year-old Edward Evans in their home on the Hattersley Estate. Hindley and Brady were found guilty of Edward's murder, as well as of two other children whose bodies were found buried on Saddleworth Moor. As one of these victims had also been killed at their house, it was later demolished to prevent it ever becoming a location for sightseers. The pair later confessed to killing two more children.

As if that isn't enough for one town, Hyde was also the location of Britain's most prolific serial killer – this being Dr Harold Shipman. The majority of his several hundred victims were murdered at his surgery in Hyde, and whom he systematically killed between 7th August 1978 and 24th June 1998. For the record, though, Shipman wasn't a Hyde man – he was born in Nottingham in 1946 and had lived in West Yorkshire before moving to Hyde. Originally charged with just 15 murders, a later inquiry after his conviction confirmed that he had murdered at least 218 people. Shipman hanged himself in his cell in January 2004.

Hyde Famous Residents

There are so many famous Hyde residents, that a section is required rather than a list. First, Dr Ron Hill (b.1938) is a former European gold-medallist marathon runner, who also held World Records for 10 miles, 15 miles and 25 kilometres in the mid-1960s. He later went on to become a major clothing entrepreneur and pioneer of sportswear, following the creation of Ron Hill Sports in 1970. His other extraordinary fact is that he has run at least a mile every day since December 1964 – even after a serious car-crash in 1993 when he broke his sternum! On 20th December 2014, Hill completed Manchester's 5 km Heaton Park run, achieving his goal of running at

Left: *Hyde Town Hall (north-east face) forms the front-piece of a quadrangle of impressive 19*th* century buildings, built in 1883-84. The large bell in the clocktower is known as Owd Joss (Old Josh), named after Joshua Bradley, a former poor child worker in one of the 19*th* century mills at Hyde. Right: This is the north-west face of the quadrangle, and includes the former police station with the original blue lamp still there (above the door to the left of the photograph). However, this building is now the location of the town library after the previous building was closed down.*

least a mile a day for 50 years, by which stage his total logged lifetime mileage was well over 159,000 miles!

Former World Champion boxer Ricky "The Hitman" Hatton (b.1978) was brought up on Hyde's Hattersley Estate. Hatton held multiple world titles at light-welterweight and one at welterweight, and won 45 of his 48 professional fights. He is ranked by the website *BoxRec* as the best British light-welterweight of all time, the second best in Europe, and seventh best in the world. In 2005 he was named Fighter of the Year by The Ring magazine and the Boxing Writers Association of America (BWAA). Hatton's connection with Hyde also led to the creation of a state-of-the-art boxing gym and health club in the town.

Other current or former high-profile Hyde residents include singers Brian and Michael, BAFTA-winning screenwriter Danny Brocklehurst (b.1971), musician Wayne Fontana (b.1945), artist Trevor Grimshaw (1947-2001), broadcaster Stuart Hall (b.1929), boxer Matthew Hatton (b.1981), Lancashire and Test cricketer Len Hopwood (1903-1985), famous artist L.S. Lowry (1887-1976), broadcaster Timmy Mallett (b.1955), Manchester United footballer Lee Martin (b.1968), and comedian Justin Moorhouse (b.1970).

Hyde Quirk Alert: Water Polo, Jekyll and Hyde and Life on Mars

Hyde's most famous claim to film fame is that the dance scene from the 1979 film *Yanks*, which starred Richard Gere, was filmed in Hyde Town Hall. As for Hyde's most famous claim to *TV* fame, this is probably from the BBC drama series *Life on Mars*, first broadcast in January 2006. Having apparently travelled back in time to 1973, the leading character, Sam Tyler, claimed to have transferred from C Division Hyde, to the City Centre's CID "A" Division. There are theories that his choice of Hyde is a clue that his 1973 persona is an alter ego – this alluding to Robert Louis Stevenson's *Strange Case of Dr Jekyll and Mr Hyde*. Talking of which, there used to be a club in Hyde called Jekyll's of Hyde, while "Dr Jekyll of Hyde" was also a moniker attributed to the mass serial killer, Harold Shipman.

Finally, did you know that Hyde was home to one of the most successful water polo teams ever? Well, from 1904 to 1914, the Hyde Seals water polo team were the finest in the world, winning the world championship in 1904, 1905 and 1906.

Left: *Hyde Library was built in 1897 and opened in 1899 as Hyde Technical School and Free Library. The building replaced the former Mechanics Institute. However, Hyde's library has recently been moved to the Town Hall.* Right: *The Grade II listed Hyde Theatre Royal was built by S. Robinson & Sons of Hyde. It opened in November 1902 and has seen many famous acts including the legendary Laurel and Hardy.*

NAME (STATUS):	**KECKWICK** (Village)
POPULATION:	c.250
DISTRICT:	Halton
EARLIEST RECORD:	*Kekewich*, 1086 (Domesday Book)
MEANING:	Probably dairy farm belonging to a man called Kek
DERIVATION:	Probably from the Old Scandinavian personal name *Kek*, plus the Old English word *wīc* (earlier Romano-British settlement, dwelling, specialised farm or building, dairy farm, trading or industrial estate, or harbour)

The Bridgewater Canal seen from Keckwick Bridge, which takes Keckwick Lane over the canal.

Keckwick Bridge.

Keckwick Geographic Trivia: Keckwick Springs

Keckwick lies within the unitary authority of Halton on the south side of the River Mersey, and is situated in the middle of the three Cheshire towns of Runcorn, Widnes and Warrington – although the latter two were in Lancashire prior to 1st April 1974! Keckwick is also intersected by the Birmingham to Liverpool railway line and is located alongside the Bridgewater Canal – the latter being England's first canal, opened on 17th July, 1761. Finally, the area is also traversed by the Keckwick Brook, while the place-name appears again some 9,000 miles away – as Keckwick Springs in Northern Territory, Australia!

Keckwick Church: All Saints

The ancient parish church for the township of Keckwick was Runcorn All Saints, while its ancient parochial chapel was Daresbury All Saints and which was also the village's district church from 1880.

Keckwick Historic Trivia: Administration

Keckwick was a township of the ancient parish of Runcorn, and part of the chapelry of Daresbury, with both areas having been part of the even older Anglo-Saxon hundred of Bucklow. Keckwick was then made a civil parish in 1866, but this was eventually abolished in 1936 when Keckwick became part of the parish of Daresbury.

Throughout the 19th century, the population of Keckwick remained fairly stable, having been registered as 69 in the first Census of 1801, as 89 in 1851, but having fallen to 65 by 1901, and even further to 54 by 1931. Ever since Keckwick was absorbed by Daresbury in 1936, though, there haven't been any further recordings of the Keckwick population, but due to an increase in modern housing towards the end of the 20th century, the village is now home to considerably more inhabitants.

Keckwick Quirk Alert: The Witches of Keckwick

The usage of Keckwick in the Cheshire Shire-Ode title is, of course, a play on words based on the 1988 film, *The Witches of Eastwick*, which starred Cher, Susan Sarandon, Michelle Pfeiffer and Jack Nicholson. And tenuous thought this connection is, Kenny Wax, the British theatrical producer was born in Bowdon, less than ten miles from Keckwick – and Kenny went on to produce a touring version of *The Witches of Eastwick*, starring Marti Pellow!

Sculpture in the centre of Keckwick village.

Three's-Up!

	MUDD	ROACHES	ROSE HILL
STATUS:	Hamlet	Residential Area; Pub; Lock	Residential Area
POPULATION:	c.10	c.1000	1435
DISTRICT:	Tameside, Greater Manchester	Tameside, Greater Manchester	Stockport, Greater Manchester
EARLIEST RECORD:	*The Mudd*, 1795	*Roaches*, 19th century	*Rose Hill*, 19th century

Three's Up Trivia!

To get to the tiny hamlet of **Mudd**, you have to leave the B6174 in Mottram in Longdendale and climb up Church Brow, from where you soon reach Mottram's 15th century parish church of St Michael and All Angels – unsurprisingly, at the brow of the hill. This particular cluster of houses around the parish church is known as Warhill, a medieval settlement of the church and a couple of isolated farmsteads. Heading out of Warhill in a southerly direction along Littlemoor Road, you could be forgiven for missing Mudd completely – as it simply amounts to a handful of houses, including Littlemoor Cottage, plus Parsonage Fields Farm and Lower Mudd Farm.

As for the 1795 reference to Mudd, this is down to a book called *Description of the country 30 to 40 miles round Manchester* by Aikin, and which includes a map showing how the roads ran over The Mudd from Mottram and down Gorsey Brow to the old packhorse bridge built in 1683. A few decades later, the 1841 census refers to a certain William Shaw, who was a weaver and a widower, and who is recorded as living at The Mudd with his wife and son, James.

Finally, Mottram was designated as a Conservation Area in 1973, and by 1986, the Conservation Area boundary had been extended to the south along Littlemoor Road to include Mudd.

Next, **Roaches** is a residential area a mile north of Mossley. It is named after Roaches Lock on the Huddersfield Narrow Canal, while also alongside the lock and canal is the Roaches Lock Inn which sits in between the canal and the River Tame. As for the Huddersfield Narrow Canal, this was built following the passing of an Act in 1793, but although construction commenced in 1794, the project was beset by problems and budgetary constraints and wasn't actually completed until 1811. The canal runs for just under 20 miles (32 km) from Aspley Basin at Huddersfield to the junction with the Ashton Canal at Whitelands Basin in

The impressive sundial on Church Brow at Warhill, only yards from the hamlet of Mudd.

Church Brow at Warhill, Mottram in Longdendale, with the parish church of St Michael and All Angels visible. Meanwhile, the hamlet of Mudd is…

…a few yards further up Littlemoor Road, with this particularly delightful little cottage proclaiming itself to be "43 THE MUDD".

The Roaches Lock Inn at Roaches, a mile north of Mossley.

View from the Huddersfield Narrow canal towards the Roaches Lock Inn.

Ashton-under-Lyne. It crosses the Pennines by means of 74 locks and climbs to 438ft at its summit where it passes through the Standedge Tunnel.

Finally, **Rose Hill** is a residential area at the western edge of Marple, and is represented by Rose Hill Marple railway station – the latter being one of two stations serving the small town of Marple (the other being Marple railway station). Rose Hill Marple is actually the terminus of, and the only station on, a 1.5 mile spur of the Hope Valley Line, enabling locals to easily get to Manchester Piccadilly. The other Marple station is actually *on* the Hope Valley Line, which connects Manchester Piccadilly with Sheffield across north Derbyshire and the Peak District, via the Hope Valley.

As well as connecting locals to Manchester Piccadilly, Rose Hill Marple is also one of three stations on the ten-mile walking and riding trail known as the Middlewood Way, which follows the course of the former Macclesfield, Bollington and Marple Railway which operated between 1869 and 1970. This also explains the 1.5 mile spur of the Hope Valley Line, as it

is a remnant of the former Macclesfield to Marple route which merged with the Hope Valley Line prior to 1970. Rose Hill Marple is therefore twice a terminus – the northern walking terminus in the Middlewood Way's case – with the other stations based at Middlewood and at the southern end of the path at Macclesfield.

As for the Rose Hill railway station, it was originally called Marple (Rose Hill) when opened in 1869, was later changed to Rose Hill (Marple), before eventually adopting Rose Hill Marple. The entirety of the Macclesfield to Marple line was proposed for closure by the Beeching Report of 1963, primarily due to the fact that most travellers, heading into Manchester Piccadilly from the south, preferred the faster West Coast Main Line route via Stockport. However, Rose Hill survived thanks to its high volume of commuters and which is now badged as an official Park & Ride station – and hence the 1.5 mile spur on the Hope Valley Line. There is also talk of Rose Hill Marple being used as a future terminus for the Metrolink tram service.

NAME (STATUS):	**LYMM** (Village)
POPULATION:	12,350
DISTRICT:	Warrington
EARLIEST RECORD:	*Lime*, 1086 (Domesday Book)
MEANING:	The noisy stream or torrent
DERIVATION:	From the Old English word *hlimme*, which is likely to derive, in turn, from its former Celtic name which probably referred to an ancient stream that ran through the centre of the village

Lymm Geographic Trivia: Lymm Dam and Warrington Connections

The civil parish of Lymm incorporates the hamlets of Booths Hill, Broomedge, Church Green, Deansgreen, Heatley, Heatley Heath, Little Heatley, Oughtrington, Reddish, Rushgreen and Statham. Both the village and civil parish are located in the greenbelt area between the towns of Warrington to the west and Altrincham to the east. Meanwhile, just to the south of the village is Lymm Dam, which was dammed in 1824 during the construction of the road which became a predecessor to today's A56.

Traditionally just inside Cheshire's northern boundary, Lymm became part of the non-metropolitan borough of Warrington on 1ˢᵗ April 1974. Warrington had previously been a county borough in Lancashire from 1900, and the town had belonged to the county of Lancashire for around a thousand years before 1974. However, the new non-metropolitan borough introduced in 1974 saw both town and borough moved from Lancashire to Cheshire – this following lobbying by the former borough council to prevent their town going to one of the new metropolitan counties of Merseyside or Greater Manchester. Given that the new county map would see Warrington cut off by a considerable distance from the new and smaller Lancashire, Cheshire became their only option. This is still the case today, with St Helens (Merseyside) to the west of Warrington, and Wigan, Salford and Trafford (all Greater Manchester) to the north and east.

Thus it was that the 1974 reforms saw Warrington incorporate the former Lymm Urban District and part of Runcorn Rural District from Cheshire, along with part of the former Warrington Rural District from Lancashire, as a new borough within Cheshire County Council. However, that's not quite the full story, as on 1ˢᵗ April 1998, Warrington – including Lymm – became an independent unitary authority – although both are still part of the ceremonial county of Cheshire and are still served by Cheshire Police and the Cheshire Fire and Rescue Service.

Lymm Church: St Mary's

The Grade II listed St Mary's church is located on the north-eastern shore of Lymm Dam, and the current incarnation is thought to be at least the fourth. Certainly, there was a Saxon church recorded in Domesday Book (1086), which was replaced within the next century by a Norman church. The third church was probably built in the 14ᵗʰ century, while the current church was largely built/re-built between 1850 and 1852 to a design by John Dobson of Newcastle. Further alterations and additions were made to St Mary's between 1870 and 1872 by the architect John Douglas of Chester, while the tower was rebuilt between 1888 and 1890 by J. S. Crowther. As for the mid-19ᵗʰ century rebuild, this had necessitated the blowing up with gunpowder of the 14ᵗʰ century nave and aisles before the rebuild could commence – although the 1521 tower was retained at this stage, and actually raised. John

Lymm Dam. The lake was dammed in 1824 during the construction of the road alongside it, and which is now the A56.

St Mary's church, Lymm, was largely rebuilt in the 19ᵗʰ century, but has at least three predecessors, with the Saxon incarnation recorded in Domesday Book.

Dobson's 1850s replacement consisted of a five-bay nave with a clerestory, along with north and south aisles, a north porch, transepts, a chancel, and a vestry. However, some features were retained such as an ogee-headed tomb recess dating from about 1322, the pulpit which is dated 1623 and the font which probably dates from the 1660s, while the stone sedilia and piscina are "new" and date from the 1870 John Douglas design. Finally, there is a ring of eight bells which were cast in 1891 by John Taylor and Company.

Lymm Historic Trivia: Lymm Hall and Lymm Grammar School

The early medieval manor of Lymm, which included a manor house and estate, belonged to the de Limm family. However, possession passed to the Domville family through marriage in 1342, and they continued to own the manor for the next 500 years. The current Grade II listed and moated Lymm Hall was built in the late 16th century for the Domville family, with service wings added in the late 18th century, while the stepped gables and mullioned windows were added in around 1840. By this stage, as well as the Hall, the estate comprised 564 acres, 18 cottages, two public houses, four farms, a corn mill, a slaughter house, and a smith's and wheelwright's shop. However, six years later (in 1846), the estate was sold off, piecemeal – this following the death of the Reverend Mascie Domville Taylor. The Hall and adjacent buildings have had several owners since then, and recently, both Hall and stables have been divided into private homes and the grounds reduced to just 10 acres. The moat is now dry, but is still traversed by the mid-17th century bridge (which is also Grade II listed), while the moated site on which the Hall stands, together with an ice house, are a Scheduled Monument.

Lymm has so many surviving historic buildings that the village centre is now a designated conservation area. As well as Lymm Hall, these include the former town hall, St Peter's church, Oughtrington Hall and Lodge (now Lymm High School), and fustian cutting cottages that belonged to the now defunct Foxley Hall, while the centrepiece of the conservation area is the Grade I listed Lymm Cross which sits at the centre of the village. The sandstone cross dates from the early 17th century and is mounted on an artificially stepped natural outcrop of red sandstone. Its shaft stands in a square pavilion, while the cross is topped off with an extension which carries a stone ball and an impressive weather vane.

Today, Lymm High School is an independent state secondary school and sixth form with academy status. The original school, however, was founded some time before its earliest known reference, which is in a church document dated 1592, and which mentions the "Master of Lymm School". The next reference is from 1601, when it was reconstituted as Lymm Grammar School following the granting of a royal charter. The school survived for several centuries on its Damside site, close

The Golden Fleece, Lymm.

The Bull's Head, Lymm

to St Mary's church, until it was forced to sell its land in 1881 after a series of financial difficulties. However, five of the eleven lots of land were bought by G. C. Dewhurst, who also happened to be a member of the board of governors, and in February 1882, he proposed a new site near Higher Lane for a school and school house along with an access road – which became Grammar School Road. An appeal was launched to raise the necessary funds for the new buildings and was so successful that the new buildings were built and opened on 12th July 1885.

The next progression was the introduction of co-education in June 1902, with the first female students starting three months later, while 1945 saw the purchase of Oughtrington Hall by Cheshire County Council for use as an annexe. This was initially used from 1945 to 1957 by the junior forms, after which the whole school was transferred to Oughtrington, with the older buildings in Grammar School Road becoming the site of the newly formed Lymm Secondary Modern School. Lymm Grammar School eventually admitted students without payment of fees, but the two institutions continued to remain separate organisations until they were amalgamated under the Comprehensive system in the early 1980s – after which the Grammar School Road buildings were sold and demolished to make way for housing. Since then, the Oughtrington site has expanded with the purchase of surrounding farmland for playing fields, and many of the existing playing fields being built on,

Left: The Grade I listed Lymm Cross is located in the centre of the village and dates from the early 17th century. The cross shaft is protected by a square pavilion with a pedimented gable on each side. Three of the gables include bronze sundials dating from 1897 and contain inscriptions: "We are a Shadow", "Save Time" and "Think of the Last", respectively. Right: Looking across the base of the cross steps to where the A56 crosses the Bridgewater Canal.

including the build of and opening of a new Sixth Form Building in 2002.

Today, ex-pupils are known as Old Lymmians, and include among their ranks Tim Curry (actor), George Davey Smith (epidemiologist), Neil Fairbrother (Lancashire and England cricketer), Maurice Flanagan (founding CEO of the Emirates airline) and David Strettle (England rugby union international).

In terms of other Lymm history, the canals first came to Lymm in the late 18th century in the form of the Bridgewater Canal, Britain's first canal, constructed by James Brindley. However, the heyday of the canal only lasted for 50 years or so, before waterway transport was superseded by the trains. Lymm railway station was opened on 1st November 1853 by the Warrington and Stockport Railway, before being absorbed by the London and North Western Railway (LNWR). Lymm Station was on the southern-most railway line between Liverpool to Manchester, but eventually its passenger service fell to the Beeching Axe in September 1962 – although the line remained open to freight until its official closure in July 1985. The Manchester Ship Canal also passes to the north of Lymm, and was constructed between 1887 and 1893.

More recently, Lymm has been the location for the filming of the 2011 television series *Candy Cabs* and the 2015 Sky 1 television series *After Hours*.

Lymm Quirk Alert: Lymm Ducks and Stan Oldport

Each Easter Monday, at noon, Lymm is home to a tradition involving around 1,000 yellow plastic ducks. They are released into Lymm Dingle, by the Lymm & District Round Table, as the prelude to a race to the bottom of Lymm Lower Dam, all as part of fund raising for local charities. This is because the ducks have all been

LYMM FAMOUS RESIDENTS (PAST AND PRESENT)

Resident	Occupation	Born	Died
Chris Bisson	Actor (Coronation Street, Shameless)	1975	-
Tim Booth	Musician (lead singer with James)	1960	-
Ian Brown	Musician (lead singer with Stone Roses)	1963	-
Sir Bobby Charlton	Legendary English footballer and 1966 World Cup winner	1937	-
Peter Collins	Former World Speedway Champion	1954	-
Matthew Corbett	TV Entertainer (think Sooty)	1948	-
Martin Edwards	Crime novelist (Harry Devlin novels, Lake District novels, etc.)	1955	-
Suranne Jones	Actress (Coronation Street, Scott & Bailey, Doctor Foster, etc.)	1978	-
Sammy McIlroy	Legendary Northern Ireland and Manchester United footballer)	1954	-
Mike Sheron	Former footballer (Manchester City, Stoke City, QPR, etc.)	1972	-
Walter Smith	Former footballer and football manager (Rangers, Everton, etc.)	1948	-
Sir John Stalker	Former Deputy Chief Constable of Greater Manchester Police	1939	-
David Strettle	England and former Saracens Rugby Union player	1983	-
David Weir	Former Scotland, Everton and Rangers footballer	1970	-
Robert Westall	Prolific author (largely of teenage fiction)	1929	1993

purchased, with a standard duck costing £1 (Racing Ducks), a selection of larger ducks sponsored by local businesses costing £30 (Corporate Ducks), and around 15 super-sized ducks priced at £60 each (Super Ducks). Also present is an eight foot-long bright yellow Mega Duck. Prizes are awarded to the winner, runners up and finally, for the slowest duck of the day – an award which is fiercely contested! Meanwhile, other Lymm traditions include carol singing at the Lymm Cross on Christmas Eve, the May Queen Festival on May Day, the Rush-bearing festival in summer (including traditional Morris dancing), and Dickensian Day – another Christmas tradition and fair, this time with a Victorian theme.

Finally, we pay a visit to number 77 Higher Lane, Lymm, for this is the location of some very strange goings-on indeed. The house dates from the 1850s, and was a school in the 19th century before it later became a private residence – which explains some of the hauntings, which include a young schoolboy wailing for his mother on the first floor and a silent and elderly schoolmaster on the ground floor whose stare "freezes you to the spot". However, the most common apparition is thought to be an owner from the 1920s, Stan Oldport, who worked for local firm, SARM Accountants. Oldport was one of three partners, along with Robert Gee and Phillip Davison, who were running the firm

when it got into financial difficulties. The problems began thanks to non-payment for services from some of their local business clients who, in turn, were suffering as a result of the national recession. SARM's vindictive response, allegedly instigated by Oldport (but who was later cleared of any involvement), was to submit doctored accounts to the Inland Revenue, over-stating the earnings of their defaulting clients – and thus rendering them subject to more tax than they were due to pay – and substantially more than they could afford. The stress incurred by this heartless ploy led to one client, George Gregory, committing suicide. The actual perpetrators, Davison and Gee, then managed to divert the blame onto the unsuspecting Oldport, who was then murdered in his own home, one June evening, by the vengeful widow of Gregory, armed with her favourite carving knife and accompanied by her dog, Bobby. Hence it is that on certain evenings in June, poor Oldport's ghost can be seen in various emotional states, ranging from confused and bewildered, to horrified and beseeching!

Left is a photo of 77 Higher Lane, Lymm, taken thanks to kind permission of the owner, Roland Potts, seen here with three of his children and family dog. The house is rumoured to be home to a number of hauntings, the most prevalent being accountant Stan Oldport who was murdered here in the 1920s having been framed by his partners.

The Bridgewater Canal as it passes through the centre of Lymm.

NAME (STATUS):	**MANLEY** (Village)
POPULATION:	614
DISTRICT:	Cheshire West and Chester
EARLIEST RECORD:	*Menlie*, 1086 (Domesday Book)
MEANING:	Common wood or clearing
DERIVATION:	From the Old English words *(ge)mæne* (held in common or communal), and *lēah* (wood or woodland clearing)

The original Manley Mere.

St John's church, Manley. There was also a Primitive Methodist church in Manley which was built in 1859, but which closed in 1970.

Manley Geographic Trivia: Manley Mere

Manley is a village and civil parish around seven miles north-east of Chester. Just to the west of the village is Manley Mere where you will find Manley Mere Sail Sports and Adventure Trail. The lake is man-made and is home to a number of water-sports, although the original (and natural) Manley Mere still survives alongside. Meanwhile the adventure trail is around 1.5 miles long and serves up numerous obstacles to contend with. Apparently, a cold water hose is offered at the end to remove all of the mud before you get back in your car…

Manley Historic Trivia: Manley Knoll

In 1912, the Grade II listed house known as Manley Knoll was designed for Llewellyn Jones in what is known as the Arts and Crafts style, having an irregular linear plan with an asymmetrical frontage of two storeys including an off-centre porch. To the left of the porch is a timber-framed projection, and to the right is a staircase bay and a service bay, while the rear of the property has four timber-framed gables with a central loggia over which is a balcony; each of the gables is decorated with different Cheshire patterns. The house interior was remodelled in 1922 for the Demetriades family by the Manchester architect James Henry Sellers. The Demetriades family lived at Manley Knoll until 1946 and developed the gardens also along Arts and Crafts lines, with one of the three quarries developed into an unusual quarry garden.

Also during the 20th century, Manley was home to television writer and novelist Cyril Abraham, until his death in 1979. Born in Liverpool in 1915, Abraham was most noted for creating the popular BBC drama *The Onedin Line*, which ran from 1971 to 1980 during which time he wrote the scripts for 22 episodes and also wrote five novels based on the series. His other television credits include *Coronation Street* (1960), *Z-Cars* (1967), *Dixon of Dock Green* (1969), *Paul Temple* (1969-1970) and *Owen, M.D.* (1971-1972).

The part of Manley Mere used for Sail Sports.

NAME (STATUS):	**MARPLE** (Town)
POPULATION:	23,686, which is comprised of: 12,277 (Marple North); 11,409 (Marple South)
DISTRICT:	Stockport, Greater Manchester
EARLIEST RECORD:	*Merpille*, early 13th century
MEANING:	Pool or stream at the boundary
DERIVATION:	From the Old English words *(ge)mære* (boundary) and *pyll* (tidal creek, pool or stream)

Marple Pub: The Navigation

The Navigation is located on the Peak Forest Canal and dates from around 1790. It was so-named as it was built to cater for the navvies (navigation engineers) who built the Marple section of the Peak Forest Canal between 1794 and 1796 – or the Peak Forest Navigation as it was known in those days. The Navigation pub is located close to Lock No. 13, one of 16 locks that stretch for around a mile and which raise the canal by 209 feet (64 metres). The promoter and largest shareholder of the Peak Forest Navigation, was local cotton mill owner Samuel Oldknow. In order to get the locks finished on schedule, and for his boats to be the first to use the canal, Oldknow served the navvies with possets, a milk drink curdled with ale and often spiced – basically as an incentive to make them work harder. The possets were actually served up by the Navigation Pub, and made such an impression that the bridge alongside The Navigation has always been known as Posset Bridge.

The Navigation at Marple was built in around 1790 and was so-named as it catered for the navvies building the Peak Forest Canal alongside which the pub is positioned.

Marple Church: All Saints

The Grade II listed All Saints' church is the 3rd known church on the Church Lane site to the south of the town. The first was a small black and white timber-framed church built towards the end of the 15th century. By the early 19th century, though, the building was little more than a ruin and was reputed to have "blown down in a gale" in 1804. As a result, a new church was built between 1808 and 1811 by architect Richard Goldsmith at a cost of £4,000 – and once again, local cotton mill owner Samuel Oldknow was a major financier, contributing roughly three quarters of the funds, with the other quarter coming from local parishioners. However, by 1870, Goldsmith and Oldknow's Georgian Chapel was proving too small for the congregation, and hence a third church was built around 100 feet (30 metres) to the south of the second. This church was built by architects Medland Taylor and Henry Taylor and consists of a three-bay nave with a clerestory, north and south aisles, and a two-bay chancel, and cost £6,056 to build. However, although a bell-tower had been included in the plans, it was never constructed (to save on costs) and the bells remained in the Georgian Chapel. The new All Saints' church was consecrated on 30th June 1880, although some services were still being held at the old church.

By 1964, though, the by-now neglected Georgian

The Grade II listed St Martin's church at Marple Bridge was built between 1869 and 1870 for Maria Anne Hudson who lived in nearby Brabyns Hall. The church was designed by John Dando Sedding.

Chapel was in a dangerous condition and most of it was demolished. However, the Grade II listed four-stage tower was saved following appropriate strengthening. At the same time, the six original bells of 1816 were re-hung with two new ones, cast in 1963 by John Taylor and Company, thus giving Marple All Saints an appealing ring-of-eight! Today, the isolated tower somewhat unusually stands 30 metres from the newer All Saints' church, while both churches are approached via two separate lych-gates; the later lych-gate, dating from 1893, is also Grade II listed. The older church still contains memorials, too, including a fine tablet by John Flaxman in memory of Rev. Kelsall Prescot, who died in 1823. Also present is a monument to Samuel Oldknow, who died in 1828, and which was sculpted by famous 19th century sculptor, Francis Legatt Chantrey.

All Saints' church, Marple, dates from 1880, but doesn't include a tower and bells. This is because…

…the tower of its predecessor, built between 1808 and 1811 was retained in 1880, and also survived demolition in 1964 when the rest of the early 19th century church was demolished.

Marple Historic Trivia: Marple Aqueduct, Marple Lock Flight, Samuel Oldknow and John Bradshaw

The land around Marple was acquired by the Vernon family in 1220 and remained under their ownership for several generations, while the villagers were mainly employed in agriculture with a few others eventually specialising in linen weaving and hat-making. That all changed at the end of the 18th century, though, as the Industrial Revolution came to the area in the form of water-powered cotton mills. The main benefactor in the area was Samuel Oldknow who constructed mills and kilns in and around Marple in the 1790s, and also contributed financially to local schemes like the construction of the Peak Forest Canal, the Macclesfield Canal and All Saints' church. As a result, the industry of Marple changed from agriculture to manufacture, and the population began to grow, bringing many new houses, mainly terraces of mill cottages for the mill workers – many of which were also built by Oldknow.

One of the most spectacular builds of this time was the Marple Aqueduct (see page 55 for photos), which was built between 1795 and 1799 to carry the Peak Forest Canal over the River Goyt – although seven men

lost their lives during its construction. The aqueduct was designed by prolific engineer Benjamin Outram and constructed by another engineer, Thomas Brown. It opened in 1800, becoming the highest canal aqueduct in England (above sea level) as well as the highest masonry-arch aqueduct in Britain. Furthermore, the difference in water levels between river and canal is 90 feet (27.4m), which is only exceeded in Britain by the Pontcysyllte aqueduct in Wales over the Dee Valley, where the difference is 126 feet (38.4m). The Marple Aqueduct comprises three semi-circular arches with spans of around 60 feet (18.3m) and contains 8,000 cubic yards (6,000 m³) of masonry.

Marple Aqueduct has had two crisis points in its lifetime. The first occurred in 1860 when repeated frost led to an urgent repair where a number of two-inch bolts and plates had to be fitted to secure two parts of the structure together. Then in January 1962, the outer face of the north-east arch collapsed. British Waterways initially wanted to demolish the aqueduct which would have meant closure of the Lower Peak Forest and Ashton Canals. However, Geoffrey Rippon, Minister of Public Buildings and Works intervened and facilitated a repair in conjunction with Cheshire County Council. Shortly afterwards, the aqueduct was scheduled as an ancient monument and, in 1966, was listed as a Grade I structure.

Also on the Peak Forest Canal at Marple is the Marple Lock Flight, a series of 16 canal locks which

Ruins of Samuel Oldknow's Mill, on the outskirts of Mellor. Built between 1790 and 1793 it was the largest cotton mill of its time but was destroyed by fire in 1892.

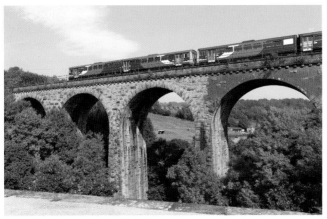

A train crossing the viaduct over the River Goyt, as seen from Marple aqueduct.

A barge exiting Lock No 6 at Marple and heading on up to Lock No 7.

raise the canal by 209 feet (64m) over a distance of around one mile (1.6km). By 1796, the Upper and Lower sections of the Peak Forest Canal had been constructed, but initially there were insufficient funds to complete the necessary flight of locks to connect the two halves; instead, a temporary tramway ferried goods and people between the two. It wasn't until 1804 that Marple Lock Flight was completed, with its 16 locks forming three definable sections; the lower section (locks 1-8), a middle section (locks 9-12), and the top section (locks 13-16), with the latter closely-spaced locks raising the canal steeply to arrive at Marple Junction, where the Peak Forest Canal meets the Macclesfield Canal. The latter canal was constructed later in the late 1820s by Thomas Telford to connect the Trent and Mersey Canal to Manchester, and opened in 1831. As for Marple Lock Flight, by the early 1960s the flight had become impassable, but pressure from the Peak Forest Canal Society and the Inland Waterways Association resulted in appropriate restoration and the flight was re-opened in 1974.

The canals that Samuel Oldknow helped finance clearly accelerated the growth of Marple, but they were soon superseded by the railways when they arrived in 1865. After that, the canals gradually fell into disrepair until the late 20th century revival for leisure. Today, the

Peak Forest Canal and Macclesfield Canal form part of what is known as the Cheshire Ring along with the Bridgewater, Rochdale, Ashton and Trent and Mersey canals.

Returning to Samuel Oldknow (1756-1828), not only did he donate much of his money to Marple causes, but he also built a six-storey mill between 1790 and 1793 at nearby Mellor (a village and civil parish in Derbyshire until 1936 when it was transferred to Marple Urban District in Cheshire). What became known as Oldknow's Mill was six storeys high, and was powered by diverting the course of the River Goyt. At that time, it was the largest cotton mill to be worked on the Arkwright system and by 1804 was employing around 550 people – many of them from Marple – who operated 10,080 spindles. The central six-storey building was also 210 feet long and 42 feet wide, with three-storeyed extensions at each side, making the total length about 400 feet. Alas, the mill suffered a catastrophic fire in 1892 and the remaining ruins were largely demolished in the 1930s, after which the site was pretty much reclaimed by nature – although the wheel pit that housed what was known as the Wellington Wheel in Oldknow's day has recently been restored.

Marple was presented with a cinema in 1932, but the building on Stockport Road actually started life in 1878

Left: *This stunning house is located opposite the junction of the Peak Forest and Macclesfield Canals, and adjacent to Marple Top Lock, which sits at the top of an impressive flight of 16 locks known as Marple Lock Flight.* Right: *A barge exits the Macclesfield Canal and joins the Peak Forest Canal.*

as a place of worship and refuge. However, it was purchased in 1932 by the Marple Cinema Company and converted into a cinema. Today, it is known as the Regent Cinema and remains an independent business. Meanwhile, at around the same time (1930s), the house known as Brentwood was converted into a holiday home for – as Arthur Mee puts it – "women who have forgotten (if they ever knew) what it is to have a holiday, women who are unemployed themselves or are wives of unemployed men, and for children of drab streets".

Finally, gone now is Marple Hall, built in the 17th century on the foundations of the former medieval manor of the Vernons, but demolished in 1959. Back in the 17th century, John Bradshaw, of Marple Hall, became the unwilling president of the court that tried King Charles I and sentenced him to death. His was also the signature that headed the king's death warrant. Fortunately for Bradshaw, he died of the plague before the Restoration, but King Charles II still had his bones dug up and hanged at Tyburn gallows for his sins. However, most remarkable of all, is a verse that young John Bradshaw wrote as a boy:

My brother Henry shall heir the land,
My brother Frank shall be at his command.
While I, poor Jack, will do that
Which all the world shall wonder at.

Looking down from Lock No. 15 to Lock No. 13 of the Peak Forest Canal at Marple.

Marple Quirk Alert: Death by Bell-ringing and The Body in the Library

When the early 19th century Georgian Chapel was built in Marple, it was completed in 1816 when six bells were hung in the church tower. However, these six bells were actually cast by Rudhall of Gloucester much earlier, in 1731, for Stockport St Mary's church, but were taken down in 1810 following the partial collapse of the Stockport church's tower. The reason for mentioning this is that it is believed that Stockport St Mary's tower was fatally damaged by over-enthusiastic bellringers, celebrating Admiral Nelson's victory at Trafalgar in 1805!

Finally, the reference to *The Body in the Library* is courtesy of Agatha Christie's fictitious elderly spinster and amateur consulting detective, Miss Marple. This is because the most commonly held belief is that Christie named the character of Jane Marple, after Marple railway station, where she was once forced to wait following an unscheduled delay to her train journey!

Marple Famous Residents

Past and present residents of Marple include illustrator **Stephen Bradbury** (b.1954), judge **John Bradshaw** (1602-1659), prolific novelist and poet **Edmund Cooper** (1926-1982), novelist **Christopher Isherwood** (1904-1986), TV presenter **Timmy Mallett** (b.1955), industrialist **Samuel Oldknow** (1756-1830), author and MP **Edward Parrott** (1863-1921), multiple paralympic medallist **Matt Walker** (b.1978), and journalist and record label owner **Tony Wilson** (1950-2007).

NAME (STATUS):	**MERE** (Village)
POPULATION:	657
DISTRICT:	Cheshire East
EARLIEST RECORD:	*Mera*, 1086 (Domesday Book)
MEANING:	Place at the pool or lake
DERIVATION:	From the Old English word *mere* (pond, pool or lake)

Mere Pub: The Swan

The Swan is located on a spot that was once home to a long-since vanished medieval monastery or an old hostelry established in around the 14th century by the monks for travellers. More tangible historic evidence is provided by a Roman milestone, which has been set into the side of The Swan under a double chimney arch.

Mere Historic Trivia: Romans, Halls, Golf and the R&A

A mile north-east of Mere is Rostherne Mere where evidence of prehistoric activity was found in the form of two flint flakes, while aerial photography has pinpointed a barrow cemetery in a field just north of Rostherne church, bordering the lake. A single fragment of Roman pottery from the late first or early second century has also been found on the south-east side of the mere, while in a field across the road from The Swan, aerial photographs have revealed crop marks suggesting an ancient cemetery. There is also evidence of a medieval moated site in the back garden of a nearby cottage, while the area adjacent to Mere is thought to mark the site of the lost medieval village of Strettle. Mere also boasts two halls, with Mere Old Hall dating from the 18th century, and Mere New Hall dating from 1834 – although the architect built it in an Elizabethan style, both outside and inside.

Mere is also home to The Mere Resort and Spa, built in 1934 after the estate was purchased by Edgar Hart for development as a country club. In more recent years, huge investment has expanded the country club into a health club and spa, while an 81-bedroomed hotel was added in 2012. The Mere is still one of the best golf clubs in the country, though, and hosts some of the best golfers of Cheshire. It has also hosted the R&A Open Qualifier for seven consecutive years – which for those that don't know, is a major privilege – as this is the Royal & Ancient Golf Club of St Andrews, and the competition being qualified for is the British Open Championship.

Mere Quirk Alert: Legends and an AA box

Local legend has it that Rostherne Mere is bottomless. Another legend tells of a foolish workman who apparently cursed a church bell as it was being conveyed to Rostherne St Mary's – at which point the bell came loose and knocked the man into the mere where he drowned. The bell was said to have followed him into the mere never to be seen again – which, of course, it wouldn't as the mere is clearly bottomless!

The Swan Inn at Mere.

The entrance to The Mere Resort and Spa (formerly Mere Golf and Country Club).Originally an entrance arch and lodge of Mere Hall, it was built in c.1840.

Another legend suggests that the mere is connected to the Irish Sea by an underground channel and that every Easter a mermaid swims upstream to the lake and rings the previously lost bell. As a result, the place became a magnet for locals every Easter Sunday, hoping to catch a glimpse of the mermaid or hear the strains of the underwater bell. Now you may well be shaking your head at this latest legend, but...at least one part of it may be true. This is because the mere was once the only known location in Britain for a form of freshwater smelt, an esturine fish of the salmon family, which may indeed indicate a former connection to the sea via an estuary. Alas, the last known specimen of this fish was caught at Rostherne Mere in 1922.

Finally, at the busy crossroads of the A50 and the A556, there stands a Grade II listed AA Box (shown top right), originally built in 1956 as a telephone booth to assist stranded motorists.

NAME (STATUS):	**MIDDLEWICH** (Town)
POPULATION:	13,595
DISTRICT:	Cheshire East
EARLIEST RECORD:	*Mildestuich*, 1086 (Domesday Book)
MEANING:	Middlemost salt-works
DERIVATION:	From the Old English words *midlest* (middle-most) and *wīc* (earlier Romano-British settlement, dwelling, specialised farm or building or dairy farm, or trading or industrial settlement or harbour)

The Kings Lock at Middlewich alongside the Trent and Mersey Canal.

The White Bear at Middlewich, which dates back to 1625.

Middlewich Pub: The White Bear

The White Bear dates from around 1625, and became an important coaching inn on the route from London to Chester. The pub takes its name from bear baiting which used to take place in the Bull Ring at Middlewich, with onlookers placing bets on the winner. The town also had an inn called The Black Bear, so the rumours that a black bear used to fight a white bear here aren't too difficult to believe, particularly if bear baiting was a regular "pastime". Anyway, the last bear associated with The White Bear Inn went by the name of Nell. Poor Nell!

Middlewich Church: St Michael and All Angels

The oldest parts of the Grade II listed St Michael and All Angels' church date from the 12th century, and include the lower part of the tower and the arcade of the east bay. However, the majority of the church was

built between 1480 and 1520, when the clerestory was added, and the Lady Chapel was built at the east end of the south aisle, while a two-storey porch was added to the south side. However, the church was badly damaged during the English Civil War, particularly during the First Battle of Middlewich in March 1643, when the Royalists used the church as a place of sanctuary. The church then underwent several restoration periods during the 19th century.

Middlewich Historic Trivia: Salinæ

The mining of salt at Middlewich goes back to pre-Roman times, but the place became home to a major saltworks under the Romans, who named the settlement as *Salinæ* – although the mining was actually centred on the township of Kinderton, about a quarter of a mile north of the current town. The Romans also

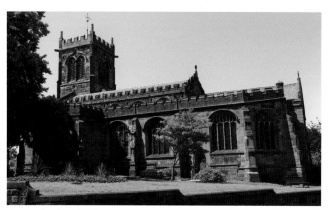

St Michael and All Angels' church at Middlewich, the oldest parts of which date from the 12th century.

St Michael's as seen from the north, beyond Middlewich's amphitheatre, which is on the site of the town's former Bull Ring.

The Wardle Canal at Middlewich is the shortest canal in Britain at just 154 feet long (47m), and links the Trent and Mersey Canal to the Middlewich Branch of the Shropshire Union Canal. This is the first lock after the Wardle Canal's junction with the Trent and Mersey Canal.

The saltworks at Middlewich is still a huge business, and the salt industry here has been buoyant for over two thousand years! The plant today is run by British Salt Limited, now owned by TATA Chemicals, and is seen here alongside the Trent and Mersey Canal.

built a fort in Middlewich at Harbutts Field and excavations to the south of the fort have found further evidence of Roman occupation, including a well.

Prior to the Norman Conquest of 1066, it is thought that there was only one brine pit in Middlewich, located between the River Croco and the current Lewin Street. As for the rest of the town, it was one of the many ravaged by William I during his "harrying of the North" campaigns of the late 1060s, while Gilbert de Venables was made first Baron of Kinderton shortly after the Conquest. The Venables family established their seat at a manor house located to the east of the town.

During the English Civil Wars of the mid-17th century, Middlewich fared pretty badly with two battles fought here. The first Battle of Middlewich took place on 13th March 1643, with the Parliamentarians led by Sir William Brereton, and the Royalists by Sir Thomas Aston. Aston had marched into Middlewich on 11th March, with 500 mounted troops and around 1,000 foot-soldiers, under instructions to "summon in the King's friends". Choosing Middlewich, in between the Parliamentarian-held towns of Northwich and Nantwich was a brave move, and when the Parliamentarians advanced on Monday 13th March, they did so from three directions, forcing the majority of Aston's troops to fall back to St Michael and All Angels' church. In the resulting battle,

the church was taken by the Parliamentarians as part of an emphatic victory. As for the Second Battle of Middlewich, that took place 26th December 1643, with the Parliamentarians again under the command of Sir William Brereton and the Royalists led by Lord John Byron. This time, the boot was on the other foot, and around 200 Parliamentarians were killed, whilst several hundred others took refuge in the church and grounds, having abandoned their canon following a Royalist cavalry charge. They later surrendered.

Middlewich expanded rapidly throughout the 19th century, partly due to the influx of people to work in the town's expanding salt and chemicals industries, and partly due to absorbing outlying areas – for example parts of Newton were added to Middlewich in 1894, with Sutton having previously been added to Newton in 1892. Other businesses that flourished in the town were a silk factory, a heavy cotton works, along with a healthy trade in fruit and vegetables, while the early 20th century saw the arrival of a chemical works and a company that manufactured condensed milk.

During World War I, Middlewich lost 136 men and another 42 during World War II. In between, the town increased in size due to extensive housebuilding, particularly to the north, west and south of the town, while the 1980s saw a significant boom in new housing. Meanwhile, today, Middlewich is famous for its folk and boat festival which has been run in the town every year since 1990, except for 2001 when it was cancelled because of the foot and mouth crisis. The three-day festival attracts around 30,000 visitors and 400 narrowboats!

The Trent and Mersey Canal at Middlewich. Following a petition in 1766, the canal was diverted from its original course to provide transport to the town.

Black and white timbered houses in Lewin Street.

NAME (STATUS):	**MOORE** (Village)
POPULATION:	768
DISTRICT:	Halton
EARLIEST RECORD:	*Mora*, 12th century
MEANING:	The marsh
DERIVATION:	From the Old English word *mōr*, meaning moor, marshy ground or barren upland

Moore Geographic Trivia:
Moore Nature Reserve

Moore Nature Reserve is located a mile to the north of Moore between the Manchester Ship Canal and the River Mersey, and comprises almost 200 acres of woodland, meadows, lakes, ponds and bird hides. The reserve is home to many diverse species of plants (including many different types of orchid), animals, insects (including many different type of dragonfly) and birds, with the latter comprising all-year residents as well as seasonal visitors. Somewhat surprisingly, though, the reserve is privately run by FCC Environment, a waste management company who also own the adjacent Arpley Landfill site.

Moore Historic Trivia: Moore Hall

The Grade II listed Moore Hall was built in the early 18th century, and consists of three storeys and five bays. The hall belonged to the Heron family from around 1755, after they bought the manor of Daresbury, including Moore Hall, with Peter Heron (1770-1848) incumbent in the early 19th century during which time he was a Member of Parliament for Newton between 1806 and 1814.

Moore was later the location of two railway stations. The first was part of the Grand Junction Railway which opened on 4th July 1837, while the second was on what eventually became known as the Birkenhead Railway in 1859, but which was jointly taken over a year later by the London and North Western Railway (LNWR) and the Great Western Railway (GWR). Opened in 1850, this second station was initially called Moore but was changed to Daresbury in April 1861. The station eventually closed to passengers in 1952 and to freight in 1965. During its heyday, though, Daresbury was a second class station at which a first class train would not stop!

Lapwing Lake at Moore Nature Reserve.

The Red Lion at Moore.

The main road through Moore.

View westwards along the Manchester Ship Canal, from Moore Lane Swing Bridge on the outskirts of Moore.

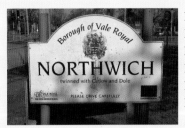

NAME (STATUS):	**NORTHWICH** (Town)
POPULATION:	19,924
DISTRICT:	Cheshire West and Chester
EARLIEST RECORD:	*Norwich*, 1086 (Domesday Book)
MEANING:	North salt-works
DERIVATION:	From the Old English word *north* (north) and *wic* (earlier Romano-British settlement, dwelling, specialised farm or building or dairy farm, or trading or industrial settlement or harbour)

Northwich Pub: The Penny Black and The Swinging Witch

The beautiful pub known as The Penny Black has that classic Tudor look. However, it was only built in 1914 – and as Northwich's main post office, too – so hence the later pub name, named after the world's first-ever adhesive postage stamp, introduced in Great Britain on 1st May 1840, sporting a profile of Queen Victoria. The conversion to a pub happened, much later, in the 1990s.

A plaque on the Witton Street frontage states: "Designed by HM Office of Works in 1914, as a purpose-built post office to serve Northwich and District, it is the town's largest liftable building". What they mean by that is, if necessary, it can quite simply be lifted and moved. This is because in the Northwich area, there is so much subsidence due to historical salt mining that important buildings used to be designed in this way. This was particularly the case in the 19th century, as this was when salt extraction began to use the more economic extraction method of brine pumping, which weakened the salt mines and actually caused many areas of Northwich to collapse! Had this occurred to the Penny Black, though, it would have been jacked up, moved, and re-located somewhere safer!

Meanwhile, the Swinging Witch was formerly known as The Old Crown until its recent name-change in late 2011, albeit back to one of its earlier names. Interestingly, during its refurbishment in 2011, the decorators uncovered an anonymous rhyme about the pub's history when stripping away old wallpaper – and which once again refers to Northwich's famous subsidence. The old verses went as follows:

The Penny Black in Northwich town centre may look old, but actually dates from 1914 when it was built as the town's main post office.

The Swinging Witch, Northwich.

> *Many a name has had this inn*
> *So many I don't know where to begin*
> *It started out as a single Crown*
> *But that was before it was sinking down.*
>
> *Six steps we had to get a drink*
> *But now they've gone it makes you think!*
> *The "Swinging Witch" was next to be*
> *The name of this hostelry.*
>
> *Years went by and lots went on*
> *From which we named it "Brasserie Couronne"*
> *But times have changed but please don't frown*
> *They've cleaned us up and renamed us The Old Crown.*

The new owners, Amber Taverns, therefore felt obliged to add a fourth verse, as follows:

> *In times of trouble with worries to share*
> *The Crown was closed and in despair*
> *A magic spell cast over the Crown*
> *The hanging sign came crashing down*
> *The Swinging Witch breathed life anew*
> *With frothy pints for me and you!*

Northwich Church: St Helen Witton

Before we address the church, it is worth pointing out that during medieval times, Northwich only covered a fairly small area at the confluence of the Rivers Weaver and Dane. To the east of the settlement was the much larger township of Witton cum Twambrooks – and it was here that St Helen Witton church was located. Also

St Helen Witton church in Northwich, also known as Northwich Parish church. It is part-named after the village in which it used to reside.

The Weaver Hall Museum at Northwich was originally the Northwich Union Workhouse when it was opened in 1837.

known today as Northwich Parish Church, St Helen Witton is Grade I listed and takes its name from when it was a chapel of ease known as the Chapel of Witton. At this time, the chapel was affiliated to St Mary and All Saints in the parish of Great Budworth, and the immediate area around the chapel was known as Witton. However, the *parish* of Witton wasn't formed until 7th August 1900, when it was formed from parts of Great Budworth, Davenham and other surrounding parishes. The parish name was something of a mouthful though: "the District Chapelry of St Helen Witton otherwise Northwich".

The original chapel is thought to date from the 13th century, although none of that build survives today; the current church dates from the 14th century, with additions in the 15th, 16th and 19th centuries. In terms of ongoing development, the original 14th century church had transepts and a chancel, while the north and south aisles were added in the 15th century along with a tower which was built (or rebuilt) in around 1498; the inscribed name "Thomas Hunter" suggests that he was the mason – a name that was associated with nearby Norton Priory at this time. The aisles were then rebuilt and widened between 1536 and 1549, thus incorporating the Lady Chapel into the body of the church, while the clerestory was added in around 1550. A major restoration was carried out in 1841, including the addition of a grand west door, and the chancel was rebuilt between 1861 and 1862. A further restoration took place between 1883 and 1886, including the creation of a baptistry inside the church.

St Helen Witton is included in Alec Clifton-Taylor's list of the "best" English parish churches. Meanwhile, Northwich Methodist chapel was opened in 1990, whereas John Wesley himself laid the foundation stone of the original Methodist chapel back in 1774.

Northwich Historic Trivia: Origins, Salt and Subsidence

The second part of the place-names Northwich and Middlewich means "salt-works" – so, the "north salt-works" and the "middlemost salt-works" in these particular cases. Recent excavations have also confirmed that salt-working at both places dates back to Roman times – although Northwich was known by the Roman name of *Condate* back then and Middlewich as *Salinae*. The Roman name for Northwich is probably a Latinisation of a Brythonic name meaning "confluence" – in this case, the confluence of the rivers Dane and Weaver. *Condate* is recorded in both the 3rd century *Antonine Itinerary* and the 7th century *Ravenna Cosmography*.

As well as the Roman salt mines, there is also evidence that suggests a Roman auxiliary fort was built at Northwich, which probably dated to the late 1st century as the Romans consolidated their grip on their north-western stronghold of Chester (*Deva*). Certainly Northwich was on a couple of Roman roads, and today, the A556 and A559 follow the route of the Roman road that ran from Chester (*Deva*) to York (*Eboracum*). The nearby A530 also follows the route of the Roman road that connected Warrington and Middlewich.

Following the Norman Conquest, Northwich belonged to the Earls of Chester until 1237, after which the town became a royal manor; Northwich was then recognised as a borough from around 1288. By the 15th century, the manor of Northwich belonged to the Stanley family, who later became Earls of Derby in 1484, and the manor stayed with the Stanleys until the late 18th century.

For centuries, salt mining remained the most important local industry, although traditional salt-making was more-or-less replaced with rock-salt mining in the 18th century. Exports were given a boost when the River Weaver was improved from Frodsham Bridge to Winsford Bridge in the 1730s, eventually allowing vessels of up to 160 tonnes (160,000 kg) to travel as far as Northwich Bridge. Then once the Trent and Mersey Canal had arrived in 1775, passing to the north of Northwich, many of the later salt mines, including the Lion Salt Works, based themselves along its banks to allow a convenient method of export.

During the 19th century, salt mining became uneconomical and, instead, hot water was pumped into the

This area of Northwich on the approach to Town Bridge from the east is known as the Bullring.

The Edwardian Dock Road Pumping Station. Built by Northwich Urban District Council in 1913, it was used for over sixty years to pump sewage from parts of Northwich to the Wallerscote Treatment Works. Prior to its build, sewage had been pumped directly into the River Weaver!

mines to dissolve the salt and the resultant brine was pumped out, after which the salt was extracted. Alas, it was this practise that weakened the mines and led to the subsidence issues discussed earlier. A phenomenon known as the Witton Flash was formed in 1880, when subsidence forced the River Weaver to flow into a huge sinkhole. As mentioned earlier, buildings were built to be liftable, including many of Northwich's timber-framed houses from the 16th and 17th centuries; as such., they could be jacked up to balance the house appropriately over the ever-changing surface.

Northwich joined the railway revolution of the 19th century relatively late, in 1863, when the Cheshire Midland Railway constructed a 12-mile (20.6km) line from Northwich to Altrincham. At around the same time, Northwich also found itself at one end of the West Cheshire Railway which ran from Northwich to Helsby, while passenger trains from Northwich to Chester via Delamere commenced in 1875.

By 1887, Northwich had its own swimming baths known as the Verdin Baths which were located in Verdin Park and were named after Robert Verdin; they were created as part of Queen Victoria's Golden Jubilee commemorations. The baths were used annually by around 20,000 people, but alas, the baths also became victim to the subsidence scourge in 1911 and had to be

closed; they were demolished the following year. The Verdin Baths were, however, succeeded by the Northwich Public Baths which opened in August 1915.

It was during the 19th century that Northwich began to expand and absorb the places around it. In 1875 Northwich and Witton cum Twambrooks had converged and the resulting district expanded further in 1880 when all of Castle Northwich was absorbed, along with parts of Hartford, Winnington and Leftwich. It wasn't until September 1894, though, that all of these areas were united as the civil parish of Northwich which, in turn, was served by Northwich Urban District Council.

The town continued to expand throughout the 20th century, with parts of Barnton, Leftwich, Lostock Gralam, Rudheath and Winnington, absorbed in 1936, and parts of Davenham, Hartford, Rudheath and Whatcroft absorbed in 1955. As for today, Northwich Town Council is comprised of five main districts: Leftwich, Northwich, Castle, Winnington and Witton. Also in the early 20th century, a bulk chemical industry became established at the three ICI sites at Lostock, Wallerscote and Winnington.

The Hayhurst Bridge (above left) and the Town Bridge (above right) were built in Northwich across the River Weaver in 1898 and 1899, respectively. Built by Colonel John Saner, they became the first two electrically-powered bridges in Great Britain. Like so many other constructions in Northwich, they were built with subsidence in mind and hence rest on floating pontoons.

The ongoing problem of subsidence in Northwich was confronted head on in February 2004, when a £28 million, three-year programme was launched to stabilise the abandoned salt mines underneath the town, and which was funded by English Partnerships via its Land Stabilisation Programme. This required the removal of millions of litres of brine from four particularly notorious mines and replacing it with a mixture of pulverised fuel ash, cement and salt. Also redeveloped more recently, to the tune of £80 million was Barons Quay.

Famous Northwichians

Sue Birtwistle (b.1945), film producer and writer; *Sir John Brunner* (1842-1919), co-founder of chemical firm Brunner Mond in 1873; *Tim Burgess* (b.1967), singer-songwriter; *Dr Harold Drinkwater* (1855-1925), physician and botanical artist; *Martin Edwards* (b.1955), crime fiction author; *John Greenway* (b.1946), M.P.; *Steve Hewitt* (b.1971), musician; *Rupert Holmes* (b.1947), composer, songwriter and author; *Charles James Hughes* (1853-1916) footballer and referee; *Diana Johnson* (b.1966), M.P.; *Matthew Kelly* (b.1950), television presenter and actor; *Matthew Langridge* (b.1983),

Olympic rower; *Ludwig Mond* (1839-1909), co-founder of chemical firm Brunner Mond in 1873; *Stuart Neild* (b.1970), horror author; *Andy Oakes* (b.1977), footballer; *Michael Oakes* (b.1973), footballer; *Jennifer Saunders* (b.1958), actress and comedian; *Robert Westall* (1929-1993), children's author.

Northwich Quirk Alert: James Boag-Munroe, Polythene and Float On

James Boag-Munroe is the fictitious creation of Northwich horror author, Stuart Neild. And, naturally, in his first novel, *A Haunted Man*, Boag-Munroe's adventures take place in the haunted salt mines of Northwich! Apparently, a Hollywood film and television series is also in development based on the books.

In 1933, Winnington became the location of the accidental discovery of the first industrially practical method for producing polythene.

Finally, until recently, Northwich was also home to the UK's only floating hotel – this being the Floatel which was moored on the River Weaver near to its confluence with the River Dane. Alas, it closed in 2009 – and then there were none!

The Bowling Green on London Road was founded in 1650.

Northwich Marina as seen from Hayhurst Bridge.

Northwich High Street.

The Brunner Library and Salt Museum was opened in 1909.

NAME (STATUS):	**OVER** (Suburb; former borough and market town)
POPULATION:	2001: 9905 (Wards of Over One [3,922] and Over Two [5983])
	2011: 13,414 (Ward of Winsford, Over and Verdin)
DISTRICT:	Cheshire West and Chester
EARLIEST RECORD:	*Ovre*, 1086 (Domesday Book)
MEANING:	Place at the ridge or slope
DERIVATION:	From the Old English word *ofer* (flat-topped ridge, hill or promontory)

Over Geographic Trivia

Over is a former borough and market town that now forms the western part of the town of Winsford – this following the expansion of Winsford in the 19th century which led to it eventually absorbing the smaller town of Over. As its name derivation suggests, Over is located on a ridge fashioned during the Ice Age. This happened when melt-waters from the last ice sheet left a long sandstone ridge from near Frodsham in the north to beyond Nantwich in the south. As it passes through Over, this ridge is largely marked by the B5074 which runs at a height of around 200 feet (61m) above sea level.

Over Church: St Chad's

The Grade II listed St Chad's church dates from the 14th century, and was built in red sandstone. The original build consisted of a tower, a nave with a narrow north aisle and a wide south aisle, plus a two-tier porch and the chancel. The south aisle was added in 1543 by Hugh Starkie, who lies at rest in the sanctuary, while the church was restored by Ewan Christian and W. Milford Teulon in 1870. The vestries and organ chambers were added in 1897–98 by the Lancaster architects Austin and Paley, and then the north aisle was widened in 1904 by John Douglas of Chester with further restoration carried out by Austin and Paley in 1906. The octagonal font dates from 1641 while there is a Grade II listed cross base in the churchyard that dates from around 1543.

Over Historic Trivia: Hunting, Abbey's, Coins and China Clay

Although Over appears in Domesday Book, we know that the place was settled in Saxon times thanks to a Saxon stone cross fragment, which was found in the early 20th century when St Chad's church was altered. It resides today in the chancel of St Chad's.

Sometime after the Norman Conquest, the Normans established a hunting lodge or summer palace at Darnhall in Over parish, which included an enclosed area where deer and wild boar were hunted by the Earls of Chester and his guests. The brook here was also dammed in order to drive three water mills and to create pools in which fish were kept. One of the later 13th century Earls of Chester was thought to have been poisoned by his wife in the hope that her father, the Prince of Wales, would favour the husband of her daughter with the manor. However, this all backfired as

St Chad's church, Over.

The cross base in St Chad's churchyard dates from around 1543.

these events took place during the Second Barons' War (1264-1267), and therefore King Henry III was about to take control of the county for himself, and thus of Over manor, even spending time at Darnhall himself.

Henry III (1216-1272) was succeeded by his son, Edward I (1272-1307), and the latter therefore acquired the title of Earl of Chester. He also founded an abbey in the 1270s at the secluded Darnhill, as a site for Cistercian monks, and which was initially populated by monks from Dore Abbey in Hertfordshire. The monks subsequently cleared the forest and turned the land to farming, but then moved to a better site three miles to the north of Over where Vale Royal Abbey was established – to which the parish of Over would pay tithes, as well as to the convent at Chester.

The second Abbot of Vale Royal Abbey then laid out land on either side of today's Delamere Street for a burgess, with each plot of land suitable for building a house and a garden, while a nearby peat bog supplied the residents with their fuel. The borough was allowed to have a weekly market as well as an annual livestock fair, while it also had to run a prison and set up a pillory for law transgressors, with the mayor acting as the judge in any borough trials. Each year, the Burgesses (those owners of each burgage plot) elected a Court Leet (a sort of town council-cum magistrates') to govern the borough, selecting one of their number to be mayor for the coming year – although the selection also had to be approved by the abbot. As for the boundary between the abbey lands and the borough, they were marked by wayside crosses, and the bases of two such crosses survive at Salterswall and Marston, with the latter known as the "wishing seat" and set up by order of Edward I.

As happened with so many religious institutions in the 14th century, the Black Death took half of Vale Royal Abbey's membership, while two centuries later the Abbey inevitably succumbed to the Dissolution of the Monasteries in the late 1530s. Vale Royal Abbey and the manor of Over were subsequently purchased by Thomas Holcroft in 1545, for £466.10s.1d, who immediately sold it on to Edmund Pershall. Over was then sold again in the mid-17th century to Thomas Cholmondeley, son of Lady Mary Cholmondeley who had already purchased Vale Royal Abbey.

During the English Civil War, Over was sacked in 1643 by retreating Royalists who had just escaped from Nantwich. It may well have been at this time that someone took the precaution of burying a little black ale mug full of silver coins, with dates ranging from the time of Elizabeth I to 1643. The coins were discovered centuries later in Nixon Drive by workmen, and now reside at the Grosvenor Museum in Chester.

In 1721, improvements were made to the River Weaver to allow large barges to reach Over and Winsford from Liverpool. Before the building of the Trent and Mersey Canal (built 1766-1777), Over was therefore the closest to the Potteries that barges could get – and hence why china clay imported from Cornwall had to be transported between Over and the Potteries by pack horses, with the finished china articles transported back similarly. During the mid-18th century, a certain George Wood made a small fortune out of this method of transportation.

The 19th century in Over was dominated by the salt industry, which became firmly established in the area in the 1830s. Interestingly, with the salt mines located to the east in Winsford, Over actually became a popular place for the more wealthy to live, as the most common winds here are westerlies! Inevitably, though, the two towns began to converge and ceased to become separate in around the 1860s. A cotton mill was then added in 1869 by Abraham Haigh at the mid-point between the two town centres. Haigh used the water supply trapped in the sand enclosed by clay on Over Ridge to power steam engines. Alas, a couple of years later, the entire building was destroyed by fire, and many of the workers who died were buried in a communal grave at St John's church. What was particularly tragic about the whole incident was that the town had ordered a fire engine but it hadn't been delivered by the time of the fire.

The Grade II listed St John's church was built in Over in 1860 when Over was separate from Winsford and was a village in its own right. The build was by architect John Dougles for Hugh Cholmondeley, 2nd Baron Delamere as a memorial to his wife, Sara.

Three's-Up!

	ROW-OF-TREES	SLAUGHTER HILL	STOAK
STATUS:	Hamlet	Road and Hill	Village
DISTRICT:	Cheshire East	Cheshire East	Cheshire West and Chester
MEANING:	A row of trees, perhaps…	Hill where sloe-trees grow, but which took on new meaning…	Usually outlying farmstead or hamlet or secondary settlement
DERIVATION:	Probably from a 19th century painting by George Sheffield	…when dozens of fleeing Royalists were slaughtered here during the English Civil War	From the Old English word *stoc* (outlying farmstead or hamlet, or secondary or dependent settlement)

Three's Up Trivia!

Row-of-trees is a distinct and sought-after residential area just to the west of both Wilmslow and Alderley Edge. The place is home to Laburnum Farm Nurseries and the Row-of-trees Women's Institute, founded in 1950, and whose sub-groups include Music Appreciation, a Book Group and a Knit and Natter Group!

The place is probably named after a 19th century painting by George Sheffield (1839-1892), which is called "Row of Trees", and is a watercolour of this very area to the west of Wilmslow. It is certainly referenced as a hamlet in the 19th century and is defined as being part of the civil parish of Chorley which was created in 1866, having previously been a township in Wilmslow ancient parish.

The prequel to, and the battle at **Slaughter Hill** in January 1644, were deeply shocking affairs. When the English Civil War commenced in 1642, the Royalist

Two rows of trees at Row-of-trees, just west of Wilmslow.

Rural scene close to Slaughter Hill.

Quirk Alert: *Slaughter Hill and the Genuine Witch Connection*

Slaughter Hill is located at the southern edge of the village of Haslington, and is the location of a bloody skirmish during the First English Civil War (1642-1646). The battle was won by the Parliamentarians, and legend has it that the battle resulted in the local brook turning red with blood – and hence some people say that this therefore lent the place its name. However, the skirmish and the place-name are probably just a coincidence, as the name of Slaughter Hill may well be a derivation of Sloe Tree Hill, itself derived from the Old English word slāh, meaning "blackthorn or sloe-tree". This theory is based upon the fact that blackthorn (which produces the sloes that contain the blackthorn's plum-like fruit), can still be found in the hedgerows down the lane named Slaughter Hill. But did you know also, that it is believed that the most effective witches' staffs and wands are made from blackthorn wood? Well, that's what they say…

The Bunbury Arms at Stoak.

St Lawrence's church at Stoak.

Dragoons were quartered at Haslington, and on the Christmas Eve of 1643, a group of Royalists attacked the village of Barthomley, which is located just over two miles to the south-east of Slaughter Hill. The locals took shelter in Barthomley church, climbing up into the steeple, but the Royalists smoked them out by burning the pews amongst other things. As the villagers emerged from the church in surrender, the Royalist soldiers stripped naked twelve of their number, and then killed them, first stabbing them multiple times and then cutting their throats. They also wounded all of the other villagers, leaving most of them for dead, while the following day, they plundered Barthomley, Crewe and Haslington as well as other surrounding settlements.

Meanwhile, nearby Parliamentarian Nantwich, had been holding out to a Royalist siege. However, towards the end of January, 1644, the siege was ended by the intervention of Sir Thomas Fairfax's army and hundreds of Royalist troops were taken prisoner – including, apparently, 120 Irish women with long knives! Some of the Royalists, however, took flight towards Slaughter Hill – perhaps the same group who had committed the atrocity at Barthomley. Their intention was probably to cross the brook to the south of Haslington via the steep-sided Haslington Gap, where the brook would ordinarily have been narrow and shallow. Alas, at this time of year, and thanks also to melting snow, the local rivers and streams were flooded, and the brook was probably a torrent. Exhausted from both the battle at Nantwich and their subsequent flight, the Royalists decided to about-turn and fight the approaching Parliamentarians, rather than be picked off crossing the flooded brook. The resulting fighting was brutal, with the Parliamentarians no doubt intent on revenge for the carnage of Barthomley. The Royalists were massacred and the dead washed away by the flooded brook, while the wounded were left lying in the melting snow which caused the brook to run red for several days afterwards.

Finally, **Stoak** is a village around five miles northeast of Chester, which sits inside a busy right-angle formed by the M56 and M53. The village is home to the

Grade II listed St Lawrence's church, which largely dates from its last rebuild in 1827 by George Edgecombe. However, it is thought that a Saxon chapel resided on this site over a thousand years ago, and which was probably succeeded by a Norman one, as indicated by fragments of Norman architecture that survived into the 19th century. Surviving the 1827 rebuild was the north wall and the Tudor hammerbeam roof of the nave while a number of fixtures and fittings pre-date 1827, too. These include two chairs which date from the early 17th century, an oak parish chest dating from 1686, some old pews, a Jacobean altar table and a Georgian pulpit, while the church bells are the oldest in the Wirral, dating from 1615, 1631 and 1642, respectively. Finally, the churchyard contains a Grade II listed sandstone sundial which dates from the 17th century and the grave of nine-year-old Nelson Burt who drowned during the River Mersey hurricane of 1822.

> **Quirk Alert:** *Urge for Offal!*
> *Both St Lawrence's church and the grave of Nelson Burt at Stoak, are mentioned in the song "The Unfortunate Gwatkin" by the band Half Man Half Biscuit. This appears on their 2014 album,* Urge For Offal!

The Shropshire Union Canal at Stoak.

NAME (STATUS):	**SALE** (Town)
POPULATION:	134,022
DISTRICT:	Trafford, Greater Manchester
EARLIEST RECORD:	*Sale*, c.1205
MEANING:	Place at the sallow-tree
DERIVATION:	From the Old English word *salh* (sallow or willow)

Sale Geographic Trivia: Switched

Sale is yet another place that was part of Cheshire from around the 11th century up until 1st April 1974, after which it became part of the metropolitan district of Trafford in the new metropolitan county of Greater Manchester. The town is located on the south bank of the River Mersey, and is prone to flooding following periods of heavy rain. However, the Sale Water Park – created in 1972 – now acts as an emergency flood basin!

Sale Church: St Anne's with St Francis and St Martin's

Sale's parish church of St Anne's is a relative newcomer, built in the 1850s. The oldest church in the parish is St Martin's in Ashton upon Mersey, although this was rebuilt in 1714 – but replaced a much older church that dated back to at least 1304, and which was built on the site of an Anglo-Saxon cemetery – meaning that there might have been an even older predecessor here. The church website states that the 1304 church was founded by Wiliemus De Salle, the first rector of St Martins. A chantry chapel to the Blessed Virgin Mary was then licensed in 1398, but was dissolved at the Reformation in 1547. The 14th century church was probably timber-based, and was destroyed in a storm in 1703 when it is believed it was set alight by a lightning strike – and hence its rebuild in 1714. An octagonal north baptistry with a pyramidal roof was then added in 1874 by W.H. Brakspear, while a new tower was built in 1887 along with a ring of 13 bells and what is now a Grade II listed lych gate.

Originally known as the White Lion, The Volunteer was rebuilt in 1898 to commemorate the Sale and Ashton volunteers of the Napoleonic Wars.

The King's Ransom pub sits on the banks of the Bridgewater Canal in the centre of Sale.

Sale's Grade II listed parish church of St Anne's with St Francis was built in 1854.

St Martin's church in Ashton upon Mersey was built in 1714, but replaced a much older predecessor that dated from the early 14th century.

Sale Historic Trivia: Through the Ages

A prehistoric flint arrowhead discovered at Sale suggests a prehistoric settlement here, while the Roman period is represented by a hoard of 46 fourth century Roman coins found at Ashton upon Mersey.

By the 12th century, the manor of Sale was held by William FitzNigel, who divided it between Thomas de Sale and Adam de Carrington, who acted as Lords of the Manor on FitzNigel's behalf. The two sub-manors soon passed to the Holt and Massey families, respectively, and remained with these two families until the 17th century, when their respective lands were sold. Just prior to this, Sale Old Hall had been built in around 1603 for James Massey, and was one of the first buildings in northwest England to be made of brick. The hall was rebuilt in 1840, but demolished in 1920. However, two of its outbuildings have survived, including the dovecote and the lodge, with the former now in Sale's Walkden Gardens, and the latter now occupied by Sale Golf Club.

The Dovecote in Walkden Gardens a survivor of Sale Hall which was demolished in 1920.

When Bonnie Prince Charlie marched southwards in 1745, a series of bridges over the River Mersey were destroyed in an attempt to halt his advance. This included Crossford Bridge at Sale which dated back to at least 1367. However, as part of a clever ruse, the Jacobites repaired the bridge and used it to send a small force into Sale and Altrincham – thus leading the English into believing the Jacobites were heading for Chester. This enabled the main Jacobite army to later march south, unmolested, through Cheadle and Stockport instead.

Also in the mid-18th century, the first turnpike road appeared in the area on a similar course to today's A56 between Manchester and Chester, and there was a toll booth on the Sale side of Crossford Bridge. Sale was also included on the Bridgewater Canal in 1765, and this transformed the town's economy by offering farmers a rapid export route into Manchester for fresh produce. Indeed, at this time, Sale was still comprised mainly of farmhouses that were clustered around today's Dane Road, Fairy Lane, and Old Hall Road. In between Sale and Ashton upon Mersey to the

This bronze bust of physicist James Joule (1818-1889) in Worthington Park was unveiled in 1905. Joule moved to Sale in the 1870s and is buried in Brooklands Cemetery.

north-west, the village of Cross Street is depicted upon a 1777 map. First referred to in 1586, Cross Street was eventually absorbed by the converging towns in the 20th century, and is today marked by a road of the same name. Back to the Bridgewater Canal, though, and "swift packet" services up the canal made commuting from Sale to Manchester both practical and convenient.

The enclosure explosion of the 18th century finally hit Sale in 1809 when 300 acres (120 ha) known as Sale Moor was enclosed and sub-divided between a number of Sale landowners – the excuse on this occasion being that common land needed to be cultivated to help counter the food shortage caused by the Napoleonic Wars. Then in 1829, Samuel Brooks acquired 515 acres (208 ha) of land in Sale, now known as Brooklands and named after its 19th century owner. Acquired from the 6th Earl of Stamford, Brooklands amounted to about a quarter of the township back then.

During the first half of the 19th century, large-scale industry was slow to develop in Sale, mainly due to the reluctance of the landowning Stamford and Trafford families to invest, and hence there was no significant expansion of the town's population. That all changed in the second half of the 19th century, though, when Sale became a key commuter town for middle class Manchester workers, particularly once Sale had been incorporated into the railway network in 1849. Of course the arrival of the railway signalled the end of both the aforementioned canal packet services and turnpike trusts, and by 1888 almost all of the local roads and highways were the responsibility of the local authority.

By the end of the 19th century, Sale's population had more than trebled in size, while a new sewerage system was added between 1875 and 1880, followed by connection to the telephone network in 1888. The town's first swimming baths and cinema followed in 1914 and 1916.

Between the two World Wars, 594 council houses were built in Sale, with additional private housing taking the total to 900, and including large housing estates like Woodheys Hall estate in Ashton. Some of those houses were damaged by German incendiary bombs during World War II, but Sale fared reasonably well compared to other areas and didn't suffer any casualties – other than the Town Hall, which was severely damaged during a three hour assault on the night of 23rd December 1943, during which time over six hundred incendiary bombs were dropped on Sale as part of the "Manchester Blitz". Meanwhile, just prior to World War II in 1933, Sale Urban District Council submitted a petition in an attempt to gain a charter of incorporation – this based in the fact that the district had the largest population and highest rateable value of any urban district in the country. As a result, Sale became a Municipal Borough on 21st September 1935.

In 1980, Sale Water Park was constructed, having previously been a 115ft deep (35m) gravel pit, but

The Grade I listed Eyebrow Cottage in Cross Street is the oldest building in Sale, and was built in around 1670. It was originally a yeoman farmhouse and is one of the earliest brick-built buildings in the Sale area. The name derives from the decorative brickwork over the downstairs windows.

Sale Town Hall was built in 1914, but was badly damaged by German bombs in December 1940 and was not completely rebuilt until 1952.

which was flooded after the extraction of the gravel that was used as part of the construction of the M63 (now the M60). Today, Sale Water Park is an artificial lake and water-sports centre, while it is also a favourite spot for fishing and bird watching.

More recently, Sale Harriers Manchester Athletics Club (formed in 1911), has produced Olympic gold medallist Darren Campbell, and Commonwealth Games gold medallist Diane Modahl. Meanwhile, the metropolitan borough of Trafford maintains a selective education system assessed by the eleven plus exam – meaning that those who pass can go to Sale Grammar School, a specialist school in science and the visual arts.

Sale Quirk Alert: By the Book and the Manchester Mummy

The rugby union team known as Sale F.C. has been based in Sale since 1861, and is therefore one of the oldest rugby clubs in the world. The club has also been based at the teams' current Heywood Road ground since 1905. Meanwhile, Sale F.C. retains its 1865 Minute Book, which is the oldest existing book in the world which contains the rules of the game.

Hannah Beswick (1688-1758), of Oldham was a wealthy woman who had a pathological fear of prema-

ture burial. Therefore on her death, her body was embalmed and kept above ground, to be periodically checked for signs of life! The reason for this was that one of Hannah's brothers, John, had shown signs of life just as his coffin lid had been about to be closed. On examination, the family physician, Dr Charles White, confirmed that he was still alive – and John subsequently regained consciousness and lived for many more years! Determined not to bow out too early as well, Hannah left a considerable sum of money to Dr White, on the proviso that she be embalmed and that the doctor and two witnesses would undertake to unveil her face once a year in order to check that she wasn't still alive! Her embalmed body was therefore kept at the Sale home of Dr White – in an old grandfather clock case! With her face covered by a veil of white velvet, she was kept during the doctor's lifetime, in the clock case, on the roof of the doctor's house! Unsurprisingly, visitors came from far and wide to view her at Dr White's house until his death in 1776. Later, Hannah's mummified body was moved to the Museum of the Manchester Natural History Society, where she subsequently earned the moniker of "The Manchester Mummy". Having later been transferred to Manchester University, Hannah was eventually buried in 1868 – presumably due to the fact that she had failed to show any sign of life in over 110 years!

Worthington Park in Sale was opened in 1900.

One part of the lovely Walkden Gardens in Sale.

NAME (STATUS):	**SOUND** (Hamlet)
POPULATION:	239
DISTRICT:	Cheshire East
EARLIEST RECORD:	*Sound*, 1310
MEANING:	Sandy place
DERIVATION:	From the Old English word *sand*, meaning "sandy place".

Sound Geographic Trivia: Sand and Sound Heath

Sound is a small settlement and civil parish around four miles south-west of Nantwich, with the parish also including the small settlements of Newtown and Sound Heath. Sound Heath is also a small Site of Special Scientific Interest and Local Nature Reserve and includes various habitats, including damp and dry lowland heath, grassland, scrub and young woodland. It is therefore an important habitat for freshwater invertebrates, including pond-dwelling species that are rare in the UK such as the mud snail, great raft spider and a species of water scavenger beetle – many of which dwell in the permanent or seasonal pools formed from past sand extraction. The snout moth is another rare UK species recorded at Sound Heath, while the area is also an important breeding site for a wide range of birds.

Sound Church: Broomhall and Sound Church

In medieval times, Sound was divided between Wrenbury chapelry (served by St Margaret's Church at Wrenbury) and Acton (served by Acton St Mary's). However, Sound got its own church in 1838, when a Wesleyan Methodist chapel was built by Joseph Cartlidge on New Town Road. Roughly halfway between Sound and Broomhall, the chapel was actually called Broomhall church. A Primitive Methodist chapel was also constructed at Sound Heath in 1875, and a Sunday school was added in the late 1930s. This chapel eventually closed in 1973, though, and the congregation united with that of Broomhall church, which was renamed as Broomhall

Broomhall and Sound church, originally built in 1838.

Sound and District Primary School is Grade II listed and was originally built in 1876, housing 58 pupils in its first year.

The Grade II listed Sound Oak Farmhouse, which dates from the early 17th century.

Sound Heath.

and Sound church and which belongs to the United Methodist Church.

Sound Historic Trivia: Malt Kilns and Beerhouses

It is thought that a hamlet existed here in the 13th century called Fouleshurst, in the vicinity of the 17th century Grade II listed Fulhurst Hall on Sound Lane. However, no traces of Fouleshurst have ever been uncovered and the settlement had been replaced by Sound by 1310. Meanwhile, the earliest landowners at Sound took their name from the village, but by the second half of the 15th century, the manor was owned by the Chetwode family.

During April 1643 it is recorded that Royalist troops "took great prey from Dorfold, Acton, Ravensmoor, Sound, and all that neighbourhood; namely, all the cows and young beasts they could find, with horses and household stuff from many, to a great value, and carried all away with them."

Much later, in the 19th century, Sound was owned by the Cholmondeleys, and by 1831 the village was home to a hopyard north of Sound Hall, which had a malt kiln. Two beerhouse keepers were also recorded in Sound in 1850, and one of the cottages adjacent to Sound Hall is believed to have been an alehouse. Finally, in 1876, Sound School opened, housing 58 pupils in its first year. During World War II, the school served as an emergency rest centre for evacuees, while the late 20th century saw the school expanded with mobile classrooms.

NAME (STATUS):	**STYAL** (Village)
POPULATION:	1051
DISTRICT:	Cheshire East
EARLIEST RECORD:	*Styhale* c.1200
MEANING:	Nook of land with a pigsty, or by a narrow path
DERIVATION:	From the Old English words *stigu* (pigsty) or *stīg* (upland or narrow path) and *halh* (nook or corner of land)
FAMOUS RESIDENTS:	Terry Waite (b.1939), humanitarian, author and hostage negotiator

Styal Pub: The Ship Inn

The Ship Inn dates back more than 350 years. It was originally known as the 'Shippon', which is nothing to do with ships at all, as a shippon was a farm building used to store manure. It became the Ship Inn when the farmer who owned the farm started brewing for the locals. Today, the Ship Inn is renowned for its 260 year old wisteria and the beautiful roses that grow up the front of the building.

Styal Church: Norcliffe Chapel

Norcliffe Chapel was built in 1823 by Samuel Greg, the owner of Quarry Bank Mill. The original Trust Deed declares the chapel as being "For the worship of God; and the furtherance of Christian life; free from the fetters of any written and unwritten; declaration of doctrine".

Styal Historic Trivia: Quarry Bank Mill

The village of Styal is dominated by the late 18th century Grade II listed Quarry Bank Mill, one of the best-preserved textile mills of the early Industrial Revolution. The mill was built alongside the River Bollin in 1784 by Samuel Greg and John Massey, and used the fast-flowing river to power the mill machinery in order to spin cotton. The mill was also connected by road to the Bridgewater Canal, which enabled the easy import of the raw cotton from Liverpool.

Samuel Greg initially leased land at Quarrell Hole on Pownall Fee from Lord Stamford, who imposed a condition that "none of the surrounding trees should be pruned, felled or lopped", thus preserving the woodland character of the area. Quarry Bank Mill was then built with four storeys measuring 90ft by 28ft (27.5m by 8.5m) and included a counting house and warehouse, while the water wheel was situated at the north end of the mill and drove 2,425 spindles. The mill was then extended in 1796 when the length was doubled to around 180ft (55m) and a fifth floor added, too, while a second water wheel was built at the southern end of the mill in 1801 – and hence by 1805, the two wheels of the mill were driving 3,452 spindles. Further extensions were built between 1817 and 1820.

Much of the housing around Quarry Bank Mill also belongs to the mill estate, the majority of which was built for the mill workers by the original mill owner, Samuel Greg. He also converted farm buildings in Styal to house his workers, while he and his family lived at Quarry Bank House alongside the mill. As for the mill houses that Greg rented to his workers, they each had a parlour, kitchen and two bedrooms, an outside privy and a small garden, while the rent due was deducted from the workers' wages. Samuel Greg also built Norcliffe Chapel for his workers which held a Sunday school, while he built Oak School to educate the children of his workers. In addition, Quarry Bank Mill initially employed child apprentices from the workhouses of Hackney and Chelsea, although later, they would come from neighbouring parishes or Liverpool workhouses. Greg provided lodgings for them, and then in 1790, he built the Apprentice House close to the factory where tutors were hired to provide his young

The Ship Inn at Styal is more than 350 years old.

Norcliffe Chapel at Styal was built in 1823 by Samuel Greg for his mill workers at Quarry Bank Mill.

Quarry Bank Mill was built in 1784 by Samuel Greg, and which today is in the hands of the National Trust. It is still a working mill, and includes the most powerful working waterwheel in Europe.

Mill workers' cottages close to Quarry Bank Mill. Like many of Styal's buildings, they were built by the Greg family during the Industrial Revolution.

The Apprentice House built in 1790 by Samuel Greg to provide his child workers with an education.

Part of Quarry Bank House and gardens in the grounds of Quarry Bank Mill.

workers with schooling. Greg was also the first mill owner to employ a mill doctor – who was responsible for the health of the children and other workers. Nevertheless, the children worked long days, which also included schoolwork and gardening after their shift at the mill had been completed. The mill work was also dangerous, with fingers liable to be lost to the machines. However, children were willing to work in the mill because life at a workhouse was much worse.

The first water wheel (1784) was a wooden overshot wheel which took water from the River Bollin via a long leat, while the second wheel (1801), which was also wooden, dammed the Bollin to increase the power, taking water directly into the mill, with the tailrace leaving the river below the dam. A third wheel was added in 1807, an iron suspension wheel with a diameter of 26ft (8m), designed by Thomas Hewes. Then between 1816 and 1820, Hewes designed a fourth water wheel which became known as the Great Wheel, and which increased the head of water despite using the same volume as its predecessors. This was achieved by sinking the wheel pit below the level of the river and taking the tail race through a tunnel to re-join the Bollin half a mile downstream. The head of water was therefore increased to 32ft (9.8 m). As well as water-power, later developments would see the mill powered also by

beam engines, horizontal steam engines and water turbines, with the steam engines offering power throughout the year, regardless of the level and flow of the river; indeed Samuel Greg purchased the first steam engine as early as 1810 as a form of auxiliary power.

When Samuel Greg retired in 1832, two years before his death, his mill was the largest such business in the United Kingdom. He was succeeded by his son, Robert Hyde Greg, who introduced power-loom weaving into the business by adding two two-storey weaving sheds in 1836 and 1838. The weaving sheds housed 305 looms and replaced hand-loom weaving in the area, which had previously been carried out in weavers' own homes or in small loom shops. The 1836 weaving shed measured 108ft by 21ft (33m by 6.5m), and the 1838 shed 98ft by 33ft (30m by 10m), and their two-storeys makes them nationally significant as most other survivors are single storey sheds with a saw-tooth roof.

Robert Hyde Greg also had to deal with a crisis when the mill was attacked on 10th August 1842 as part of the Plug Plot riots – also known as the General Strike of 1842 – and which had been started by miners in neighbouring Staffordshire who, in turn, had been influenced by the Chartist movement.

The estate and mill were eventually donated to the National Trust in 1939 by Alexander Carlton Greg with the mill actually remaining active until 1959. In 2006 the National Trust acquired Quarry Bank House and its gardens, which were followed by the gardener's house and upper gardens in 2010. As for the mill today, it is essentially a cotton mill museum, and it also houses the most powerful working waterwheel in Europe, powering the same type of looms that existed here in the 19th century. That said, the wheel isn't a Quarry Bank original; it is an iron wheel which was moved here from Glasshouses Mill at Pateley Bridge and which had been designed by an apprentice of Thomas Hewes, Sir William Fairbairn. Finally, in 2013, Channel 4 produced a docu-drama called *The Mill*, which was inspired by the history of Quarry Bank Mill.

In other brief history, Styal railway station opened in 1909 on the line linking Crewe, Wilmslow and Manchester Piccadilly, while HMP Styal is a women's prison which opened in 1962 and occupies some former buildings of the Styal Cottage Homes which housed destitute children from the Manchester area between 1898 and 1956. As for Styal's state primary school, this is located on the Styal National Trust estate.

Another view of Quarry Bank Mill.

The medieval Styal Cross, rebuilt after being demolished by a car in 1980.

Farm Fold, numbers 5 to 8.

Styal Methodist church.

NAME (STATUS):	**VICTORIA PARK** (Park)
POPULATION:	N/A
DISTRICT:	Wirral, Merseyside
EARLIEST RECORD:	1901
MEANING:	Named after Queen Victoria

Victoria Park Historic Trivia:
The Tranmere Cross

Victoria Park is an early 20th century park in Tranmere, Birkenhead. When the park was first opened in 1901, it only included the gardens of a large property called Arudy House, which had been owned by Victor Poutz, a French cotton merchant – but both house and gardens had subsequently fallen into disrepair until their overhaul in 1901.

At the top of Victoria Park is the Tranmere Cross. The remains of an ancient cross in Tranmere are first mentioned in an 1833 book by Thomas Taylor, called "Picture of Liverpool or Stranger's Guide". However, later Victorian authors tell of the cross' disappearance, with the generally agreed theory being that it disappeared around 1862. The cross was then re-discovered in 1935, masquerading as the column and base of a sundial in front of the main doorway of Tranmere New Hall; effectively hiding in plain sight! The man who recognised its true nature was local historian J.E. Allison. He had been drawn to the column height and the unusual carving, as well as the fact that such a shaded location did not seem particularly suited to a sundial. His own opinion was that it looked more like the shaft and base of an ancient cross. Mr Allison sought opinion from various authorities who all agreed that, not only was this indeed an ancient cross, but that it was also the missing *Tranmere* Cross. The date of origin was put at the turn of the 16th century, and the cross was then re-erected in Victoria Park on 18th October 1937. As to its original site, it is thought that it would not have been far from Tranmere New Hall, as a lengthy transportation would have resulted in damage to the cross. One theory is that it was originally located in Church Road, an area that was "cleared up" in 1862-63 when the old Hall was demolished and Church Road straightened out.

There is also another Victoria Park on the Wirral peninsula, a couple of miles to the north of the Tranmere version – but this one is home to Poulton Victoria Football Club, of the West Cheshire League! However, there is a *third* Victoria Park in Cheshire today, in Warrington alongside the River Mersey. It was laid out on the site of the Old Warps Estate after the local council bought it in 1897. The council converted the site into an amenity for the locals of Latchford, and named it Victoria Park as part of the commemoration of Queen Victoria's Diamond Jubilee. Within the park, the Georgian manor house called Old Warps survives, along with a modern sports stadium with a large running track that is home to Warrington Athletics Club.

Above: *Victoria Park in Tranmere was opened in 1901.It offers fine views across the River Mersey to Liverpool.* Right: *The Tranmere Cross can be found at the top of Victoria Park. This 15th century medieval cross went missing in around 1862, but was re-discovered in May 1935 and erected on this spot in October 1937.*

NAME (STATUS):	**TARVIN** (Village)
POPULATION:	2728
DISTRICT:	Cheshire West and Chester
EARLIEST RECORD:	*Teruen*, 1086 (Domesday Book)
MEANING:	Boundary stream
DERIVATION:	From the Celtic river-name, meaning "boundary stream", or possibly the Welsh word *tervyn* or *terfyn* meaning "boundary"; another theory suggests the Latin word for "terminus"

Tarvin Church: St Andrew's

Although an earlier 12th century church existed at Tarvin, the oldest part of the current Grade I listed St Andrew's church dates from the 14th century – this being the south wall and south arcade. The single-framed roof over the south aisle dates from 1380, and is the only one of its type in Cheshire, while another 14th century relic is the wooden screen to the Bruen chapel which stands south of the chancel; the chapel windows also date from this time. The rest of the church dates mainly from the 15th century rebuild, including the tower, although the north aisle was added after the tower. The octagonal font is also contemporary with the tower, and the Flemish reredos dates from around 1500. The chancel was restored in the 18th century, with further restorations following during the late 18th and 19th centuries as well as in 1908.

St Andrew's is yet another in a long line of English churches that bears the scars from the English Civil War, this in the form of cannon ball and musket shot marks on the church walls from local Civil War skirmishes. As for the five-bay nave and the two-bay chancel, they reside under the same roof and are lit by six dormer windows, while ornate nave beams rest on elaborate wooden corbels that date from around 1650.

Tarvin Historic Trivia: The Great Fire of Tarvin

When the Romans built their fortress at Chester (*Deva*) in around 76 AD, the road from Northwich (*Condate*) to Chester passed about half a mile to the north of Tarvin, and a Roman coin from the reign of Constantius 1 (AD 293–305) was found nearby. Indeed, one suggestion for the name of Tarvin (meaning boundary or terminus), is that it marked the eastern edge of the land which the Romans annexed from the Celtic *Cornovii* tribe, to support their fortress at *Deva*. Later, the River Gowy to the west of Tarvin marked the boundary between two Saxon Hundreds, and part of the Kingdom of Mercia known as the *Wrēocensǽte*. More solid Saxon evidence is provided by Anglo-Saxon cross fragments dating from the 10th or 11th century and which were found when an English Civil War trench was excavated.

Following the Norman Conquest of 1066, it was normal for the previous Anglo-Saxon incumbent of the manor to be disinvested in favour of one of William I's loyal noblemen. However, Domesday Book records the

The George and Dragon pub is located on High Street, Tarvin, and sits opposite The Red Lion which dates from the 18th century.

The Grade I listed St Andrew's church at Tarvin, the oldest part of which dates from the 14th century.

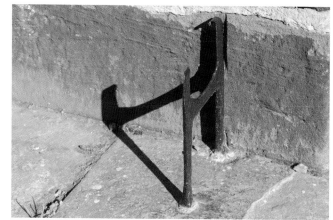

Left: These gates and gate piers that lead up to St Andrew's church are all Grade II listed, as is the sundial (right:) *which is located in front of the church porch.*

owner of Tarvin manor to be the same in both 1066 and 1086 – the Bishop of Chester St John's, in this particular case. That said, the bishop in post was a Norman bishop by 1086!

At the time of the Norman Conquest, Tarvin was within Rushton Hundred, but by the end of the 12th century it had moved to the Eddisbury Hundred. Then in c.1226, the Bishop of Lichfield founded the prebend of Tarvin, perhaps due to the village being on what was then the disputed boundary between England and Wales. Thus began a long-term relationship between Tarvin and the Bishops of Lichfield and Coventry until April 1550, when the bishop granted Tarvin to Sir John Savage.

It was during Sir John's tenure that Tarvin received its market charter and Tarvin Grammar School was founded by Randall Pickering. One of the school's 18th century masters for 36 years was John Thomasen, described by Arthur Mee as "the finest penman in England". Certainly, his penmanship graces many of our museums, and Queen Anne admired his work so much that she asked him to transcribe many Greek works by what Mee calls "the old poets". The grammar school was eventually closed in 1939, but was restored in 1997.

During the English Civil War, Tarvin was initially occupied by Parliamentarians, and two early skirmishes occurred during November 1643 and January 1644. By July 1644, the Royalists held Tarvin only for the Parliamentarians to win it back in September 1644, after which they occupied it for the rest of the war, housing a strong garrison within strong earthworks.

We now move on to noon on the 30th April 1752, for this was the day of the Great Fire of Tarvin. It broke out in the north-west part of the village, but within two hours, most of the town had been burnt down. Mercifully spared were the timber-framed buildings of Church House and Church Cottages, as well as Bull's Cottage, buildings which stood on the outskirts of the town.

During the 18th century, Tarvin found itself on the turnpike road from Lichfield to Chester, following an Act of 1769, while it was also on the road from Northwich, too. Almost a century later, Tarvin became a civil parish in 1866, while nine years later, the new civil parish found itself on the railway line from Chester to Manchester, and was served by Barrow for Tarvin station. The station was eventually closed in June 1953, but the line remains open. The 1960s then saw the village population begin to expand with many houses occupied by white-collar workers and their families.

Tarvin Quirk Alert: Last Rites

Tarvin St Andrew's church has a number of cannonball and musketball holes in the tower wall next to the west door, made during the English Civil War. The likely reason is that this is where prisoners were shot!

Church House and Church Cottages on Church Street, Tarvin.

These fine Georgian houses on Church Street date from 1756.

NAME (STATUS):	**WARMINGHAM** (Village)
POPULATION:	244
DISTRICT:	Cheshire East
EARLIEST RECORD:	*Warmincham*, 1259
MEANING:	Homestead of the family or followers of a man called Wǣrma or Wǣrmund
DERIVATION:	From the Old English personal name for Wǣrma or Wǣrmund, plus the Old English words *ing* (associated with or called after) and *hām* (homestead)

The Bear's Paw at Warmingham dates from the 19ᵗʰ century.

St Leonard's church at Warmingham dates from 1715.

Warmingham Church: St Leonard's

The Grade II listed St Leonard's church was built in 1715 from purple bricks, but of this build, only the tower remains of a purplish hue. This is because the nave and chancel were rebuilt out of sandstone in 1870, replacing an earlier timber-framed church body. The churchyard is home to an old cross dating from 1298.

Warmingham Historic Trivia: Lords of Salt

The earliest find in Warmingham parish was a gold Iron Age coin dating from the end of the 1ˢᵗ century BC, although it is thought that an urn discovered in the parish may date from as long ago as the Bronze Age, having originally thought to be Roman. Fast-forwarding over one thousand years, the settlement was home to a corn mill by 1289, which would have been contemporary with the previous church. During the medieval period, the manor of Warmingham belonged to first the Mainwaring and then the Trussell family, while the 16ᵗʰ century saw the manor part-owned by the Hatton family before it passed to Ranulph Crewe (1558-1646). Crewe was the son of a tanner, but became a judge and Chief Justice of the King's Bench, a post to which he was appointed by James I on 26ᵗʰ January, 1625 – although he was removed from that office by James' successor, Charles I in November 1626 – this for refusing to subscribe to a document affirming the legality of forced loans! Both of Crewe's sons became MP's, while the Crewe family retained control of Warmingham manor until 1918.

Two views of the Grade II listed Church House, the oldest surviving building in Warmingham parish. Dating from the late 16ᵗʰ century, the right-hand photograph reveals the typical Elizabethan timber-framed look with decorative framing in a chevron pattern. One former resident was John "Rebel" Kent, a supporter of Bonnie Prince Charlie in the Jacobite uprising of 1745.

One of the earliest finery forges (or smelting furnace) was established in Warmingham in the mid-17th century. It was still in operation in around 1750, when its annual output of bar iron was recorded as 300 tons, more than any other Cheshire forge.

However, it is inevitable that salt dominates Warmingham over the centuries, given its location on the Northwich Halite Formation, a Triassic salt field with a 558-787ft thick (170–240m) salt-bearing layer lying around 590-820ft (180–250m) below the surface. Brine has also been extracted here for centuries. Indeed, it is known that brine from Warmingham parish flashes were used to make salt in Middlewich during Roman occupation. It was in the 19th century, though, when uncontrolled brine pumping went industrial in the area, increasing further after World War I, and which led to the inevitable subsidence problems. This included the notorious Sandbach Flashes which first appeared in the early 1920s – these being pools formed by subsidence from the dissolving underlying salt, and further accelerated by salt extraction. The flashes were still expanding in the mid-20th century, but a stop was eventually put to uncontrolled brine pumping in the 1970s. The early 1980s then saw British Salt introduce controlled brine pumping at a site near Hill Top Farm in Warmingham, with emphasis on preventing further subsidence; indeed, the Warmingham site is one of only two major brine fields still being exploited in Britain. The brine extracted is processed to make white salt at British Salt's Middlewich salt works a couple of miles further north, resulting in around half of the UK's pure salt output. Since 2003, EDF has also very resourcefully stored natural gas in the Warmingham parish, in underground cavities in the salt-bearing stratum, created by the dissolving salt. As for the flashes, they now form a Site of Special Scientific Interest and a popular site for birdwatching.

During World War II, a prisoner-of-war camp was set up at the southern end of the parish, while there was a heavy anti-aircraft battery near Bottoms Farm in 1940–41 and the aforementioned corn mill was adapted to manufacture aircraft parts.

Finally, Warmingham village now comprises a conservation area that includes St Leonard's Church, Church House, Hill Top Cottage, Mill House, Island House and the Bear's Paw Hotel, while the village continues its tradition of holding Warmingham Wakes in early May.

Warmingham Quirk Alert: 3¼

Warmingham lies exactly 3¼ miles north of Crewe, 3¼ miles south of Middlewich, and 3¼ miles west of Sandbach.

Above: *Part of the brine pumping machinery near Hill Top Farm, Warmingham.*
Below: *The centre of the village of Warmingham, which is now a conservation area.*

NAME (STATUS):	**WHARTON** (Suburb and ex-hamlet)
POPULATION:	2509
DISTRICT:	Cheshire West and Chester
EARLIEST RECORD:	*Wanetune*, 1086 (Domesday Book); *Waverton*, 1216
MEANING:	Farmstead by a swaying tree or near marshy ground
DERIVATION:	From the Old English words *wæfre* (flickering, wavering or quivering) and *tūn* (farmstead)

Wharton Church: Christ Church

Christ Church was built at Wharton in the early 1840s by James France-France of nearby Bostock Hall, in the Gothic Revival style. It was consecrated on 26th June 1843 by the Bishop of Chester, John Bird Sumner which coincided with the creation of the parish of Wharton, initially as a district of Davenham parish; Wharton became an ecclesiastical parish in March 1860. The tower clock was added in 1849 as a gift from salt-works proprietor John Dudley of Wharton Lodge, in memory of his wife. Also in memorial is the east stained glass window for Revd John Lowthian, who died in 1859 after being thrown from his horse. He had been Christ Church's first vicar having taken up the post in 1845, aged only 29.

The chapel was substantially enlarged in the late 1840s to include a new nave, chancel and bell tower, with money having been raised from public subscription which included gifts from Princess Victoria of Saxe-Coburg-Saalfeld (the mother of Queen Victoria), from John Bird Sumner (who had now become Archbishop of Canterbury), and grants from the Church Building Societies. The original chapel of ease became the north and south transepts of the new building, which provided seating for 350 people.

Wharton Historic Trivia: Salt and Railways

Wharton was a hamlet until the mid-19th century, when the salt industry began to develop along the course of the nearby River Weaver. Thereafter, the place developed into a sizeable suburb of north-eastern Winsford with its population increasing from 1,400 in 1841 to 1,775 in 1851.

Wharton is also the location of Winsford railway station, originally opened in 1837 on the Grand Junction Railway. Tragically, there have been two serious rail collisions near to Winsford Station. The first in 1948 killed 24 passengers when a passenger train stopped to let a passenger alight, and the train was rammed by a following postal express. Then on 26th December 1962, 18 passengers were killed when a Liverpool Lime Street to Birmingham New Street train crashed into a stationary Glasgow Central to London Euston train which had stopped due to frozen points.

Wharton Quirk Alert: Reverends

The Revd Robert Eden Henley was Christ Church's fifth vicar, and served from 1891 to 1933 dying on 7th May 1933 on a Sunday afternoon between services. He has been described as "a natural gentleman being well

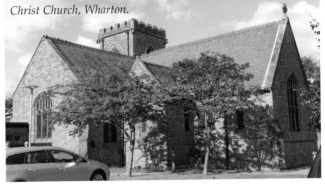
Christ Church, Wharton.

The Red Lion is located at the south-western fringe of Wharton.

Winsford railway station is located in Wharton.

connected socially and with impeccable manners". However, he was also known for hiding with the lights out in order to catch local boys' scrumping, to whom he duly delivered a quick clip around the ears!

One other vicar of note is the Revd John Higgins, who served Christ Church from 1972 to 1974. He gets a mention because 1972 was also the year that his namesake, Alex Higgins, first won the World Snooker Championship…and who was eclipsed several decades later by the reverend's *exact* namesake, John Higgins who so far has won four world titles!

NAME (STATUS):	**WHITEGATE** (Village)
POPULATION:	1172
DISTRICT:	Cheshire West and Chester
EARLIEST RECORD:	*Whytegate*, 1540
MEANING:	The white gate
DERIVATION:	From the Old English words *hwīt* (white) and *geat* (gate, gap or pass); in this particular case, it refers to the outer gate of Vale Royal Abbey

St Mary's church, Whitegate.

A Grade II listed late 17th-century timber-framed and thatched house in Whitegate.

Whitegate Church: St Mary's

St Mary's church is Grade II listed and largely dates from the 19th century. However, the chapel of the medieval Vale Royal Abbey stood on this same site, sometime after the founding of the abbey in 1277. Vale Royal Abbey was once the largest Cistercian abbey in Britain, and as the Cistercian's were known as the white monks, it is believed that a white gate between the abbey and the village resulted in the name of the latter; indeed, the 1540 reference above comes from an Act relating to a "church at the White Gate of Vale Royal Abbey". By 1715, though, the church was in a ruinous state and it was rebuilt in brick in 1728. However, in 1874–75 the church was rebuilt again by John Douglas of Chester for Lord Delamere.

Whitegate Historic Trivia: Vale Royal Abbey

For more on the history of the medieval Vale Royal Abbey, see *Quirky Cheshire (Over)*. However, following the Dissolution of the Monasteries in the late 1530s, the abbey passed to Thomas Holcroft, one of the king's commissioners. He demolished the abbey church and most of the abbey's domestic buildings, but retained the south and west cloister ranges including the abbot's house and the monks' dining hall along with their kitchen – all of which became part of a very large mansion that he built. The mansion passed to the Cholmondeley family in the early 17th century, but suffered badly during the English Civil War when the Royalist Cholmondeleys were attacked by Parliamentarians who burned down the south wing. Nevertheless, the Cholmondeleys continued to live at Vale Royal Abbey until 1907, adding a new south-east wing in 1833, while in 1860, architect John Douglas redressed the centre of the south range, which had formerly been timber-framed. Today, Vale Royal Abbey is part-golf club-house, part-apartments.

Today's Vale Royal Abbey is part-golf club-house, part-apartments. The Tudor and later mansion was built around the core of the medieval south and west ranges of the former abbey cloister and contains surviving rooms including the abbot's great hall.

The former lodge to Vale Royal Abbey in Whitegate.

NAME (STATUS):	**WOODHOUSES** (Lane, Iron Age hillfort)
POPULATION:	N/A
DISTRICT:	Cheshire West and Chester
EARLIEST RECORD:	N/A
MEANING:	Typically places named this way mean "houses in or near a wood"
DERIVATION:	From the Old English words *wudu* (wood or forest) and *hūs* (house)

Woodhouses Geographic and Historic Trivia

Woodhouses is an Iron Age hillfort that is located to the east of Helsby in north-west Cheshire and is protected as a Scheduled Ancient Monument. The hillfort rises to a height of 450ft (137m), and is located at the northern end of the Mid Cheshire Ridge – this being a range of low sandstone hills which stretch from the south of the county at Bickerton, to Woodhouse Hill and Beacon Hill in the north.

Spotting evidence of the Iron Age hillfort today isn't easy, though, as much of Woodhouse Hill has long-since been reclaimed by trees, bracken and shrubs. However, the western approach was naturally defended by a series of sharp cliffs, while a rampart was constructed to the north and the east where the ground slopes more gently. Excavations in 1951 showed that the rampart was originally 13ft (4m) high and revetted with stone on both sides. A number of small rounded stones, believed to be slingstones, have been found on the site – these having been projectiles presumably launched at the defences when the hillfort was under attack.

Today, the site and the surrounding areas form part of Snidley Moor Wood much of which is owned and managed by the Woodland Trust.

Woodhouse Hill was the site of an Iron Age hillfort and is a Scheduled Ancient Monument.

Part of the series of steep cliffs that provided a natural defence to the west of Woodhouses Iron Age hillfort.

Part of the very steep ascent to the top of Woodhouse Hill.

Some of the surviving ramparts/earthworks of the former Iron Age hillfort at the top of Woodhouse Hill. Much of the site has long-since been reclaimed by nature.

On climbing Woodhouse Hill, there are two separate and very steep climbs, in between which is this delightful path…

…and along this path, you will find two benches that offer stunning views towards Liverpool across the River Mersey.

The Best of the Rest

Name	Location and Trivia
BRICKHOUSES	A hamlet in Cheshire East, named after Brickhouse Farm at Yoxalls Corner on Holmes Chapel Road, a mile north-west of Sandbach.
BROOMHILL	A cluster of houses at the eastern end of Broomhill Lane between the villages of Great Barrow and Little Barrow, in Cheshire West and Chester. The name means "hill where broom grows" and is derived from the Old English words *brōm* and *hyll*.
BRYN	A hamlet in Cheshire East, 3 miles south-west of Northwich. The name means "hill" and derives from the Celtic word *brinn*.
CHERRY TREE	A 20th century housing estate at the eastern edge of Romiley in Stockport, Greater Manchester.
COBBS	A 20th century housing estate in the southern suburbs of Warrington.
DUNKIRK	An area just south of Ellesmere Port in Cheshire West and Chester, named after Dunkirk Lane which links the A5117 with Capenhurst.
FOLD	A residential area on the eastern outskirts of Dukinfield, Tameside. Fold is a common name in this area which includes Broadbent Fold, Leigh Fold and Hole House Fold!
GRAVEL	A residential area and ward to the east of Winsford in Cheshire West and Chester.
LITTLE MOOR	A residential area of Stockport, Greater Manchester. Little Moor clusters around the A626, wedged in between the other residential areas of Portwood and Foggbrook.
NOONSUN	Appears on the AA Close-Up Britain Road Atlas as a hamlet 3 miles east of Knutsford on Noah's Ark Lane, Cheshire East, but is actually only comprised of Noonsun Farm and its complex of farmhouses, cottages, barns and the Old Dairy.
PICTON	A hamlet located halfway up Picton Lane between Mickle Trafford and Stoak in Cheshire West and Chester. Picton was recorded in Domesday Book (1086) as *Picheton*. The name means "farmstead of a man called Pica", and is derived from the Old English personal name, *Pica*, plus the Old English word *tūn*, meaning "farmstead".
SAIGHTON	A hamlet located 2 miles south-east of the outskirts of Chester, in Cheshire West and Chester. Saighton was recorded in the Domesday Book (1086) as *Saltone*. The name means "farmstead where willow-trees grow" and is derived from the Old English names *salh* (willow-tree) and *tūn* (farmstead). Population in 2011 was 202 people.
REDDISH	A residential area a mile north-east of Lymm, first referenced as *Redish* in 1857. Also a residential area 4 miles north-east of Stockport, Greater Manchester. Historically in Lancashire, Reddish was annexed by Stockport in 1901. First referenced as *Rediche* in 1212, the name means "reedy ditch", and is derived from the Old English words *hrēod* and *dīc*.
RUSHTON	A village 5 miles west of Winsford in Cheshire West and Chester, first referenced in Domesday Book (1086) as *Rusitone*. The name means "farmstead where rushes grow" and is derived from the Old English words *rysc* (rush) and *tūn* (farmstead).
SYDNEY	A residential area at the north-eastern edge of Crewe which takes its name from Sydney Road which runs through the estate. The population is between 2500 and 3000.
TANG	Named after a narrow No Through Road in Bredbury Green called The Tang. Formerly in Cheshire, The Tang has been part of Stockport in Greater Manchester since 1974.
THE MARSH	Named after a former marshy area to the south-west of Congleton in Cheshire East, and which runs south-west of Padgbury Lane.
THE VALLEY	A residential area in the centre of Crewe named after Valley Brook which runs through the centre of the estate and through Valley Park.
WESTY	A large suburb and former ward (population 6125 in 2001) to the south-east of Warrington, located between the River Mersey and the Manchester Ship Canal.
WOODLANDS	A fairly affluent residential area just south of Stalybridge on the easternmost outskirts of Tameside, Greater Manchester.
WOODSIDE	Two separate hamlets, one in Cheshire West and Chester, the other in Cheshire East. The former is located on the western edge of Delamere Forest Park along Forest Farm Road and Yeld Road, and the other, a mile south-east of Wettenhall.
YEW TREE	A residential area to the east of the town of Dukinfield in Tameside, Greater Manchester, and which spreads out to the north of Yew Tree Lane.

This former Methodist chapel in Gravel is dated 1926.

Reddish Lane, at the tiny place called Reddish which is located around a mile north-east of Lymm.

The centre of the hamlet of Rushton.

Park Gates Farm Cottages at Rushton date from the 17th or early 18th century.

The Sydney Arms, on Sydney Road, Sydney, Crewe.

The entrance to The Tang which is on the western outskirts of Romiley. Note the post box on the outside of the house on the right – which is Victorian and has the letters V R embossed in gold either side of the golden crown. The house is known as Cobble Cottage.

Valley Park is located at the centre of the area of Crewe known as The Valley.

The entrance to Woodlands Road, from the A6018.

Bibliography

Books

Arthur Mee, *The King's England: Cheshire* (Hodder and Stoughton, 1943)
Alan Crosby, *A History of Cheshire* (Phillimore & Co. Ltd., 1996)
A.D. Mills, *Oxford Dictionary of British Place Names* (Oxford University Press, 1991)

Information panels and booklets at:

Anderton Boat Lift
Barnton and the Trent & Mersey Canal
Beeston Castle
Birkenhead Priory
Chester (various)
Chester Cathedral
Daresbury All Saints' church
Dunham Massey
Grosvenor Museum, Chester
Halton Castle
Hamilton Square, Birkenhead
Little Moreton Hall
Lyme Park
Lymm
Maiden Castle
Marple Aqueduct
Marton St James & St Paul's church
Middlewich Library
Newbridge (Weaver Parkway Trail)
Northwich
Norton Priory
Port Sunlight
Quarry Bank Mill
Runcorn Bridge
Sandbach Crosses
Styal Cross
Tatton Park
Tranmere Cross, Victoria Park
Whitegate

Websites

http://broadbottomvillage.com/
http://cheshirewi.org.uk/
https://chestercathedral.com/
http://en.wikipedia.org/wiki
http://historic-liverpool.co.uk/
https://historicengland.org.uk/
http://hydonian.blogspot.co.uk/
http://lymegreensettlement.org.uk/
http://neighbourhood.statistics.gov.uk/
http://oldhyde.blogspot.co.uk/
http://roman-britain.co.uk/
http://tattonestate.com
http://thehatton.co.uk/
http://themereresort.co.uk/
http://www.bluebellinn.net/
http://www.british-history.ac.uk/
http://www.britishlistedbuildings.co.uk/
http://www.broomedgefarm.co.uk/
http://www.cheshirearchaeology.org.uk/
http://www.cheshirelife.co.uk/
http://www.cheshirenow.co.uk/
http://www.cheshiresouth.org.uk/
http://www.chesterchronicle.co.uk/
https://www.chesterwalls.info/
http://www.chestertourist.com/
http://www.christ-church-wharton.org.uk/
http://www.discoverchester.co.uk/
http://www.domesdaybook.co.uk/
http://www.eatonandrushton.org.uk/
https://www.eatonestate.co.uk/
http://www.fccenvironment.co.uk/
http://www.floweryfieldchurchhyde.co.uk/
http://www.geograph.org.uk/
http://www.happy-valley.org.uk/
http://www.haslington.org/
http://www.hattonvillage.co.uk/
http://www.historicengland.org.uk/
http://www.historyofparliamentonline.org/
http://www.littlergrange.co.uk/
http://www.lymegreenhall.co.uk/
http://www.lymmvillage.co.uk/
http://www.manleyknoll.com/
http://www.marple-uk.com/

http://www.megalithic.co.uk/
http://www.middlewich-heritage.org.uk/
https://www.nationaltrust.org.uk/
http://www.norburychurch.org.uk/
http://www.pittdixon.go-plus.net/
http://www.poyntonweb.co.uk/
http://www.redliontarvin.co.uk/
https://www.roacheslockinn.co.uk/
http://www.stmartins-lowmarple.co.uk/
http://www.stmartinsaom.co.uk/
http://www.stmaryslymm.org/
http://www.tameside.gov.uk/

http://www.tattonpark.org.uk/
http://www.thegreyhoundashley.co.uk/
https://www.theguardian.com/
http://www.theshipstyal.co.uk/
http://www.thornber.net/
https://www.tripadvisor.co.uk/
http://www.ukbmd.org.uk/
http://www.virtual-knutsford.co.uk/
http://www.visionofbritain.org.uk/
http://www.visitnorthwich.co.uk/
http://www.warringtonguardian.co.uk/
http://www.winsfordhistorysociety.co.uk/

View towards the conical-shaped Shutlingsloe in East Cheshire.

View towards the north-east from part-way up Shutlingsloe.

View north-west towards Manchester from the trig point on Shutlingsloe.

Torside Reservoir in the Longdendale Valley – part of Cheshire for around 1000 years until ceded to Derbyshire in 1974.

A weir on the Crowden Brook at Crowden in the Longdendale Valley.

View over the Dee Estuary from West Kirby on the Wirral – another area lost to Cheshire on 1st April 1974 – this time to Merseyside.